TÍA VICTORIA'S SPANISH KITCHEN

VICTORIA SERRA

TÍA VICTORIA'S SPANISH KITCHEN

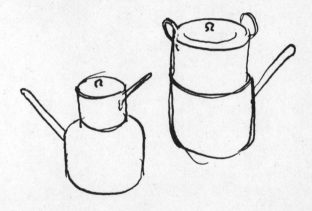

TRANSLATED AND WITH AN INTRODUCTION BY
ELIZABETH GILI
EDITED AND ADAPTED BY NINA FROUL
WITH DECORATIONS BY DRAKE BROOKSHAW

Weathervane Books
New York

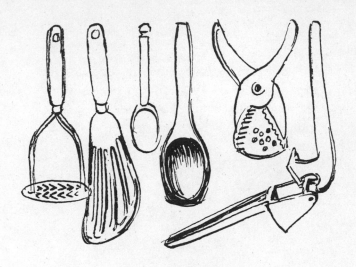

CONTENTS

To my husband Joan, who first encouraged me to do the cooking, and to my children Jonathan, Martin and Katherine who, with him, appear to have enjoyed the consequences.

E. G.

INTRODUCTION

Tía Victoria's Spanish Kitchen is a book of recipes for home cooking with a Spanish flavour, the majority of which are simple. However complicated the richer and more exotic recipes appear to be, the instructions for their preparation are straightforward and can be followed by those with only a little experience of cooking. At first sight, some of the ingredients may be unfamiliar, but there can be few towns that do not claim at least one good delicatessen shop which provides a wide selection of continental sausages and exotic foods. All the ingredients in these recipes (the quantities of which are based on an allowance for four to six people) are obtainable in this country. The less familiar fish mentioned in the fish section should not present difficulties to a worthy fishmonger. None of the fish mentioned is rare, except the *mérou*. Though difficult, even this is not impossible to get. But the recipes for this famous delicacy could not be excluded from a genuine Spanish cookery book, for the Spaniard has a particular liking for this fish, as expressed in the old Spanish saying 'of meat the lamb, of fish the mérou'. In the meat section the preponderance of recipes for veal over beef is explained by the fact that veal is more abundant in Spain than beef. Many of the veal dishes would be equally delicious made with a similar cut of beef. The section of vegetable recipes is almost as large as that for meat, and gives a refreshing variety in the manner of serving the same vegetable—potato dishes alone number more than twenty, and even cabbage is made interesting.

This book is a translation of my mother-in-law's, Victoria Serra de Gili's, Spanish cookery book *Sabores*, containing a great variety of Spanish dishes. I have omitted recipes that are not genuinely Spanish (for *Sabores* was designed not solely to equip the Spanish housewife with a simple approach to national cooking, but also to introduce her to some international dishes), but have

7

retained the recipe for *canneloni*, although this is usually considered an Italian dish, because it is so much a part of Spanish festive life. Similarly, some Spanish variations of Mediterranean and other dishes have been left in.

Among the recipes, mostly among those for desserts, there are a number bearing the name of a girl or a boy. These my mother-in-law dedicated to her daughters, daughters-in-law and grandchildren. In her Introduction she maintains that she is no more than a housewife with a flair for cooking (which not only her daughters, but also her sons have inherited!). She was persuaded to write down the recipes that delighted the family, and gradually *Sabores* was created 'to offer her many years' experience in solving the daily problem of food' in a manner attractive both to the eye and to the palate. The book was an immediate success when it was first published in 1945, and has been a best seller in Spain ever since. I can only hope that *Tía Victoria's Spanish Kitchen* may prove to others as useful and enjoyable as *Sabores* has been to my family and to me.

With a little experience, it will become obvious that Spanish cookery can compare favourably with that of any other country. It is rich and full-flavoured, its ingredients recognizable and its sauces intended not to conceal but to reveal the natural flavours of the great variety of meat, fish, vegetables and fruit of Spain. And olive oil is the basic fat used in the preparation of Spanish dishes, as it is in the cooking of all Mediterranean countries, giving a particular richness to the flavour. There are certain prejudices against Spanish cooking which I should like to try to dispel. I agree with Dionisio Pérez in his *Guía del buen comer español*, a spirited defence of cooking in Spain, that the mistrust of olive oil inspires most recriminations. In the past this criticism has too often been justified, since the oil was not refined and purified and, as the great traveller Richard Ford writes in his *Gatherings from Spain* in 1846, 'is said to be used indifferently for lamps or stews'. The traveller then might well have had memories of a home or restaurant filled with asphyxiating odours. Today this does not apply, as the best refined Spanish olive oil can be bought everywhere. Above all, it is important to remember that olive oil is *not* greasy when properly heated before use.

Another feature that has caused misgivings is the part played by garlic in Spanish cooking. It is true that it plays an important part, as it does indeed in the cooking of all Mediterranean countries. But in this book you will find many exciting dishes cooked without even a whiff of it. Even where garlic is recommended, and fortunately for those who enjoy it there are many typical dishes that require it, the amount used can be determined entirely by personal taste, though, naturally, to give the proper Spanish flavour, the amount advised is best. The reputation that Spanish cooking has acquired as uncompromising and highly spiced is questioned by Victoria Serra, and you will discover here no 'abuse of spices', as she calls it.

One of the most difficult adjustments a visitor to Spain must make is to the hours and the weight of Spanish meals. Breakfast is often no more than a token breaking of the fast, and consists of coffee, or thick chocolate, which Ford says 'is the favourite drink of the church and allowable even on fast days', into which bread, fresh or fried, may be dipped. Lunch is eaten between one and four o'clock (in Madrid it is particularly late), allowing time for a *siesta* afterwards, a necessity where the midday sun is not conducive to work. It consists of a soup, or hors-d'œuvre, a vegetable (which is always served separately, before the meat or fish course), pasta or rice dish followed by fish or meat, which may be accompanied by potatoes. Then comes a sweet, and fruit. If cheese is offered, it is most likely to be one made from goat's milk, or an excellent one called *manchego*, from La Mancha, which is a ewe's milk cheese. Wine is drunk at all meals; even the children, as in

France, drink it diluted. Between four and nine, or nine-thirty, when the evening meal is eaten, there is no official break, though tea (at about 6 p.m.) for children usually consists of a slice of bread and a bar of chocolate. The Spaniard, who finishes work at about 7 p.m., can return slowly home, by way of aperitifs and talk with his friends, to the evening meal which in form resembles lunch. Theatres, cinemas and concerts do not begin their evening performances before about 10.45 p.m., in spite of efforts to make them earlier. On feast-days and on Sundays the meal, either lunch or dinner, is crowned with *dulces*, and consists of every imaginable fantasy of cream and sponge, soaked in rum or covered with chocolate, or pastries filled with angel-hair jam and nuts, small and dainty, and bought from a pastry shop or *pastelería*, on the way home from Mass. In the past, nunneries have specialized in making many of the sweetmeats associated with particular saints' days, which are celebrated in Spain with gaiety and feasting. Originally the nuns of St Leandro made the *yemas de San Leandro* for Holy Week in Seville. Few housewives would attempt these delicacies. And while all the shops close on Sundays, and on those saints' days that are celebrated all over Spain (those of St James, St Joseph, St John, etc.), the pastry shops alone stay open. Apart from the national saints' days, every village has its own saint to celebrate in its own gay manner.

Every country owes something of its cooking, either in raw materials or confection, to its invaders, and Spain is no exception. One wonders what in fact the people of the Iberian Peninsula originally ate—for olives and garlic (now so distinctive of Mediterranean cooking) were brought by the Romans; and saffron, black pepper, nutmeg, lemons, cane sugar, rice and bitter oranges came with the Arab conquerors; the sweet orange was introduced through Portugal from China; while the taste for *garbanzos* (or chick-peas) came with the Carthaginians. And it was not until the discovery of America that Spain, and through her, Europe, first enjoyed potato, tomato, pimento and chocolate. In the varied soil and climate of Spain, most of these foreign foods found a natural home.

The Iberian Peninsula in shape likened by Strabo the Greek to a stretched bull's hide, is almost twice as large as the British Isles, and only a little smaller than France. Even apart from Portugal, it is the home of very different peoples and of four separate languages (Castilian, Catalan, Basque, Galician), as distinct from each other as Portuguese is from all four. The climate is as heterogeneous as the people, ranging from the sun-drenched south and south-east, where fertile valleys yield crops of olives, oranges, rice, figs, pomegranates, peaches, melons and many other fruits and vegetables, through the wild unpeopled wastes of the central plains, to the north-west, in agricultural Galicia, where the climate differs little in rainfall from our own, and women may be seen on their way to work in the fields carrying umbrellas, when not in use, balanced on their heads.

Each region of Spain has its specialities, or its local interpretation of national dishes. Perhaps the least original is the cooking of Madrid, which historically has always had two styles—that of the Royal and noble houses (which was eclectic and cosmopolitan), and that of the people, who lived poorly and had little to offer that is distinctive except perhaps *churros*, a doughnut mixture, fried and sold in the streets at any *fiesta* anywhere in Spain. *Sopa de ajo* (garlic soup) seems also to have originated in Madrid. But the *olla podrida*, or *cocido*, from which comes the French *pot-au-feu*, and into which Ford affirms 'the whole culinary genius of Spain is condensed', had its origins in Andalusia in the south, though every region has its own variations and we give the Catalan version as the richest. Ford tells of 'a worthy dignitary of Seville, in the good old times, before reform and appropriation had put out the church's kitchen fire . . . on feast days used turkeys instead of chickens, and added two sharp Ronda apples, and three sweet potatoes of Malaga'. Ford adds: 'His advice is worth attention; he was a good Roman Catholic canon, who believed everything, absolved everything, drank everything, ate everything, and digested everything. In fact, as a general rule, anything that is good in itself is good for an *olla*, provided, as old Spanish books always conclude, that it contains nothing contrary to the holy mother church, to orthodoxy, and to good manners.' From Andalusia comes another popular dish, of Arab origin, an iced soup for hot days: *gazpacho*. Generally speaking, 'a la Andaluza' means with tomatoes and pimentos, though the latter are even more important in dishes from Murcia. All over the southern half of Spain, the characteristic confectionary preserves the Moorish tradition, with sweetmeats made from almonds, sugar, and spices —for example the different kinds of *turrón* (Alicante, Jijona, etc.), eaten at Christmas time, and the *mazapán* of Toledo.

The land in the valley of Granada, in the south, is some of the most fertile in Spain and yields a variety and abundance of fruit and vegetables at the foot of the snow-covered mountains of the Sierra Nevada. There rich and poor alike eat *potaje de habas secas* (a vegetable dish of broad beans with garlic, tomatoes, onions and artichokes) on St Anthony's day. This is the region of *jamón serrano*, a ham like no other, sun-cured in the mountain snow.

On the south-east coast of Spain we enter another area of rich cultivation, of sweet oranges, rice, fruit and vegetables. Valencia, already famous in the fifteenth century for good eating, claims to produce the best rice in Spain, challenged only by the Catalans, and Zamora in the north. Nevertheless, it is Valencia that has given its name to perhaps the best known of all Spanish dishes— *paella* or Valencian rice. It is usual, in many parts of Spain, to have *paella* on Sundays as the first course.

The richness of Catalan cooking reflects the prosperity of this region of Spain. The olive oil, wines and meat are of excellent quality. The first cookery book known in the Peninsula, and one of the earliest in Europe, was the *Libre de Coch* by Ruperto de

Nola, written in Catalan and printed in Barcelona probably before 1500. It was translated into Spanish as *Libro de Guisado*, and in less than a century and a quarter it was reprinted more than twenty times, many more times than Cervantes' *Don Quixote* in the next century! Seafood on the Catalan coast is good, and *zarzuela de pescado* a delicious combination.

There is some difficulty in identifying what is French and what is Spanish in Pyrenean cooking, which is hardly surprising since the Kingdom of Aragon bestrode the Pyrenees in mediaeval times, and even as late as the seventeenth century the Roussillon was part of Catalonia. Lamb reared in the Pyrenees of Aragon and Navarra is singularly tasty, and the most common dish in these regions is grilled chops or *chuletas de cordero a la navarra*. But in the old Kingdom of Aragon, and especially in Zaragoza, there was no family celebration without *pollos a la chilindrón* (chicken with pimentos, tomatoes, garlic, onions and ham).

From Galicia comes *lacón con grelos* (a stew of pork with turnip tops), and typical of Asturias is *fabada asturiana* (pork with butter beans). Galicia and Asturias have a very similar type of cooking to that of Brittany and Normandy: *callos* (tripe) *a la moda de Oviedo* is the same as the French *tripes à la mode de Caen*; *and langosta* (lobster) *a la llanisca* differs in no way from *homard à la morlaisienne*. Both Normandy and Asturias use blood sausage, cook with cider, and drink cider at meals. Both Brittany and Asturias make a variety of puddings with apples.

Fish dishes abound round the coasts of Spain, though not because of any *necessity* to eat fish on Fridays, for Spain has dispensation in a Papal Bull, issued and paid for yearly, in which indulgence from Rome was granted to Ferdinand III in order to keep the Spanish Crusaders in better condition for fighting the Infidel; it is because of the abundance and variety of fish to be found there. The conveyance to the interior of fresh fish from both the north and the south is one of the best organized industries

of Spain. In many of the ports *fiestas* of fish are held, as in Cádiz,
at which all the dishes, even as many as twenty-one at a time, are
fish dishes. Along the Málaga coast, but only between Estepona
and Nerja, are found the *boquerón* (fresh anchovy) so much appreciated in the rest of Spain. Galicia, apart from the excellent fresh
fish from its ports of Vigo and La Coruña, has supplied the
interior of Spain with pickled oysters since the sixteenth and
seventeenth centuries. The *caldereta* from Asturias is a fish stew
made with the fish of the Cantabric, of the quality of which they
are very proud. The Basques have given to all Spain a dish which
is eaten at least once a week in homes, restaurants and taverns—
bacalao a la vizcaína (dried cod with onions, tomatoes, pimentos
and garlic)—a dish known not only in Europe, but also in Russia,
Poland and Japan.

In an introduction to Spanish cooking I have necessarily only
been able to give an indication of the best-known regional dishes,
the recipes for all of which can be found in this book; and I have
omitted altogether to mention the infinite variety of shellfish and
regional hams that provide a delicious richness in *tapas* which are
eaten with aperitifs all over Spain and in Córdoba, accompanied
by *Montilla* (a local white wine similar to, but lighter than sherry),
even substitutes for a meal. No one would deny the influence that
French cooking has had on Spanish cooking, as on that of other
European countries. But since perhaps not enough recognition
has been accorded to Spanish ingenuity for dishes whose origin
lay in Spain, but whose fame came through their adoption by the
French, I would like to indicate some of the ways in which
Spanish dishes, in spite of resistance from king and aristocrat,
crept into French life. In his *Guía del buen comer español*,
Dionisio Pérez maintains that the disrepute of Spanish cooking
comes from the time of Philip V of Spain and the literature of pre-
revolutionary and of Napoleonic times, when the opinion was
generally accepted that nothing but what was French was good,

whether it was ideas, cooking, customs or clothes. Yet it cannot be doubted that Spain considerably enriched French cooking, particularly during the eighteenth and nineteenth centuries. This was generously acknowledged by Maurice Cousin, Comte de Courchamps, in his Introduction to the *Dictionnaire général de la cuisine française ancienne et moderne*, 1866, when he wrote: 'Spain is a country with such a flair for creating stews, that the three best entrées of old French cooking, that is, *accolades d'anguilles à la royale*, *perdrix à la Medina-Coeli* and *ollas-podridas*, found their way into France with the retinue of Queen Ana' (Louis XIII's wife). The Spanish princesses who became queens of France took their cooks with them. And many French dishes known since as 'à l'Empératrice', or 'Eugénie', or simply 'à l'espagnole', date from the time of Eugenia de Montijo, wife of Napoleon III, some of which contain the ingredients prevalent in the Andalusian dishes of her youth—olive oil, garlic and tomato. Even Charles X imported the cook Gippini from Jerez de la Frontera to remind him of the dishes he enjoyed as Comte d'Artois in that city.

As trophies of war, France is indebted to Spain for some very fine recipes. The best trophy, the only beneficial thing that France got out of 'that unfortunate campaign' of the Napoleonic war, according to Auguste Escoffier (one-time chef to Napoleon III and of the Carlton and Savoy Hotels in London, and author of *Le Guide Culinaire*) was a manuscript of recipes salvaged by General Junot in 1807 from among the precious manuscripts of the rich and powerful monastery of Alcántara. Junot sent the manuscript to his wife Laure, later Duchesse d'Abrantès, who made good use of it, and some of these recipes appear in her *Mémoires*, including that for *consomado* or *consommé*. Thanks to the duchesse, the French have also enjoyed *faisan à la mode d'Alcántara*, *bécasse à la mode d'Alcántara* and *perdreau à la mode d'Alcántara*, distinctive of which is the use of *foie-gras* and truffles in their preparation, although these ingredients are usually considered a French speciality. We find, for instance, A. Dumas writing in his *Grand dictionnaire de cuisine*: 'France stuffs with truffles, Castile with olives, Catalonia with prunes and Galicia with chestnuts.' One of the most felicitous and widely known recipes that came to France as the result of a war is that for mayonnaise (although the famous cook Caréme includes this in his book *La Cuisine Française dans le siècle XIX* as a French invention). In the south of France, and in Spain, *all-i-oli* (made with garlic and olive oil) had been known since the tenth century, and came from Rome. But mayonnaise (made with olive oil and yolks of eggs) was first introduced into France after the subjugation of Mahon in Menorca in 1757, and took its name from that city (in Spanish it is written *salsa mahonesa*). Jean Conil, in his *Gastronomic Tour de France*, lists among the specialities of the Pyrénées-Orientales the *all-i-oli à la catalane* (which is none other than a garlic mayonnaise)—giving an indication of its origin, for, after all, Perpignan was once the royal town of the princes of Majorca.

The excellence of Spanish cooking penetrated as far north as Flanders and Germany, through the entourage of Charles V of Spain, and reached Naples and Sicily in the south with the Aragonese and the Catalans. And *sauce espagnole*, as Henry Smith says in *Classical Recipes of the World*, is one of the four sauces from which almost all other sauces are made, and according to Escoffier, came to France with the suite of Queen Ana.

I think perhaps I have said enough to suggest that Spanish cooking has had a considerable, if not always acknowledged, influence. In the same way, Spain has been enriched by her contacts, not least, as we have seen, with the Arabs, who occupied a great part of her territory for 800 years, and left an unmistakable mark on Spanish sweetmeats.

One last word: Spanish wines go very well with Spanish food.

Spain is essentially a wine-drinking country, and is the largest wine-producing country in the world, after France and Italy. Of exported wines sherry is, of course, the best-known Spanish drink, and was already famous in England in Elizabethan times. Sir John Falstaff, in *Henry IV*, Part II, speaks eloquently on the properties of 'good sherris-sack' in encouraging wit and valour—'If I had a thousand sons, the first human principle I would teach them should be, to forswear thin potations and to addict themselves to sack.' There are three basic types of sherry—*finos*, *amontillados*, and *olorosos*. The *finos* are pale and dry; the *amontillados* are medium-dry and more mature; while the *olorosos* are dark, full-bodied, but not necessarily sweet. In these three main classes there are many varieties of quality. *Manzanilla*, which is lighter than the *fino* and very dry, comes from a neighbouring district and is not, strictly speaking, a sherry, but it is equally appropriate for drinking before a meal. All sherries, to be sold as such, must come from a small area around the town of Jerez de la Frontera (from which the wine gets its name), and are completely reliable.

Of table wines the principal ones are the *riojas* from the northern half of Spain, and the *valdepeñas* from the district of La Mancha, south of Madrid. The red *rioja* wines are of a claret type, the white are rather dry. Both the red and the white *valdepeñas* wines are dry. Among Catalan wines the *alella marfil*, a hock-type white wine, a little on the sweet side, comes from a district north of Barcelona. But nearly every region in Spain grows its own wine, and there are many varieties. Generally speaking, table wines have not yet reached the reliable standardization of sherries, but are nevertheless good-quality wines.

A delectable sweet wine to serve with desserts is *moscatel*, made from the muscat grape. *Málaga* is a sweet, dark, fortified dessert wine. The best Spanish sparkling wine, although at its driest it is a little sweeter than the French champagne, bears comparison with it.

Spanish brandy, the distillation of which only began towards the end of the last century, is a little sweeter and heavier than the French, but of excellent quality. Among Spanish liqueurs obtainable in this country are the aniseed-flavoured *anís del mono*, and the sweet herb-flavoured *calisay*, both from Catalonia.

On the whole, Spanish wines are perhaps harsher, more earthy than those of France and Germany, whose subtler and more exquisite wines are lost on the full flavour of Spanish cooking. Try a Spanish wine when you cook the Spanish way, and I am confident you will not be disappointed.

Oxford   ELIZABETH GILI

ACKNOWLEDGEMENTS

I should like to express my gratitude most of all to my husband Joan, who patiently went through every word of my translation, for his help at every stage of the book. I am also deeply indebted to Nina Froud for her editing; her advice and experience have been invaluable and very much appreciated. I wish to thank my sister-in-law Núria Mestres de Gili for the addition of recipes for *Dried Cod Pil-Pil*, *Spanish Diplomatic Pudding*, *Gazpacho*, and *Romesco Sauce*; and also Catalina Cañet, wife of the proprietor, and cook of the Restaurant Reig in Palafrugell, for her recipes for *Lobster and Chicken*, *Suquet*, and *Peas a la Catalana*, among the dishes for which she is famous on the Costa Brava. I am indebted to André L. Simon for his help with a French reference. To Selwyn Jepson and to Teddy Schuller I am grateful for practical suggestions in connexion with the book; and to other unnamed friends I should like to express my gratitude here.

E. G.

USEFUL FACTS AND FIGURES

Weights and Measures

English weights and measures have been used throughout this book. In case it is wished to translate these into their American counterparts the following tables give a comparison.

Liquid Measures

One pint of liquid may be regarded as equal to two American measuring cups for all practical purposes. (American cups are standard '$\frac{1}{2}$-pint' measuring cups, but the American pint is slightly smaller than the British and American $\frac{1}{2}$-pint cups are actually equivalent to two-fifths of a British pint.)

3 teaspoons equal 1 tablespoon.

The average English teacup is $\frac{1}{4}$ pint or 1 gill.

The average English breakfast cup is $\frac{1}{2}$ pint or 2 gills.

When cups are mentioned in the recipes in this book they refer to a B.S.I. measuring cup which holds $\frac{1}{2}$ pint.

Solid Measures

English	American
1 lb. Butter or other fat	2 cups
1 lb. Flour	4 cups
1 lb. Granulated or Castor Sugar	2 cups
1 lb. Icing or Confectioners' Sugar	3 cups
1 lb. Brown (moist) Sugar	$2\frac{1}{2}$ cups
1 lb. Golden Syrup or Treacle	1 cup
1 lb. Rice	2 cups
1 lb. Dried Fruit	2 cups
1 lb. Chopped Meat (finely packed)	2 cups
1 lb. Lentils or Split Peas	2 cups

Solid Measures (cont.)

English	American
1 lb. Coffee (unground)	2½ cups
1 lb. Soft breadcrumbs	4 cups
½ oz. Flour	1 level tablespoon*
1 oz. Flour	1 heaped tablespoon
1 oz. Sugar	1 level tablespoon
½ oz. Butter	1 tablespoon smoothed off
1 oz. Golden Syrup or Treacle	1 level tablespoon
1 oz. Jam or Jelly	1 level tablespoon

* Must be proper measuring tablespoon

Metric Weights and Measures

It is difficult to convert to metric measures with absolute accuracy, but 1 oz. is equal to approximately 30 grammes, 2 lb. 3 oz. to 1 kilogramme. For liquid measure, approximately 1¾ English pints may be regarded as equal to 1 litre; 1 demilitre is half a litre, and 1 décilitre is one-tenth of a litre.

Oven temperatures

	Electricity °F.	Gas regulo	°C.
COOL oven	225 to 250	0 to ½	107–121
VERY SLOW oven	250 to 275	½ to 1	121–135
SLOW oven	275 to 300	1 to 2	135–149
VERY MODERATE oven	300 to 350	2 to 3	149–177
MODERATE oven	375	4	190
MODERATELY HOT oven	400	5	204
HOT oven	425 to 450	6 to 7	218–233
VERY HOT oven	475 to 500	8 to 9	246–260

Note: This table is an approximate guide only. Different makes of cooker vary and if you are in any doubt about the setting it is as well to refer to the manufacturer's temperature chart.

Time-table for Cooking Meat

The usual time allowed for roasting, baking and boiling meat is:
15 minutes to the pound and 15 minutes over for thin pieces of mutton, lamb or beef.
20 minutes to the pound and 20 minutes over for thick joints, with little or no bone.
25 minutes to the pound and 25 minutes over for pork and veal.

Salads & Hors-d'œuvre

ENSALADAS Y ENTREMESES

Artichoke Salad   *Ensalada de alcachofas*

Take six small, tender globe artichokes. Cut into quarters and cook in boiling salted water with a slice of lemon peel. Drain and rinse with cold water. Boil some small onions, drain and leave until cold. Put the onions and artichokes on a dish, and cover with red sauce (p. 72).

Celery Salad   *Ensalada de apio*

Wash and trim the celery. Choose the tenderest pieces and cut them into chunks $2\frac{1}{2}$ inches long. Fill the hollows with *foie-gras* and serve on a bed of watercress salad.

Cauliflower Salad   *Ensalada de coliflor*

1 small cauliflower   green sauce (p. 76)
2 hard-boiled eggs   2 cooked carrots

Wash and divide the cauliflower into flowerets. Cook in boiling salted water, drain well; leave to cool, put on a dish, and decorate with slices of carrot and boiled egg. Serve with green sauce.

Brain Salad   *Ensalada de seso*

2 sets calf's brains   2 tablespoons olive oil
1 lettuce   mayonnaise sauce (p. 74)
salt   1 tablespoon chopped parsley
juice of 1 lemon

Clean the brains, cook them in boiling salted water and leave to cool, without draining. Shred lettuce finely and season to taste with salt, lemon juice and olive oil. Put it in a dish and place the brains, cut in thin slices, on top. Cover with mayonnaise sauce and sprinkle with parsley.

Normandy Salad   *Ensalada normanda*

1 lb. diced potatoes   1 tablespoon chopped chervil
18 mussels   5 tablespoons olive oil
1 sprig thyme   1 tablespoon vinegar
2 sprigs parsley   ½ teaspoon salt
1 clove garlic   ¼ teaspoon pepper
1 diced carrot

Cook the potatoes in boiling salted water, and drain. Clean the mussels thoroughly, put in a saucepan with two tablespoons olive oil, carrot, thyme, garlic and parsley. Cover the pan and keep over very low heat for 15 minutes, then remove shells. Mix the rest of olive oil, the vinegar, salt, pepper, and the liquid from the mussels in a bowl, and whisk. Arrange the potatoes on a dish, place the mussels on top, pour the sauce over them, sprinkle with chervil and serve.

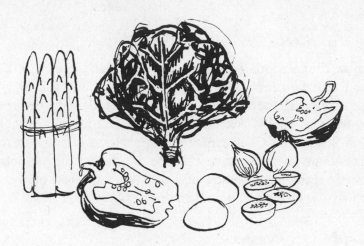

Rainbow Macédoine   *Macedonia iris*

1 lettuce	8 anchovy fillets
1 bunch radishes	1 teaspoon chopped chervil
1 bunch watercress	3 tablespoons olive oil
1 head celery	1 tablespoon vinegar
2 chopped hard-boiled eggs	½ teaspoon salt
2 oz. cooked diced ham	

Wash lettuce, radishes, the whitest part of celery and watercress and leave in cold water. A little time before serving, drain well and put in a salad bowl. Place the anchovy fillets, cut into pieces, on top, alternating with ham. Sprinkle with hard-boiled eggs. Put chervil in another bowl, add oil, vinegar and salt. Mix well and serve in a sauce-boat.

Four persons are needed to make a salad: a spendthrift for oil, a miser for vinegar, a counsellor for salt and a madman to stir it all up

Potato Boats   *Barquitas de patatas*

4 large potatoes
8 oz. fresh crayfish

3 carrots, cooked and diced
1 pint supreme sauce (p. 76)

Choose four smooth, long-shaped potatoes and cut them in half; scoop out the centres, forming little boats, and cook in boiling salted water. Remove with care so as not to damage them, drain and leave to cool. Cook the crayfish in boiling salted water for about 8 minutes. Cool, remove from shells, and cut into pieces. Mix enough supreme sauce with the crayfish to fill the potatoes. Arrange these in the centre of a dish. Mix the rest of the sauce with the carrots, pour around the potato boats and serve.

Canapés   *Canapés*

1. Remove crust from slices of bread, cut into squares, and fry in butter. Mash the yolks of two hard-boiled eggs and four anchovy fillets, adding a little butter and a few drops of oil. Blend into a smooth paste and spread on the pieces of fried bread. Sprinkle with the finely chopped whites of egg.
2. Cut and fry the bread as in the previous recipe. Spread with a mixture of grated cheese and butter. Decorate the corners with a small slice of gherkin and the centre with a disc of sweet pimento.
3. Cut and fry the bread as described and spread with *foie-gras* mixed with butter. Decorate the four corners with a disc of sweet pimento and the centre with a slice of hard-boiled egg.

Cheese and Ham Canapés   *Pastelillos de queso y jamón*

1½ oz. butter
1¼ oz. flour
½ pint milk
2 beaten eggs
8 oz. Dutch cheese

6 oz. ham
olive oil for frying
1 bunch watercress
bread

Make a thick *béchamel* sauce (p. 70) using the butter, flour and milk. Cut bread into round slices ¼-inch thick; cover with sauce, put a round of cheese on top, follow with a slice of ham of similar size, and cover with another layer of sauce. Carefully coat the savouries with egg, fry in hot olive oil until golden and serve on a bed of watercress.

Spanish Canapés   *Canapés a la española*

Slice a sandwich loaf and cut off the crusts. Pound anchovy fillets in a mortar with butter (allowing 4 oz. of butter to twelve fillets). Spread this paste over slices of bread. Put a line of sieved hard-boiled yolks in the centre and a strip of sweet pimento on each side.

Fried Sandwiches   *Emparedados*

1. Cut some ¼-inch thick slices of bread from a sandwich loaf and remove the crusts. Moisten one side lightly with milk, place a slice of ham on top and cover with another slice of bread moistened on the inside. Cover the sandwiches with a cloth, leave under a weight for a little while, then coat in beaten egg and fry in hot olive oil until golden.

2. Prepare bread as above, but instead of ham use cream cheese, then proceed to coat the sandwiches in beaten egg and fry as described.

3. Prepare the bread as described. For filling make a paste of *foie-gras* and butter. Spread it on one side of each slice of bread, press together, then coat in beaten egg and fry as above.

St George Rolls   *Panecillos de San Jorge*

6 round bread rolls   2 hard-boiled eggs
1½ lb. spinach   12 oz. tomatoes
4 oz. hake   2 tablespoons olive oil
1 tablespoon butter

Cut the tops off the rolls in a circle, to be used as 'lids', and very carefully scoop out the crumb, leaving a crust shell. Boil the spinach in salted water, drain and chop. Fry the hake in butter, chop it together with the hard-boiled eggs and mix with the spinach. Sieve the tomatoes and cook with olive oil until the purée thickens. Put a little of the purée at the bottom of each roll, fill with the spinach mixture, cover with the 'lids', put on a baking tray, sprinkle with olive oil and bake in the oven until they are golden.

Monk-fish Fillets   *Filetes de rape*

12 oz. monk-fish	2 leaves tarragon
1 hard-boiled egg	parsley
4 anchovy fillets	1 tablespoon vinegar
10 capers	3 tablespoons olive oil

Clean the fish and remove skin and bones. Cut into strips and cook in boiling salted water. Drain and place in an oval dish. Pound the hard-boiled egg, anchovies, capers, tarragon and parsley together in a mortar, adding vinegar and oil. Blend well and put this dressing on the fish. Prepare this in advance to let the fish become permeated with the dressing.

Egg Hors-d'œuvre   *Huevos para entremés*

1. hard-boiled eggs   pimentoes, peeled and seeded
   butter   watercress

Hard-boil as many eggs as required, shell them and cut off the tips so that they stand up. Cut in half horizontally and remove the yolks, taking care not to damage the whites. Pound sweet pimentoes in a mortar (allowing one for four eggs), add the yolks and a little butter, season with salt and mix well. Fill the whites with the mixture. Place them on a dish, and decorate with watercress.

2. tinned tunny   mayonnaise sauce (p. 74)
   hard-boiled eggs   watercress

A delicious alternative filling for the egg-whites (prepared as above) is tinned flaked tunny pounded with the yolks and mixed with mayonnaise sauce. Serve on a dish decorated with watercress.

Do not forget to drink with salad, and let there be no water in it

Potato Medallions   *Medallones de patata*

1.   4 large, long potatoes   3 chopped hard-boiled eggs
     20 anchovy fillets   butter

Boil the potatoes in their skins in salted water, drain and cool. Peel them and cut into rounds, about ½-inch thick. Cover each round of potato with a good layer of butter, top with a little mound of chopped hard-boiled egg and twist an anchovy fillet like a turban round the eggs.

2.   4 large, long potatoes   butter
    sobrasada   sweet pimento
    green olives

Prepare the potatoes as above. Mix sobrasada with butter. Spread each round of potato thickly with the mixture. Decorate with two criss-cross strips of sweet pimento. Place a slice of green olive in the centre.

Anchovy Rolls   *Rollos de anchoas*

24 anchovy fillets   8 oz. tomatoes
2 hard-boiled eggs   8 oz. olives stuffed with pimento
vinaigrette sauce (p. 76)

Roll the anchovy fillets, arrange on a dish, and place an olive in the centre of each. Decorate the dish with alternate slices of tomato and hard-boiled egg, and dress lightly with a vinaigrette sauce.

American Tomatoes   *Tomates a la americana*

1 lettuce   1 tin tunny
4 large, ripe, firm tomatoes   mayonnaise sauce (p. 74)
salt

Cut off the tops of tomatoes, remove seeds and sprinkle with salt. Blend mayonnaise sauce and flaked tunny into a smooth paste with a fork and fill the tomatoes. Arrange each tomato on a lettuce leaf.

Tomatoes Mimosa   *Tomates a la mimosa*

4 large, ripe, firm tomatoes
1 lettuce
8 anchovy fillets
½ teaspoon salt
1 tablespoon olive oil

4 oz. stoned olives
4 oz. cooked ham, cut thick
1 hard-boiled egg

Cut the tops off the tomatoes, remove seeds, season with salt and sprinkle with oil. Wash the lettuce, shred, drain well, and put on a flat dish. Cut each anchovy fillet in two. Dice the ham. Fill the tomatoes, first with olives, then with anchovies and ham. Sprinkle the tops with chopped hard-boiled egg. Arrange the tomatoes on the lettuce, and the result is a dish no less agreeable to the eye than to the palate.

Spring Tomatoes   *Tomates primaverales*

8 large tomatoes
8 oz. peas
4 oz. French beans
mayonnaise sauce (p. 74)

8 oz. diced potatoes
2 diced carrots
1 hard-boiled egg
1 bunch small radishes

Cook the peas, potatoes and carrots in salted water. Cut the beans in ½-inch pieces and cook in the same way. Drain and leave to cool. Mix all vegetables with mayonnaise sauce. Cut off the tops of tomatoes, scoop out the pulp with a spoon, season with salt and fill with the vegetables. Decorate with slices of hard-boiled egg, and surround with small radishes. Serve in a glass dish.

Stuffed Tomatoes   *Tomates rellenos*

6 large, ripe, firm tomatoes
12 oz. prawns
mayonnaise sauce (p. 74)
¼ teaspoon pepper

vinegar
12 anchovy fillets
1 lettuce

Cut off the tops of the tomatoes, remove the seeds, and season with salt. Shell the prawns, chop them up with the anchovies, add a little mayonnaise sauce, a few drops of vinegar, and pepper. Mix well and fill the tomatoes. Serve on a foundation of crisp lettuce leaves.

Baked Tomato Custards   *Flanes de tomate*

1½ oz. butter	1 teaspoon sugar
1½ lb. tomatoes	3 eggs
½ teaspoon salt	

Grease some small moulds with butter. Boil the tomatoes until soft, sieve into a small pan containing the butter. Add salt and sugar, and simmer gently for 10 minutes. Beat the eggs and season with salt. Add to tomatoes and mix well. Fill the moulds with the mixture and cook in a *bain-marie* in the oven until set. These baked tomato custards may be used as hors-d'œuvre or to accompany a dish of meat or vegetables.

Baked Cheese Custards   *Flanes de queso*

½ pint milk	2 oz. diced ham
4 beaten eggs	1¼ oz. butter
3 oz. grated cheese	breadcrumbs
salt and pepper	

Boil the milk. When it is cold, add eggs, cheese, seasoning and ham. Butter several small moulds, sprinkle with breadcrumbs, fill with the mixture, cook in the oven in a *bain-marie* until set, cool, turn out and serve.

SOPAS, CALDOS Y PURÉS

Chicken Broth   *Sopa de gallina*

wing and breast of chicken   1 stick celery
2½ pints water   salt
1 onion   4 oz. rice flour
1 carrot

Put chicken in a pan of boiling water. Add whole onion, carrot, celery and salt to taste. Cook for 3 hours over a moderate heat. Strain the broth, bone the chicken and chop up the flesh. In another pan dilute the flour with a little cold stock, gradually add the rest of the broth, stirring continuously. Add chopped chicken, cook for 10 minutes and serve.

Consommé   *Consommé*

1 lb. lean veal	1 carrot
1 wing and breast chicken	1 stick celery
1 ham bone	5¼ pints water
1 turnip	sugar
1 large onion	1 egg
1 leek	

Clean and wash the ingredients and put them, except the egg and sugar, in a saucepan of cold water. Boil for 3 hours, skimming well from time to time and adding a little burnt sugar to give it colour. Strain, leave to cool, carefully remove all fat from the surface, put in an egg with its shell and return the pan to the fire. As soon as it begins to boil, draw the pan to the edge of the burner, so that it will simmer slowly and on one side only. After 5 minutes the egg will rise to the surface, drawing all the impurities with it. Strain the clarified broth through a clean cloth moistened with cold water and the result will be a completely clear *consommé*. Serve in soup cups with *croûtons* of fried bread, or with finely chopped hard-boiled egg and a little diced ham, or with diced stock custard (p. 50). There is an endless variety of garnishes to suit all tastes.

Consommé with Eggs   *Consommé con huevos*

bread	*consommé*
eggs	

Put a toasted slice of bread into each large soup cup and break a fresh egg on top. Pour the boiling *consommé* (see previous recipe) over it and serve.

Between the hand and the mouth the soup is lost

Duchess Soup   *Sopa a la duquesa*

4 pints boiling water
2 breasts of chicken
1¼ lb. veal bones
1 onion
8 oz. tomatoes

4 oz. tapioca
3 yolks
2 tablespoons milk
2 oz. butter

Put the chicken, veal bones, onion and tomatoes in a pan of boiling water and cook gently for 3 hours. Strain through a sieve into another pan. Dice the chicken and keep. Bring the broth to the boil and sprinkle in tapioca, stirring constantly. Cook gently until the tapioca becomes transparent. Dilute the yolks with milk in a soup tureen. Add butter, chicken and, finally, the tapioca broth. Stir well and serve.

Queen Soup   *Sopa a la reina*

2½–3 pints chicken broth
    (p. 35)
4 oz. rice flour

2 yolks
cooked diced chicken

Prepare a good chicken broth. Mix the rice flour with a little cold broth in a saucepan. Keep a little cold broth for diluting yolks. Add the rest of the broth, stirring all the time, to prevent formation of lumps. Cook for 10 minutes. Put the yolks into a soup tureen and dilute with cold broth. Pour in the thickened broth, add diced chicken and serve.

Giblet Soup   *Sopa de menudillos*

giblets
2 tablespoons butter
1 chopped onion
1 peeled and chopped tomato
6 oz. bread

2½–3 pints water
1 clove garlic
parsley
1 hard-boiled egg
salt

Fry chicken, turkey, goose or duck giblets in butter, remove and, in the same pan, fry onion and tomato. Slice bread, add to pan, fry lightly, pour in boiling water and add the giblets cut up into small pieces. Pound garlic, parsley and hard-boiled egg in the mortar. Dilute with two to three tablespoons cold water and add to the soup. Season with salt and simmer gently for 45 minutes.

Garlic Soup   *Sopa de ajo*

6 oz. stale bread	½ teaspoon paprika
2 tablespoons olive oil	2 pints salted water
3 or 4 cloves garlic	1 egg

Slice bread very thinly and put in a soup tureen. Heat oil in a pan and fry garlic until golden. Add paprika, stir and immediately remove from heat, otherwise paprika will go black and taste bitter. Pour boiling salted water over the bread. Cover and leave to stand a few minutes. Beat the egg with a little milk or water, to prevent it curdling, add to soup. Remove garlic and serve.

Meat Ball Soup   *Sopa de albóndigas*

4 oz. meat (veal or pork)	salt
2 oz. fat salted pork	2 oz. flour
1 large diced onion	oil or lard for frying
4 oz. chopped and peeled tomatoes	4 oz. sliced bread
sprig parsley	2½–3 pints salted boiling water
2 oz. breadcrumbs	1½ oz. chopped roasted almonds
1 egg	

Mince the meat, pork, a little onion and parsley. Add bread-crumbs, egg and salt to taste. Shape into balls the size of a hazel-nut, roll in flour and fry in very hot olive oil or lard. Drain. In the same fat fry the onion and tomatoes. Put bread into a pan of boiling water. Add onion, tomatoes, meat balls and finely chopped almonds. Check seasoning. Simmer on a low heat for 45 minutes, stirring occasionally, taking care not to damage the meat balls.

Rice Soup Mercedes   *Sopa de arroz Mercedes*

4 oz. pork
lard
2 chicken livers
1 chopped onion
1 chopped tomato
2 finely shredded carrots
1 chopped chervil

1 tablespoon chopped parsley
1 thinly sliced turnip
2 chopped leeks
8 oz. rice
3½ pints boiling water
salt

Fry the pork in lard. Remove, and in the same fat fry the livers. Drain and in the same fat fry onion and tomato. Add carrots, chervil, parsley, turnip and leeks and fry well. Cut the livers and pork into small pieces. Stir in rice, mix well, pour in water, add salt to taste and simmer until the rice is cooked.

Hazel-nut Soup   *Sopa de avellanas*

2 cloves garlic
2 tablespoons olive oil
2 pistils toasted saffron

5 oz. sliced bread
2 oz. roasted hazel-nuts
2½ pints boiling water

Fry the garlic and one slice bread in oil until golden. Put the garlic in a mortar with saffron, fried bread and hazel-nuts. Pound into a smooth paste and put into a pan of boiling water, with salt, bread and the oil in which the garlic was fried. Simmer on a low heat for 1 hour.

Onion Soup   *Sopa de cebolla*

1. 1 large onion
    2½ pints water
    6 oz. thinly sliced bread

olive oil
salt

Put one large finely sliced onion in a pan of water. Cook for 30 minutes. Add bread, olive oil and salt to taste. Cook for another 30 minutes. Whisk until smooth and serve.

2. 8 oz. chopped onions
    1½ oz. butter
    2½ pints water

6 oz. thinly sliced bread
1 teaspoon salt
1 egg

Fry the onions in the butter until golden. Put in a pan of hot water. Add bread and salt, and cook for 45 minutes. Beat the egg in the soup tureen, dilute with a little water or milk, pour the contents of the pan over it, stir well and serve.

Thyme Soup   *Sopa de tomillo*

6 oz. bread
2–3 tablespoons olive oil
2–3 sprigs thyme
1½ teaspoons salt

2½ pints water
2 eggs
2 tablespoons milk

Slice bread very thinly, put it in a soup tureen and sprinkle with olive oil. Put thyme and salt in a saucepan of boiling water. Boil for 5 minutes, then strain it on to the bread. Beat eggs, dilute with milk, add to the soup, stir and serve.

Soup Mimosa   *Sopa mimosa*

4 oz. French beans
salt
3 oz. potato flour

2½ pints stock
1¼ oz. butter
3 hard-boiled eggs (yolks only)

Choose small and tender beans, cook them in salted boiling water, drain and keep. Dilute the flour with a little cold stock. Heat the rest of the stock and add it, gradually, to the flour paste, stirring continuously. Simmer gently for 10 minutes, pour it over the butter in the soup tureen, mix well; scatter the beans on top and sprinkle with yolks of the hard-boiled eggs rubbed through a large-holed sieve. In this way the egg will fall in the shape of tiny balls and give the appearance of mimosa flowers.

Spring Soup   *Sopa primaveral*

4 oz. tender French beans
4 carrots
4 turnips
1 medium-sized cabbage
8 oz. potatoes
4 leeks
1 stick celery

1 chopped onion
2 oz. lard
3½ pints water
salt
4 oz. rice
4 oz. peas (shelled)

Clean all the vegetables and shred into long thin strips. Melt the lard in a saucepan and fry the onion until golden. Add all the other vegetables, except the peas, stirring to coat them all with the lard. Pour boiling water over them, add salt to taste and simmer for 2 hours. Add rice and peas, cook until ready and serve.

Lightning Soup   *Sopa relámpago*

6 oz. bread
2 oz. butter
6 eggs

2 pints water
salt

Cut bread into thin slices, line with it six individual soup bowls, divide the butter into equal portions and add to bread. Add a fresh raw egg to each bowl, taking care not to break yolks. Pour lightly salted boiling water into bowls and serve.

Catalan Cocido   *Cocido catalán*

8 oz. chick-peas
1 teaspoon bicarbonate of soda
5¼ pints water
1 breast and wing of chicken
8 oz. skirt of veal
8 oz. neck or loin of mutton
1 ham bone
1 large onion

1 carrot
1 stick celery
4 oz. piece fat salted pork
1 meat ball (p. 38)
8 oz. black sausage
1½ lb. potatoes
1 cabbage
rice and vermicelli or macaroni

Soak the chick-peas overnight in cold water with bicarbonate of soda. Rinse and put them in a saucepan of boiling water, together with the chicken, veal, mutton, ham bone, onion, carrot and celery. Simmer for 2 hours. Put in the fat salted pork in one piece and the mince meat ball (made as described in the recipe for meat ball soup, except that it is made as one big elongated floured ball). Cook for 30 minutes, add the black sausage whole, and potatoes and cabbage cut up into fairly large pieces. When these are cooked, strain into another pan as much stock as is needed to make the soup and cook in it some rice and vermicelli, or macaroni, or any other *pasta*. When these are ready, pour them into the soup tureen and add the rest of the stock. As a second dish, serve all the meat on one plate and all the vegetables on another. This makes a substantial meal, in addition to rich soup, and both are traditionally served on Christmas day, before the turkey.

Cauliflower Soup   *Sopa de coliflor*

1 medium-sized cauliflower	1 peeled and chopped tomato
flour	3 oz. diced bread
olive oil for frying	1½ oz. butter
1 chopped onion	

Cut up the cauliflower, wash it and cook for 10 minutes in salted water, being careful not to overcook. Drain, keeping the water. Dip the cauliflower in flour, fry in oil, remove and in the same oil fry onion and tomato. Reheat the cauliflower water, add bread, fried cauliflower, onion and tomato. Simmer for 1 hour, adding water if the soup is too thick. Sieve the soup into the tureen, blend in the butter and serve.

No olla *without fat pork, nor wedding without a tambourine;*
No olla *without fat pork, nor sermon without St Augustine*

Cream Soup   *Sopa de crema*

6 hard-boiled eggs	2 oz. butter
2½ pints milk	4 oz. cooked peas
salt	

Remove the yolks and pound in a mortar, adding a little milk to make a smooth paste. Pour it into a pan and cook over a low heat. Add milk gradually, stirring constantly to achieve the consistency of a thin cream. Season with salt. Remove from heat, add butter in very small pieces and blend well. Chop the whites of egg minutely, put in a soup tureen, add peas, pour the contents of the pan over them and serve.

Chick-pea Soup   *Sopa de garbanzos*

8 oz. chick-peas	1 chopped onion
1 teaspoon bicarbonate of soda	1 chopped tomato
5½ pints water	salt
1 slice bread	8 oz. macaroni
2 tablespoons olive oil	

Soak the chick-peas overnight in water with bicarbonate of soda. Rinse, put in a pan of cold water, bring to the boil, skim, cover, simmer for 1½ hours. Fry bread in olive oil. In the same oil, fry the onion and tomato. Pound the fried bread in a mortar, add it together with onion and tomato to the chick-peas. Salt to taste. Continue to simmer for 1½ hours. Once cooked, rub the chick-peas through a sieve into another pan, straining through all the liquid. Reheat, put in macaroni, bring to the boil, simmer until macaroni is done to your liking and serve.

Of soup and of love the first is the best

Macaroni Soup with Meat Balls

Sopa de macarrones con albóndigas

1 chopped onion	4 oz. veal or pork
1 chopped tomato	2 oz. fat salted pork
1 tablespoon lard	1 egg
2½–3 pints stock	8 oz. macaroni

Fry onion and tomato together in lard. Add to stock. Make the meat balls as described in the recipe for *Meat ball soup* (p. 38). Bring stock to the boil, add macaroni and meat balls, cook until the macaroni is ready and serve.

Mayonnaise Soup   *Sopa de mahonesa*

5 oz. bread	6 oz. hake
8 oz. potatoes	oil for frying
2 pints water	mayonnaise sauce (p. 74)

Cut up the bread and put it into a pan of water. Fry the fish, skin, bone, cut up and add to the bread. Peel and slice potatoes finely. Add to pan. Salt to taste and simmer for an hour. Whisk until smooth (or rub through a sieve). Make a garlic flavoured mayonnaise sauce. Pour the soup into the tureen. Stir the sauce into it just before serving. This is a delicious soup.

Mint Soup   *Sopa de menta*

1 oz. olive oil (or butter)	2½ pints hot water
1 chopped onion	salt
2 peeled, chopped tomatoes	mint leaves
6 oz. bread	

Heat oil in a pan and fry onion and tomatoes. Add bread cut into chunks, stir once or twice, pour in water, season with salt to taste, add a handful of mint leaves. Simmer for an hour and serve.

Grated Potato Soup   *Sopa de patata rallada*

2½ pints stock   salt
2 large potatoes   grated cheese

This soup can be made with any kind of stock, including fish stock.
Strain the stock into a pan. Peel the potatoes and grate them into
it, stirring well to prevent formation of lumps. Season with salt to
taste, simmer 15–20 minutes. Serve with grated cheese.

Catalan Soup   *Sopa de payés*

4 oz. chick-peas   8 oz. sliced potatoes
1 teaspoon bicarbonate of soda   1 small sliced cabbage
1¼ lb. veal bones   1 sliced onion
1 ham bone   4 oz. blood sausage
5 pints water   4 oz. rice
salt   4 oz. thick vermicelli

Soak the chick-peas overnight in water with bicarbonate of soda.
Check the bones carefully and remove all splinters, as this soup is
not strained. Put the bones into a pan with water, add chick-peas;
skim it as it comes to the boil and simmer for 2 hours. Add salt
to taste, potatoes, cabbage and onion and simmer for another hour.
Add the sausage, rice and vermicelli. Cook for 12–15 minutes,
remove bones and black sausage. Slice the sausage. Pour soup into
a tureen, add sausage and serve.

Costa Brava Soup   *Sopa Costa Brava*

10 oz. monk-fish   4 oz. potato flour
16 oz. hake   ½ cup cold fish stock
3½ pints water   3 egg yolks
1 sliced onion   1–2 tablespoons milk
2 teaspoons salt   2 oz. butter
1 lb. tomatoes

Wash the fish but do not cut. Put whole in a pan of water, with onion and salt. Boil tomatoes until soft and sieve into the pan. Cook together for ½ hour. In another saucepan, mix the flour with fish stock. Strain soup, add to flour, etc. Mash hake, add to soup, simmer 15 minutes, stirring continuously. Dice the monk-fish. Dilute the yolks with milk in the soup tureen. Blend in butter, adding it in small pieces. Put in monk-fish, pour in soup, mix well and serve.

Monk-fish Soup   *Sopa de rape*

1¼ lb. monk-fish head
1 head hake
4 pints water
bouquet-garni
4 cloves garlic
2 teaspoons salt
1 chopped onion

8 oz. peeled and chopped tomatoes
3 tablespoons olive oil
1½ oz. pine kernels
6 oz. sliced bread
saffron
2 egg yolks

Cut the monk-fish head into pieces and put it to boil in a saucepan, together with the head of hake, *bouquet-garni*, two cloves of garlic and salt for half an hour. When cooked, strain and keep the stock. Skin and bone the fish, detach the small pieces of flesh, and add to the stock. In another saucepan, fry the onion and tomatoes in two tablespoons oil. Pound the pine kernels in a mortar (if a little monk-fish liver could be added, it would be an improvement). Add to tomato and onion and mix well. Add bread, turning the slices over, to flavour both sides. Pour the whole into the fish stock. Pound the rest of garlic in the mortar, with a few saffron pistils and a little olive oil. Stir the mixture into the soup and leave to simmer for 45 minutes. Dilute yolks in the soup tureen with a little water, to prevent curdling. Pour in the soup, stir well and serve.

Catalan Lent Soup   *Sopa de vigilia a la catalana*

4 oz. dried haricot beans
4 oz. dried conger-eel
3½ pints water
1 chopped onion
1 peeled and chopped tomato
2 tablespoons olive oil

½ lb. spinach
1 sliced onion
1 sliced potato
salt
3 oz. rice
3 oz. vermicelli

Soak the haricot beans and the conger-eel overnight. Rinse them and put in a saucepan of cold water. Cook on a medium heat for 2½ hours. Fry chopped onion and tomato in oil and add to the soup. Wash the spinach carefully and shred it. Add sliced onion, potato and spinach to the rest. Season with salt to taste, simmer 20 minutes, add rice and vermicelli. When these are cooked, the soup is ready.

Mussel Soup   *Sopa de mejillones*

24 big mussels
1 chopped onion
1 chopped tomato
2 tablespoons olive oil
½ teaspoon salt
¼ teaspoon pepper

2½ pints water
6 oz. sliced and toasted bread
1½ oz. roasted almonds
2 cloves garlic
1 sprig parsley
1 hard-boiled egg

Clean the mussels well and place in a frying pan over the fire to open. Remove shells and set the mussels aside with their juice. Fry the onion and tomato in oil, add salt, pepper, mussels and their juice and fry together for a few moments. Add hot water. Bring to the boil, add bread. Pound the almonds, garlic and parsley in a mortar. Chop hard-boiled egg and add with the almond mixture to the soup. Salt to taste, simmer for 45 minutes and serve.

Crayfish Soup　　　*Sopa de cangrejos de río*

1 sliced onion	4 tablespoons sherry
2 sliced carrots	pinch pepper
4 oz. butter	3 oz. rice flour
1 bay leaf	2½ pints milk
1 sprig thyme	4 oz. cream
30 small crayfish	2 yolks
2 tablespoons brandy	

Put onion and carrots in a saucepan with half the butter, bay leaf and thyme and cook lightly. Wash the crayfish and remove intestines by grasping the middle of the tail and pulling: as each one is thus cleaned, put it at once into the saucepan so as not to lose the juice. Cover the pan and cook for 5 minutes. Add brandy and sherry, stir, add pepper, cook 10 minutes, then remove from heat. Extract the meat, cut into pieces and keep. Pound the heads, legs and shells in a mortar and return to the pan with a tablespoon of water. Cook 10 minutes. In another pan, mix the flour and milk, cook a little. Rub the contents of the other pan through a sieve, pressing well, and add to milk and flour mixture. Cook for 10 minutes, stirring continuously. Remove from heat, add remaining butter and cream. Dilute the yolks with a little water in a soup tureen, add a pinch of pepper, crayfish and the contents from the pan. Stir well and serve.

NOTE. Very small crabs are also used in Spain for making this delicious soup, which is then called *Sopa de cangrejos*.

He that will look into his neighbour's pots must not cover his own

Soup Montserratina *Sopa montserratina*

4 oz. dried conger-eel
4 oz. dried haricot beans
4 oz. chick-peas
5¼ pints water
1 sliced onion

8 oz. sliced potatoes
1 medium-sized cauliflower
3–4 tablespoons olive oil
salt
4 oz. rice

Soak the conger-eel, haricot beans and chick-peas overnight. Rinse and put into a saucepan of cold water. Boil for 2 hours. Divide the cauliflower into flowerets. Heat oil and fry onion lightly. Add onion, potatoes and cauliflower to the soup. Simmer until all the vegetables disintegrate. Then sieve them into another saucepan, straining through all the soup, salt to taste, reheat, add rice. Simmer until rice is cooked and serve.

Bouillabaisse *Bullabesa*

2 lb. fish
4½ pints water
12 oz. tomatoes
1 carrot
2 large onions
3 or 4 cloves garlic
bouquet-garni
1 sprig mint
1 gill dry sherry

1 lemon
salt
8 oz. prawns
12 large clams
4 oz. olive oil
1 oz. flour
saffron
bread *croûtons*

The best fish for bouillabaisse are, among others, the John Dory, monk-fish, red mullet and hake, but the greater the variety the better. Put the fish into boiling water, with the peeled and quartered tomatoes, sliced carrots and onions, garlic, *bouquet-garni*, mint, sherry, a slice of lemon and salt to taste. Boil fast for 15 minutes; add whole prawns, clams and a little sauce, made by pounding some garlic with a little olive oil and stirring into it a pinch of saffron. Brown the flour lightly in a little olive oil in a frying pan. Add to soup. Cook 10 minutes and strain into another pan. Remove the bones and skin from the fish, cut the flesh into big chunks and put them on a serving dish. Remove the shells of the clams and prawns, cut into pieces and add them to the fish. Pour the very hot soup into a tureen and serve accompanied by the fish and *croûtons* of bread fried in oil.

Baked Stock Custard　　　*Flan de caldo*

3 egg yolks　　　　　　　　½ pint stock
1 egg

Beat together three yolks and one whole egg. Little by little, add stock, stir well and pour into a greased mould. Bake in the oven in a *bain-marie*, taking care that the water does not bubble. When cooked, allow the custard to cool, turn out of the mould and dice if it is to be added to a soup or a consommé. If it is intended as garnish for another dish, the custard is made in small individual moulds.

Potato and Tomato Soup　　　*Sopa de patatas y tomates*

2 lb. peeled potatoes　　　　1 teaspoon sugar
1 lb. tomatoes　　　　　　　1½ oz. butter
2 pints water　　　　　　　salt

Cook the potatoes and tomatoes, cut into pieces, in a saucepan of boiling water. When cooked, sieve the vegetables into another saucepan and add as much of the liquid in which they were cooked as necessary to obtain a purée consistency. Season with salt to taste, add sugar, simmer for 10 minutes. Remove from heat, stir in butter, adding it in small pieces, and serve.

Bread Croûtons   *Pan frito*

Slices of bread used as a foundation for certain preparations and as garnish. Cut thin slices of bread, remove crusts and cut slices into triangles, rounds, hearts, diamonds, crescents, dice, etc. Special cutters are available for fancy shapes. Fry in hot fat and drain well. They may be fried in butter, oil or other fat, depending on the nature of the dish for which they are intended.

Purée Soup, Country Style   *Puré a la campesina*

2 lb. potatoes   4 carrots
1 lb. onions   1 stick celery
1½ oz. butter   2 pints water

Cut up the vegetables and cook them in boiling salted water, rub through a sieve into another pan and add as much of the liquid in which they were cooked as required to obtain purée consistency. Reheat, pour into a soup tureen and blend in butter, adding it in small pieces.

Fresh Pea Soup   *Puré de guisantes tiernos*

2¼ lb. peas (shelled)   2 tablespoons olive oil
1 lb. sliced potatoes   1 chopped onion
2 sliced carrots   2 oz. butter
2 pints water   bread *croûtons* (see above)

Put the peas, the potatoes and carrots into salted boiling water. Fry the onion lightly in oil and add to the pan. Cook until the peas are tender. Rub through a sieve into another pan and reheat. Blend in the butter. Serve with *croûtons*. This soup must be of the consistency of thin cream.

Haricot Purée Soup   *Puré de judías blancas*

1¼ lb. white haricot beans
1 head garlic
1 sliced onion
2 tablespoons olive oil

½ teaspoon paprika
salt
2 oz. ham in one piece
1½ oz. butter

Cook the beans and garlic in water for about 2 hours. Fry the sliced onion in oil until golden, add paprika, stir well and add to beans. When the beans are almost cooked, season with salt to taste, rub all through a sieve. Keep hot. Dice the ham, fry lightly in butter and add to soup just before serving.

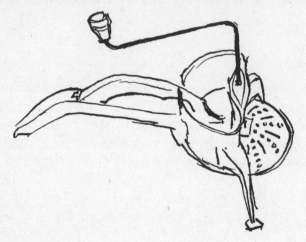

Vegetable Purée Soup   *Puré vegetal*

bicarbonate of soda
4 oz. dried peas
4 oz. dried broad beans
4 oz. dried haricot beans
4 oz. dried chick-peas
4 oz. lentils
5¼ pints water
1 ham bone
2 sticks celery

1 sliced onion
1 sliced tomato
2 sliced potatoes
2 sliced turnips
2 sliced carrots
2 leeks
2–3 tablespoons oil
salt
bread *croûtons* (p. 51)

Put all the dried vegetables to soak overnight in a pan of cold water with a little bicarbonate of soda. Rinse and put them in a saucepan of cold water, with the ham bone, potatoes, turnips, carrots and celery and simmer for $1\frac{1}{2}$–2 hours. Fry onion and tomato, add to soup, season with salt to taste, continue to cook for $1\frac{1}{2}$ hours. Rub through a sieve, reheat and serve with *croûtons* of bread fried in butter.

Gazpacho   *Gazpacho*

1 onion	white pepper
vinegar	4 tablespoons olive oil
5 slices crustless bread	peeled and seeded tomatoes
1 clove peeled garlic	green seeded pimento
1 large tin tomato juice	cucumber
$\frac{1}{2}$ pint iced water	hard-boiled egg
salt	croutons

Slice the onion, sprinkle with vinegar and leave to marinate. Soak the bread in water. Pound the garlic in a mortar, whisk it together with the tomato juice, bread, water, salt and pepper. Add oil drop by drop. Chill in the refrigerator. Dice the tomato, pimento, cucumber, hard-boiled egg and drained onion finely. Serve this garnish and *croûtons* in separate dishes with the chilled gazpacho. Just before serving add ice and, if necessary, more iced water. If a mixer is available, put all ingredients, except the diced garnish, into it, with oil. Season to taste, chill and serve as above.

ARROZ Y PASTAS ALIMENTICIAS

BEFORE cooking rice wash it well in a colander under a jet of water, until the liquid runs completely clear. Drain well. Sprinkle into plenty of salted boiling water. For plain boiled rice, cook for 15–20 minutes. Strain, rinse with boiling water to separate grains.

Catalan Rice   *Arroz a la catalana*

1 tender chicken	18 mussels
2 oz. lard	8 oz. peas (shelled)
thyme	1¼ lb. rice
½ gill white wine	salt
2 tablespoons olive oil	3 or 4 cloves garlic
1 lb. squid	saffron
8 oz. finely chopped onions	1–2 teaspoons olive oil
8 oz. tomatoes, peeled and chopped	1 pimento

Clean and joint the chicken and fry in lard in a saucepan until golden. Add a small sprig of thyme and a little white wine. Cover, leave until almost cooked and remove, as it will finish cooking with the rice. In another pan heat the oil. Clean and cut up squid, add to oil, cover and cook on a very low heat until soft. Add onions, brown lightly, add tomatoes, then the mussels. Cover the pan until the mussels open, shaking it from time to time. Transfer the contents of this pan to the pan containing the chicken, and add rice. Let it fry a little, pour in boiling water (two cups to every cup of rice) and add the peas. Season with salt. Pound garlic in a mortar with a little saffron, bind with olive oil and add to pan. Cook for 20 minutes. Decorate with strips of pimento and serve.

Spanish Rice   *Arroz a la española*

3 heads hake	1 chopped onion
1 sliced onion	1 tablespoon lard
4 cloves garlic	1¼ lb. rice
1 bay leaf	2–3 tablespoons olive oil
parsley	4 oz. diced loin of pork
thyme	4 chicken livers
salt	3 oz. butter
water	1½ oz. flour
pinch sugar	½ pint milk
12 oz. tomatoes	1 egg yolk

Make a fish stock using the heads of hake, one onion, two cloves of garlic, a sprig of parsley, a bay leaf, a sprig of thyme, salt and sufficient water for the quantity of rice (allowing a little more than two cups for every cup of rice). While this is boiling, prepare tomato sauce (p. 71) using tomatoes, two cloves of garlic and sugar, and put it aside. In another saucepan, fry chopped onion in lard. When it begins to colour, add well-rinsed rice, let it fry a little, then pour in strained fish stock. Cook for 15 minutes, when the liquid will have evaporated. While the rice is cooking, heat olive oil in a frying pan and fry the pork and chicken livers. Remove, and using the same pan make a *béchamel* sauce (p. 70) using $1\frac{1}{2}$ oz. butter, flour and milk. Cut chicken livers into small pieces, and add, together with pork, to the sauce. Remove from heat, mix in an egg yolk and the rest of the butter. Butter a ring mould, put in the rice, pressing it down a little, and put in the oven for 5 minutes. Turn out on to a round dish, cover with tomato sauce and fill with the pork and chicken liver mixture.

Milan Rice   *Arroz a la milanesa*

4 oz. ham in one piece	$1\frac{1}{2}$ lb. rice
1 onion	boiling water
1 bay leaf	4 oz. grated cheese
2 oz. lard	1 tablespoon chopped parsley
8 oz. tomatoes, peeled and chopped	$1\frac{1}{2}$ oz. butter
8 oz. cooked peas	1 teaspoon salt
pinch pepper	1 sweet pimento

Cut the ham and onion into small pieces and fry in lard with a bay leaf. When the onion begins to colour, add tomatoes, peas and pepper. Cook for a moment, add rice and stir until it begins to colour. Pour in boiling water (allowing two cups for every cup of rice), add cheese, parsley, butter and salt. Cook for 15 minutes (when all the water will have evaporated). Remove from heat, decorate with strips of pimento, put in the oven for 5 minutes and serve in the cooking dish.

Montesina Rice   *Arroz a la montesina*

1 jointed rabbit
2 oz. lard
8 oz. sliced mushrooms
2 tablespoons olive oil
1 sliced onion
4 cloves chopped garlic
8 oz. tomatoes, peeled and chopped

1 teaspoon salt
½ teaspoon pepper
1½ lb. rice
2 diced pimentos
1½ oz. pounded roasted almonds

Heat the lard in a saucepan and brown the rabbit lightly. Add mushrooms, simmer for 10 minutes and remove pan from heat. In another saucepan, fry the onion in oil. When it begins to colour, add garlic and fry a moment without browning. Add tomatoes, season with salt and pepper; cook lightly, add rice, fry it a little, add rabbit and mushrooms, stir well, pour in two cups of boiling water for every cup of rice, taste, add more salt if necessary. Add almonds and pimentos. Cook for 20 minutes, leave for 5 minutes on the side of the stove and serve.

Rice Bellavista   *Arroz bellavista*

1½ lb. rice
salt
1 bay leaf
2½ pints boiling water
3 pig's kidneys
1 teaspoon flour

1 gill white wine
3 cloves garlic
chopped parsley
3 oz. butter
6 eggs
pimento (optional)

Cook the rice in boiling salted water with bay leaf and drain. Prepare *sauté* kidneys (p. 216), using kidneys, flour, wine, garlic and parsley. Scramble the eggs lightly with half the butter and a little salt, taking care to keep them creamy. Grease a ring mould, blend the rest of the butter into the cooked rice, press it into the mould and put in the oven for a moment. Turn out on to a round dish, garnish the borders with kidneys, fill the centre with scrambled eggs. To make the presentation of the dish more complete, put strips of pimento around the top of the rice ring.

White Rice with Eggs   *Arroz blanco con huevos*

1 finely chopped onion
3 tablespoons olive oil
4 oz. peeled and chopped tomatoes
pinch salt
pinch paprika

12 oz. raw blood sausage
1½ lb. rice
4 cloves peeled garlic
6 eggs

Fry the onion in one tablespoon oil until golden. Add tomatoes, season with salt and paprika, stir. Skin and mash sausage with a fork, add to pan and fry lightly. Cook the rice in boiling salted water with whole cloves of garlic. Drain, remove garlic, and immediately add two tablespoons of olive oil. Mix well, put out on to a round dish and spread the contents of the frying pan on top of the rice. Finally, place a fried egg in the centre and the other fried eggs around it.

Rice with Pigeon   *Arroz con pichón*

2 tablespoons lard
1 jointed pigeon
2 oz. diced fat salted pork
1 chopped onion
chopped garlic

1–2 tablespoons chopped parsley
8 oz. peeled and chopped tomatoes
boiling salted water
1 lb. rice
1 pimento

Heat lard in a saucepan and fry the pigeon. Add pork, onion, garlic to taste, parsley and tomatoes. Fry lightly. Pour in boiling salted water (allowing a little more than two cups of water for every cup of rice). Boil until the pigeon is almost cooked. Add rice and cook for 15 minutes. Turn out on to a dish and decorate with strips of pimento.

Rice with Dried Cod   *Arroz con bacalao*

8 oz. dried cod
2 tablespoons olive oil
1 finely chopped onion
1 chopped green pimento
8 oz. peeled, chopped tomatoes
8 oz. shelled peas
18 mussels

3 cloves garlic
1½ lb. rice
boiling water
1 tablespoon chopped parsley
salt
pinch saffron

Place the cod on a hot grill to loosen skin. Remove skin and bones, break cod into small pieces, wash well to take the salt out, squeeze and put it aside on a plate. Heat olive oil in a saucepan and fry the onion and the pimento. When they begin to colour, add tomatoes, peas, cod and well washed mussels. Fry lightly, add rice, stir, pour in boiling water (allowing two cups to every cup of rice). When it begins to bubble, stir in parsley, salt to taste, garlic, pounded in a mortar with saffron and bound with a little olive oil. Simmer 15–20 minutes and serve.

Lent Rice   *Arroz de vigilia*

3 large heads of hake
24 mussels
½ gill white wine
4 cloves garlic
bouquet-garni

2 gherkins
1½ lb. rice
1 egg
olive oil for mayonnaise sauce

Wash the heads of hake and the mussels thoroughly and put them in a saucepan with enough cold water to cover, add wine, three cloves garlic, *bouquet garni* and salt to taste. Bring to the boil then simmer for 30 minutes. Strain into another saucepan, and cook the rice in this liquid for 20 minutes. Put cooked rice on a dish and cover with mayonnaise sauce (p. 74) made with one clove of garlic and one egg. Take mussels out of their shells. Decorate rice with mussels, alternating with discs of gherkin.

Economical Rice   *Arroz económico*

1¼ lb. rice	3 cloves garlic
2 oz. butter	18 large mussels
3 oz. grated cheese	breadcrumbs
1 lb. tomatoes	chopped parsley

Cook the rice in boiling salted water, drain, mix in butter and cheese and press it into a mould for 5 minutes. Make tomato sauce (p. 71) using 1 lb. tomatoes and two cloves garlic. Prepare mussels *au gratin* (p. 168) using one clove of garlic, breadcrumbs and parsley. Turn out the rice on to a dish, cover with tomato sauce, garnish with mussels and serve.

Scarlet Rice   *Arroz escarlata*

2–3 tablespoons olive oil	salt
1 finely chopped onion	½ gill sherry (or brandy)
2 diced carrots	1 tablespoon flour
8 oz. large prawns	8 oz. peeled and sliced tomatoes
1 bay leaf	2 oz. butter
1 sprig thyme	8 oz. rice

Heat oil in a saucepan and fry the carrots and onion lightly. Add prawns, bay leaf and thyme. Season with salt, sprinkle with sherry and cook gently for 10 minutes. Extract the prawns and remove heads and shells; pound these latter in a mortar and return them to the saucepan. Add flour, tomatoes and half cup water. Simmer for 30 minutes, stirring from time to time to prevent sticking. Rub the purée through a sieve to make a thick sauce. Add half the butter and keep the sauce hot without allowing it to boil. Cook the rice in boiling salted water as described, drain, and mix in the rest of the butter. Divide the rice into small individual dishes, cover with the sauce, put a prawn in the centre of each and serve.

Costa Blanca Rice — *Arroz Costa Blanca*

2 oz. lard
3 tablespoons olive oil
8 oz. cuttle-fish or squid
8 oz. finely chopped onions
1 sliced pimento
8 oz. tomatoes, peeled and chopped
1 sprig parsley
pinch pepper
pinch paprika
8 oz. shelled peas

3 globe artichokes
1 lb. clams
1½ lb. rice
boiling water
salt
8 oz. conger-eel
8 oz. large prawns
3 or 4 cloves garlic
pinch saffron

Heat lard and olive oil in a saucepan and add the cuttle-fish or squid, well cleaned and cut into pieces, but without salt, as it hardens the fish. Cover the pan and leave it to cook on the lowest possible heat until the fish is soft. Add onions and pimento. When the onions become golden, add tomatoes, parsley, pepper and paprika. Put in peas, artichokes, previously cooked until tender and quartered, and, lastly, the well washed clams. Cook gently together for a few moments, then add the rice, measuring it out in cups. Fry a little, pour in boiling water (two cups for every cup of rice) and season with salt. When it begins to bubble, add the conger-eel (cut into pieces, rolled in flour and fried), the raw prawns, and three or four cloves garlic pounded with saffron and bound with a little olive oil. Season with salt and cook 15–20 minutes.

Rice María   *Arroz María*

8 oz. hake	1 bay leaf
8 oz. monk-fish	1 sprig thyme
8 oz. large prawns	1 sprig mint
24 mussels	salt
2 tablespoons dry sherry	1½ lb. rice
garlic	tomato sauce (p. 71)

Boil all the fish, prawns, mussels with sherry, garlic to taste, bay leaf, thyme, mint and salt in water for 20 minutes. Strain into another saucepan and use the stock for cooking the rice. Prepare tomato sauce using 1¼ lb. tomatoes. When the rice is cooked, turn it out on to a dish, cover with the fish, skinned, boned and cut up into small pieces. Remove the head and shells of the prawns, cut into pieces and mix them with the fish. Pour the tomato sauce over the dish, decorate with shelled mussels and serve.

NOTE. The amount of water should be carefully measured out so that, allowing for evaporation, there will still be two cups of liquid for every cup of rice.

Rice Margarita   *Arroz Margarita*

1¼ lb. veal bones	3 oz. grated cheese
1 onion	4 chicken livers
1 carrot	2 tablespoons olive oil
1 turnip	12 oz. tomatoes
3 oz. butter	pinch salt
1 sliced onion	½ teaspoon sugar
1½ lb. rice	

Make a stock using veal bones, one onion, carrot and turnip. Heat half the butter in a saucepan and fry the sliced onion. Add well rinsed and drained rice, fry with the onion, and add the strained stock (allowing two cups of liquid to one of rice). Cook the rice for 10 minutes, add half the cheese and finish cooking. Turn out on to a heat-resisting dish. Drop the tomatoes into boiling water, simmer for a few minutes, peel and rub through a fine sieve. Fry the chicken livers in oil, remove and in the same pan cook the tomato purée. Cut up the livers, return them to the frying pan, add salt and sugar, cook for 5 minutes, then pour this sauce over the rice, sprinkle the rest of the grated cheese on top, and add the rest of the butter in small pieces. Put in a hot oven for a few minutes and serve.

Rice Mignon   *Arroz Mignon*

2 tablespoons lard	½ teaspoon salt
1 tender jointed chicken	1 chopped truffle
1 finely chopped onion	1½ lb. rice
1 tablespoon flour	2 oz. butter
½ pint water	2 raw yolks

Heat the lard in a pan and lightly brown the chicken. Add onion. When the chicken is almost cooked, remove it and put the flour into the pan. Fry it lightly, add water, salt and truffle. Return the chicken to the pan and finish cooking on a very low heat. Boil the rice in salted water, strain, and mix in the butter. Put it in a mould for 5 minutes, turn it out on to a round dish and surround it with chicken pieces. Add yolks to the sauce in the pan, blend well and pour over the rice.

Beef in peace and quietness is better than chicken with sour sauce

Paella Valenciana   *Paella Valenciana*

1 tender chicken
salt
½ pint olive oil
8 oz. loin of pork
8 oz. chipolata sausages
8 oz. squid
4 oz. finely chopped onions
1 sliced pimento (or small tin of
    pimento)

12 oz. tomatoes
8 oz. mussels
1½ lb. rice
1 lobster or 8 oz. large prawns
8 oz. French beans
8 oz. peas (shelled)
4 cloves garlic
saffron

Joint and salt the chicken. Heat five to six tablespoons oil in a large saucepan and fry the chicken until golden. When it is half cooked, add the pork, the sausages and the squid, all cut into pieces, cover the pan and leave to cook on a very low heat. When it is ready, add onions and pimento (if tin pimento is used, do not add it until after the water has been poured into the rice). When they begin to colour, add the peeled and chopped tomatoes, fry together and add the mussels. As soon as the mussels open out remove pan from heat.

Heat the rest of the oil in a large two-handled frying pan (or *paella*), put in the rice, fry lightly, and immediately mix in all the contents of the saucepan. Stir well, and pour in boiling water (two cups of water to one cup of rice); add raw prawns (or lobster), the beans and peas, and four cloves garlic, pounded together with some saffron pistils and bound with a little olive oil. Bring to the boil, simmer for 15 minutes and remove the pan from heat.

Before serving allow to stand for 5–10 minutes. Another equally successful way of cooking a *paella* is by using a boiling fowl instead of a roasting chicken and letting the stock cool to skim off the fat, when it can be warmed and used for cooking the rice instead of boiling water.

Rice Mould   *Pastel de arroz*

1 lb. hake	salt
1 carrot	1 lb. rice
1 bay leaf	oil for mayonnaise sauce
1 sprig parsley	1 egg
1 stick celery	1 clove pounded garlic
1 sprig thyme	

Boil the hake, carrot, bay leaf, parsley, celery and thyme in salted water for 10 minutes. Strain into another pan, and boil the rice in this stock. When cooked, drain, put half the rice in a greased mould. Skin, bone and cut up the hake into small pieces. Put the fish on top of rice in mould, cover with a layer of mayonnaise sauce (p. 74) made with one clove garlic and one egg. Cover with the rest of the rice and press it down well. Put the mould in the oven to heat it through. Turn the rice out of the mould and cover it with the rest of the mayonnaise.

Canneloni   *Canalones*

24 *canneloni pasta* squares	4 oz. butter
1 chopped onion	2¼ oz. flour
2 tablespoons lard	1¼ pinto milk
8 oz. lean diced pork	2 tablespoons olive oil
1 set diced lamb's brains	1 lb. tomatoes
3 diced chicken livers	2 oz. grated cheese
1 small truffle	

Make the filling for the *canneloni* in the following way: lightly fry the onion in lard, add pork, brains and chicken livers. Fry for a few minutes and mince them with the truffle. Using the same frying pan add two tablespoons butter, stir in a heaped tablespoon flour, cook lightly, dilute with a cup of milk and cook for 5 minutes. Mix in the minced ingredients, cook for another 5 minutes, and remove from heat.

Cook the *canneloni pasta* in boiling salted water with two tablespoons olive oil for 10 minutes, putting them in one by one to prevent sticking. Strain, rinse under the cold tap, place separately on a clean cloth, put a tablespoon of filling in the centre of each and roll. Make a *béchamel* sauce using the rest of the flour, butter and milk. Cover the bottom of an oven-proof oblong dish with a layer of the sauce and place the *canneloni*, side by side, in the dish. Make a sauce by boiling the tomatoes and pressing them through a sieve and pour over the *canneloni*. Cover with the rest of the *béchamel* sauce, sprinkle with grated cheese and a little melted butter. Put in the oven to brown the top.

Fish Canneloni   *Canalones de pescado*

24 *canneloni pasta* squares	2 hard-boiled eggs
8 oz. monk-fish	1 truffle
8 oz. prawns	4 oz. butter
1 bay leaf	2½ oz. flour
olive oil	½ pint milk
2 tablespoons white wine	1 lb. tomatoes
1 teaspoon salt	2 oz. grated cheese
boiling water	

To prepare the filling, put the monk-fish, prawns, bay leaf, a tablespoon olive oil, wine and salt into a saucepan with enough boiling water to cover the fish, and simmer for 15 minutes. Strain the fish and keep the stock. Skin and bone the monk-fish, shell the prawns, and chop them together with eggs and truffle. Melt half the butter in a small saucepan and stir in 1 oz. flour, gradually adding 8 oz. milk, making a thick *béchamel* sauce. Mix in the chopped ingredients and season with salt. Cook all together for 12–15 minutes and fill the *canneloni*, then proceed as in recipe for *Canneloni*, using fish stock for making the *béchamel* sauce.

Catalan Vermicelli   *Fideos a la catalana*

12 oz. rib of pork	parsley
2 oz. lard	4 oz. sausages
1 chopped onion	1¼ lb. vermicelli
8 oz. tomatoes	

Cut the pork ribs into small pieces and fry in lard until golden. Add onion, brown lightly. Peel the tomatoes, chop together with the parsley and add to onion. Halve the sausages and add to pan. As soon as the sausages are cooked, put in broken up vermicelli, fry for a few moments then pour in a little boiling water and add salt to taste. When the vermicelli is cooked, serve immediately.

Vegetable Macaroni   *Macarrones a la jardinera*

8 oz. string beans	1 sliced red pimento
4 carrots	4 oz. butter
8 oz. peas (shelled)	2 lb. tomatoes
1¼ lb. macaroni	pinch pepper
salt	3 oz. grated cheese
1 chopped onion	

Cut up the beans and the carrots and cook them together with the peas in boiling salted water. Drain. Cook the macaroni in boiling salted water and drain. Fry the onion and pimento in a little butter. When the onion becomes golden, add half the tomatoes, peeled and chopped. Fry a little, then mix in boiled vegetables, cover the pan and leave to cook over a moderate heat for 10 minutes. Season with salt and pepper. Add macaroni and mix well.

Butter an oven-proof dish and turn the contents of the pan into it. Sprinkle with grated cheese and cover with tomato sauce (p. 71) made with the rest of the tomatoes. Scatter with pieces of butter, and put in the oven to brown the top.

Macaroni with Fillet of Pork   *Macarrones con lomo*

1¼ lb. macaroni
1½ oz. butter

sauce for meat (p. 75)
1 lb. fillet of pork

Cook the macaroni in boiling water with salt, drain and mix in the butter together with the sauce. Blend well and turn out on to a dish. Cut the pork into strips, fry and arrange on top of the macaroni. Pour the fat in which they were fried over the dish.

Macaroni Stew   *Macarrones guisados*

8 oz. diced lean pork
3 chicken livers
2 tablespoons lard
1 chopped onion
8 oz. tomatoes, peeled and chopped

1¼ lb. macaroni
boiling water
salt
3 oz. grated cheese

Fry the pork and chicken livers in lard, remove, and in the same fat fry the onion. When this begins to colour, add tomatoes, fry lightly. Chop the livers and pork finely and add to pan. When all the ingredients are cooked, break up and add the macaroni, fry together for 5 minutes, pour in enough boiling water to cook the macaroni, simmer season with salt, remove from heat, add grated cheese, stir well and serve.

Spanish Noodles au Gratin   *Tallarines al gratín*

3 oz. butter
2 oz. flour
1 pint milk
3 chicken livers

1¼ lb. noodles
2 oz. finely chopped ham
3 oz. grated cheese

Make a *béchamel* sauce (p. 70) using half the butter and all the flour and the milk. Chop chicken livers finely and add to sauce. Put a saucepan with plenty of water on the fire, bring to the boil, add salt, toss in noodles. Cook for 15 minutes, drain, return noodles to pan, add ham, half the cheese and the *béchamel* sauce, stir well and turn out into an oven-proof dish. Sprinkle with the rest of the cheese, dot with butter and brown lightly in the oven.

SALSAS

All-i-oli   *Salsa all-i-oli*

4 cloves garlic   4 tablespoons olive oil
pinch salt

Pound garlic in a mortar and season with salt. Mash to a paste, add olive oil drop by drop, stirring continuously in the same direction, until a smooth sauce is obtained. If, for whatever reason, the *all-i-oli* does not thicken, or if it gets thin after it has thickened, remove it from the mortar, pound a teaspoon of bread-crumbs in the mortar and add the sauce mixture drop by drop, stirring as before.

NOTE. This is the original recipe for *all-i-oli* which means garlic-and-oil in Catalan, not to be confused with garlic mayonnaise (p. 74).

Béchamel Sauce　　　*Salsa béchamel*

1½ oz. butter　　　　　½ pint milk
2 tablespoons flour　　 salt

Melt butter in a saucepan and stir flour into it. Cook carefully without allowing the flour to brown, add milk gradually, to prevent formation of lumps. Season with salt to taste, and simmer gently for 10 minutes. The consistency must be smooth and creamy.

White Sauce　　　*Salsa blanca*

White sauce is made in the same way as *béchamel* sauce with the sole difference that stock or water is used instead of milk.

Villeroi Sauce　　　*Salsa a la Villeroi*

Reduce *béchamel* sauce (p. 70) to concentrate and thicken the consistency and add finely chopped truffle. Use for coating various foods intended for dipping in egg and breadcrumbs and frying.

Colbert Sauce　　　*Salsa Colbert*

½ pint stock or meat glaze　　　1 tablespoon chopped parsley
2 oz. butter　　　　　　　　　　1 tablespoon sherry
juice of ½ lemon

Heat stock in a saucepan. Remove from heat, blend in slightly softened butter and beat well, add lemon juice, parsley and sherry, Keep it hot in a *bain-marie*. This sauce must not boil.

Cream Sauce　　　*Salsa crema*

Make this in the same way as *béchamel* sauce, but when removed from heat stir in a yolk of egg and a little butter.

Mushroom Sauce   *Salsa de champiñones*

1 tablespoon olive oil   ½ teaspoon salt
1 oz. butter   ¼ teaspoon pepper
1 finely chopped onion   1 clove pounded garlic
1 tablespoon flour   4 oz. finely chopped mushrooms
1 gill white wine   1 teaspoon chopped parsley
1½ gills water

Heat oil and butter in a saucepan; fry the onion, and when it begins to colour, add the flour. Cook until golden, gradually pour in the wine and water, stirring continuously. Season with salt and pepper. Add garlic and cook gently for 10 minutes. Add mushrooms and parsley and simmer for a further 10 minutes.

NOTE. If fresh mushrooms are used, parboil them for 10 minutes. Tinned mushrooms need only be rinsed.

Mushroom (or Truffle) Fumet

Fumet de champiñones o de trufas

This *Fumet* (see note in Glossary) is used to enhance the flavour of certain sauces. Simmer mushroom or truffle peelings in Madeira (or similar heavy wine), boiling the liquid down almost to nothing. This fumet is usually made when the mushrooms or truffles are being used for some other purpose.

Tomato Sauce   *Salsa de tomate*

1 lb. ripe tomatoes   1 teaspoon sugar
½ cup water   ¼ teaspoon pepper
2 tablespoons olive oil   1 tablespoon butter (optional)
2–3 cloves garlic   1 teaspoon chopped parsley (op-
½ teaspoon salt   tional)

Cook tomatoes with a little water until soft. Drain and rub through a fine sieve. Heat oil in a pan. Crush the garlic slightly and fry until golden, then remove and pour in the tomato purée. Add salt, pepper and sugar, and cook for 10 minutes. If desired, chopped parsley and a little butter may be added.

Egg Sauce   *Salsa de huevos*

3 hard-boiled eggs
1–2 tablespoons olive oil
1 teaspoon vinegar
½ teaspoon salt

¼ teaspoon pepper
1 teaspoon chopped parsley
milk

Shell the eggs when cold and separate the yolks from the whites. Mash the yolks with a fork, and bind them with a little olive oil until they form a thick and smooth paste. Add vinegar, salt, pepper, parsley and enough milk to give the sauce the consistency of cream. Chop the whites and stir them into the sauce; mix well.

Katherine Sauce   *Salsa Katherine*

½ gill tarragon vinegar
3 raw yolks
3 oz. melted butter

salt
pepper
1 tablespoon chopped chervil

Pour vinegar into a small saucepan and bring it to the boil, remove from heat and cool, add yolks, re-heat in a double saucepan, keeping the water just below boiling point, stir vigorously until the sauce thickens. Add butter by degrees, season with salt and pepper to taste, add chervil and serve.

Red Sauce   *Salsa encarnada*

1 large ripe tomato
1 clove pounded garlic
1 tablespoon grated breadcrumbs
1 tablespoon vinegar

pinch paprika
pinch salt
olive oil

Scald tomato, peel, and remove seeds. Pound in a mortar with garlic and breadcrumbs previously soaked in vinegar. Season with paprika and salt. Mix well, then add the olive oil little by little until the desired consistency is reached.

Scarlet Sauce   *Salsa escarlata*

1 tinned red pimento	olive oil
1 egg yolk	juice ½ lemon
pinch salt	

Pound the red pimento in a mortar, add yolk of egg, salt and olive oil, little by little, stirring all the time until the required quantity is reached. Finish off with lemon juice.

Spanish Sauce   *Salsa española*

2 tablespoons olive oil	1 tablespoon chopped parsley
1 tablespoon flour	1 bay leaf
1 gill white wine	1 clove
1 sliced onion	salt and pepper
1 crushed clove garlic	1 pint water
1 sliced carrot	1 ham bone

Heat oil in a saucepan and fry the flour until golden. Add wine, bring to the boil and add onion, garlic, carrot, parsley, bay leaf and clove. Season with salt and pepper to taste. Cook lightly together, add water and ham bone, cover the pan, simmer for 1 hour, strain through a fine strainer and serve.

Hollandaise Sauce   *Salsa holandesa*

4 oz. butter	3 egg yolks
1 tablespoon vinegar	salt and pepper

Melt butter in a *bain-marie*, add vinegar and yolks, stirring them in one by one. Be very careful not to let the sauce boil, otherwise it will curdle. Stir well until it thickens to the consistency of cream. Season with salt and a little pepper. If the sauce is too thick, dilute with a teaspoon of warm water. Keep hot in a *bain-marie*.

English Sauce   *Salsa inglesa*

1 tablespoon butter	1 tablespoon dry sherry
2 tablespoons flour	2 tablespoons mushroom *fumet*
1 gill white stock	1 tablespoon tomato purée
pinch salt	

Make a white sauce (p. 70), add sherry, mushroom *fumet* (p. 71) and tomato purée. Season with salt.

Mayonnaise   *Salsa mahonesa*

1–2 yolks of egg	olive oil
salt and pepper	lemon juice or vinegar

Put the yolk (or yolks, depending on quantity of sauce required) into a bowl, add salt and pepper, stir well, start adding olive oil drop by drop, stirring all the time in the same direction. When the sauce thickens sufficiently, add vinegar (or lemon juice). Continue to stir and add oil until enough sauce is obtained. Should the sauce fail to thicken, or curdles half way through, a few drops of cold water will set it right. If this does not help, begin the operation all over again. Take another bowl, rinse it out with cold water and, *without drying the bowl*, put in a fresh yolk and add the curdled mayonnaise drop by drop, stirring all the time and in the same direction until all is used up.

Garlic Mayonnaise   *Salsa mahonesa con ajo*

Add one pounded clove garlic to the egg yolk in the bowl and proceed as for ordinary mayonnaise sauce.

Muselina Mayonnaise   *Salsa mahonesa muselina*

Make an ordinary mayonnaise sauce. Beat the egg whites until very stiff and fold them into the sauce. Prepared in this way the sauce is lighter and more frothy.

Maître d'Hôtel Sauce   *Salsa a la maître d'hôtel*

3 oz. butter   1½ tablespoons chopped parsley
¼ teaspoon salt   ½ tablespoon lemon juice
pinch pepper

Cream the butter in a bowl. Season with salt and pepper. Add parsley and mix well. Slowly add lemon juice, stirring all the time.

Mornay Sauce   *Salsa Mornay*

Make a *béchamel* sauce (p. 70) and add to it 2½ oz. grated Gruyère cheese and a tablespoon finely chopped parsley.

Muselina Sauce   *Salsa muselina*

4 oz. butter   3 yolks
1 teaspoon rice flour   salt and pepper
1 tablespoon vinegar   2 tablespoons whipped cream

Melt butter in a *bain-marie*, blend in rice flour, add vinegar, stir in yolks one by one, season to taste, stir until the sauce thickens, incorporate whipped cream. Keep hot in a *bain-marie* and on no account allow sauce to boil. Whisk vigorously before serving.

Sauce for Meat   *Salsa para carnes*

1 tablespoon lard   4 oz. sliced mushrooms
1 truffle   1 tablespoon flour
½ wineglass dry sherry   ½ pint stock
2 oz. diced ham

Heat lard in a small saucepan and lightly fry a truffle cut into strips. Pour in the sherry and simmer to reduce a little. Add ham and mushrooms, blend in the flour, cook until it browns lightly, gradually add stock and cook gently for 5 minutes.

Spanish Supreme Sauce   *Salsa suprema*

Pound a little lemon peel and a small piece of onion in a mortar. When well pounded, mix in the yolk of an egg, then, little by little add olive oil, stirring vigorously; when the sauce is almost made add a few drops of vinegar and salt.

Tartare Sauce   *Salsa tartara*

Make a mayonnaise sauce (p. 74); add to it 10 capers, and a gherkin and chervil, both well chopped. If the sauce is too thick, add a few drops of tepid water.

Green Sauce   *Salsa verde*

Pound in a mortar a crustless slice of bread, soaked in vinegar, with a few sprigs of parsley to a smooth paste. Season with salt. Gradually, add olive oil until a fairly thick sauce is obtained.

Victoria Sauce   *Salsa Victoria*

Make a mayonnaise (p. 74) flavoured with two tablespoons tomato sauce (p. 71), a little chopped truffle and grated peel of half an orange.

Spanish Vinaigrette Sauce   *Salsa vinagreta*

1 onion	salt
1 hard-boiled egg	oil
1 tablespoon chopped parsley	vinegar

Chop an onion very finely, add a hard-boiled egg and parsley and chop well together. Put in a bowl, season with salt and mix in olive oil and vinegar in the required quantity, allowing one tablespoon vinegar to three tablespoons oil.

Clam or Mussel Butter   *Manteca de almejas o de mejillones*

2 dozen clams   4 oz. butter

Boil clams, remove shells and pound them in a mortar into a smooth paste. Add butter and mix well. Mussels can be used instead of clams.

Anchovy Butter   *Manteca de anchoas*

Wash and bone the anchovies, pound in a mortar into a smooth paste; mix in butter in the proportion of six anchovies to 4 oz. butter.

Crayfish Butter   *Manteca de cangrejos de río*

6 oz. crayfish   4 oz. butter

Wash and boil crayfish, pound in a mortar. Melt butter in a saucepan, add crayfish, stir a few times, remove from heat and rub through a sieve. Store in a jar with a well-fitting lid.

Pimento Butter   *Manteca de pimiento*

2 tinned sweet pimentos   seasoning
4 oz. butter

Pound pimentos in a mortar. Add butter, season to taste and mix well.

NOTE. These butters are used in some sauces, or as *canapés* spreads.

Romesco Sauce   *Salsa romesco*

2 large peeled tomatoes
6 cloves garlic
12 roasted almonds
olive oil

1 teaspoon vinegar
½ teaspoon salt
1 dessertspoon paprika

Pound tomatoes and garlic together in a mortar with almonds. Bind with olive oil, adding it gradually to desired consistency. Add vinegar, salt and paprika. Mix well and rub through a sieve. Serve with hot or cold lobster, or with any other fish, especially grilled fish.

Samfaina Sauce   *Salsa samfaina*

Chop, not too finely, some aubergines, tomatoes, pimentos and marrow, season and fry lightly in oil. This sauce is typical of the Spanish eastern seaboard, and delicious with chicken (p. 224), or pork. The proportions of ingredients can be varied, according to taste.

The best sauce is hunger and a good appetite

VERDURAS Y LEGUMBRES

Spinach with Eggs *Acelgas con huevos*

3½ lb. spinach
2 oz. butter
1 oz. flour

½ pint milk
3 hard-boiled eggs
1 oz. grated cheese

Cut the spinach and rinse well to remove all dirt. Cook fast in boiling salted water for 5 minutes. Drain and chop finely. Make *béchamel* sauce (p. 70) using 1 oz. butter, the flour and the milk. Put half the spinach in an oven-proof dish, and cover with slices of hard-boiled egg. Cover with the remaining spinach, pour *béchamel* sauce over it, sprinkle with cheese and the rest of the butter and put in the oven to brown the top.

79

Spinach and Ham   *Espinacas con jamón*

2¼ lb. spinach
salt
1 oz. lard

2 oz. ham in thick slices
2 chopped hard-boiled eggs
noisette potatoes (p. 112)

Pick over, wash and boil the spinach in salted water. Rinse under a cold tap, drain well and chop. Heat lard in a frying pan. Dice and fry the ham. Remove the ham and in the same fat lightly toss the spinach. Put the spinach on a dish, sprinkle with chopped hard-boiled eggs, scatter the fried ham on top and garnish with fried *noisette* potatoes.

Creamed Spinach   *Espinacas a la crema*

2¼ lb. spinach
salt
2 oz. butter
1¾ oz. flour

1 pint milk
2 raw yolks
croûtons

Boil the spinach in salted water, drain, press to extract all the water and chop very finely.

Make *béchamel* sauce (p. 70) using the butter, flour and milk. When it is cooked, add spinach, mix well, cook gently for 10 minutes, remove from heat, add yolks and stir well. Put the spinach in a dish with small *croûtons* of bread fried in butter.

Spinach Fritters   *Fritos de espinacas*

1½ lb. spinach
1 cup olive oil
4 oz. butter
1 finely chopped onion

½ teaspoon salt
¼ teaspoon pepper
8 eggs
2 oz. breadcrumbs

Wash the spinach and cook in plenty of boiling salted water. Drain and chop. Heat one tablespoon oil and 1 oz. butter in a frying pan. Fry the onion lightly. Add spinach, season with salt and pepper, fry for a couple of minutes. Make some omelettes using this mixture and six beaten eggs, put on a plate and, when cold, cut into triangles. A few moments before serving, dip the spinach omelette triangles in beaten egg and grated breadcrumbs, fry in the rest of the butter mixed with olive oil. This dish makes an excellent accompaniment to meat.

Boiled Artichokes   *Alcachofas hervidas*

Choose good, firm globe artichokes. Remove outside leaves, cut off the points and cook the artichokes in boiling salted water with half a lemon, a teaspoon of flour and a tablespoon of olive oil. Drain, and leave to cool. Cut into four or six pieces and arrange on a dish. Serve green sauce (p. 76) in a sauce-boat.

Fried Artichokes   *Alcachofas rebozadas*

Boil the artichokes as described in the previous recipe. Drain well; if small leave whole, if large cut into pieces. Roll in flour and beaten egg and fry in very hot olive oil until golden.

Artichokes à la Barigoule   *Alcachofas a la barigoule*

8 globe artichokes	1 chopped onion
4 oz. ham	1 wineglass white wine
8 oz. mushrooms	½ teaspoon salt
1 sprig parsley	8 oz. bread
10 oz. fat salted pork, or bacon	flour
olive oil for deep frying	1½ oz. butter
2 chopped carrots	

Remove the hard outer leaves of the artichokes and cook in boiling salted water for 10 minutes. Drain and leave to cool. Chop ham, mushrooms and parsley and mix together. Remove chokes and stuff the artichokes with the ham and mushroom mixture. Cover with two slices of fat salted pork or bacon rashers, tie with thread and deep fry in olive oil.

Heat two tablespoons olive oil in a saucepan and lightly fry the onion and carrots. Pour in the wine, stir well, add half cup water and salt. Transfer the contents of the saucepan to an ovenproof dish with a lid. Put in the artichokes, cover and cook in the oven for ½ hour. Fry eight slices of bread and arrange on a dish; on top of each put an artichoke, having removed the thread. Add a heaped teaspoon of flour to the pan juices, if necessary dilute with a little water, add butter in small pieces, stirring constantly to blend well. Strain the sauce over the artichokes.

Grilled Artichokes   *Alcachofas asadas*

Choose large, tender globe artichokes. Cut off the stalks and separate the leaves with care so as not to break them. Sprinkle with salt and between the leaves brush with a little olive oil and vinegar. Grill them on or under a gentle heat, otherwise they will burn, while the centres remain hard. Remove the burnt leaves, if any, and serve with grilled chops. Artichokes can also be roasted in the oven.

Braised Artichokes   *Alcachofas rehogadas*

Remove hard outside leaves and cut off the points almost to half
the artichoke; quarter them and leave in water with a sliced lemon
for an hour. Heat some olive oil in a saucepan. Drain the artichokes well and put in the pan. Season with salt, stir carefully and
cover. Cook on a moderate heat, adding a little water from time
to time. Ten minutes before they are cooked, add chopped garlic
and parsley to taste and the juice of half a lemon, stirring carefully
so that the artichokes do not disintegrate.

Stuffed Artichokes   *Alcachofas rellenas*

8 globe artichokes	olive oil for deep frying
2 oz. ham in one piece	1 chopped onion
4 cloves garlic	4 oz. chopped tomatoes
4 or 5 sprigs parsley	1¼ oz. pounded roasted almonds
2 tablespoons breadcrumbs	1 cup water
flour	salt

Prepare the artichokes as described. Cook in boiling salted water
for 10 minutes. Drain and leave to cool. Make a stuffing, using
ham chopped with garlic and parsley, and mix in breadcrumbs.
Take the artichokes and with great care distribute the stuffing
between the leaves. Squeeze them a little to make the leaves stick
together, roll in flour and deep fry in olive oil. Heat two tablespoons oil in a saucepan and fry the onion and tomatoes. Add
almonds and water. Season with salt. When boiling is established,
put in artichokes, cover the pan and cook on a moderate heat until
done.

Hunger, thirst and cold drive a man into the house of his enemy

Grilled Aubergines   *Berenjenas asadas*

Wet the aubergines and grill them on hot coals, or on the gas flames, or directly on the hot plate, turning them frequently to ensure even grilling, until they are very soft. Never put them under a grill or in an oven: pimentos, on the contrary, are very good cooked under the grill or in the oven. After grilling peel and wash the aubergines. Cut them into strips and season with salt and olive oil. Serve cold.

Aubergines with Cheese   *Berenjenas con queso*

6 big aubergines
salt
6 tablespoons olive oil
2 oz. butter

1¾ oz. flour
1 pint milk
2 oz. grated cheese

Peel the aubergines, cut them into rounds, put in a colander, sprinkle with salt and leave to stand for about an hour to drain the liquid from them. Fry in hot olive oil. Make a *béchamel* sauce (p. 70) with a little of the butter, the flour and the milk. Put a layer of aubergines in an oven-proof dish, sprinkle with cheese and cover with *béchamel*. Continue alternating the layers, ending with a layer of *béchamel*, sprinkle with cheese, top with small pieces of butter and put in the oven to brown the top.

Aubergines with Almond Sauce
Berenjenas con salsa de almendras

8 aubergines
1½ teaspoons salt
4 oz. flour
olive oil
1 chopped onion

1 peeled, chopped tomato
1 cup water
2 oz. roasted pounded almonds
1 teaspoon sugar

Peel the aubergines and cut lengthwise into slices $\frac{1}{2}$ inch thick. Season with salt and leave in a colander for about an hour. Dip in flour and fry in hot olive oil. Heat some olive oil in a saucepan and fry the onion. When it is golden, add tomato and fry together. Pour in sufficient water for the sauce. Add almonds and sugar, check seasoning, adding salt if necessary. Cook for a few moments, add aubergines, cover the pan and simmer gently for half an hour.

Aubergines with Tomatoes — *Berenjenas con tomate*

8 aubergines
2 teaspoons salt
1 cup olive oil
1 finely chopped onion
1 clove chopped garlic

1 lb. tomatoes
1 pinch sugar
2 tablespoons breadcrumbs
1¼ oz. butter
1¼ oz. grated cheese

Peel and slice the aubergines, sprinkle with salt and leave in a colander for an hour to drain off the liquid. Then fry them in hot olive oil and put in an oven-proof dish. Fry the onion. When it becomes transparent, add garlic. Cook the tomatoes with a little water, rub through a sieve and add to onion. Season with salt and sugar and leave to cook gently. When ready, pour over the aubergines, sprinkle with breadcrumbs, grated cheese and melted butter and put in the oven to brown the top.

Fried Aubergines — *Berenjenas fritas*

6 aubergines
salt

2 oz. flour
1 cup olive oil

Peel the aubergines, cut them in round slices, sprinkle with salt and leave in a colander for an hour to drain off the liquid. Dip in flour, fry in very hot oil and serve as a garnish for a meat dish.

Stuffed Aubergines   *Berenjenas rellenas*

6 broad, straight aubergines	1 egg
8 oz. pork	flour
2 oz. fat salted pork	olive oil for frying
1 onion	1 tomato
salt	1½ oz. roasted pounded almonds
2 tablespoons grated breadcrumbs	1 teaspoon sugar

Cut off the ends of the aubergines and scoop out pulp, taking care not to break the skins. Chop the pork and salted pork (or bacon) with a few slices of onion and a pinch of salt. Put in a bowl, mix with breadcrumbs and bind with an egg. Blend well. Stuff the aubergines with this mixture, roll them in flour and fry in oil. Chop the rest of the onion. Peel and chop tomato. Heat some olive oil in a saucepan and fry the onion and tomato. Add almonds and sugar. Pour in sufficient water to cook the aubergines. When it begins to boil put them in, cover the pan and simmer until soft.

Aubergine Soufflé   *Berenjenas suflés*

6 broad, short aubergines	1 oz. flour
salt	½ pint milk
3–4 tablespoons olive oil	2 oz. grated cheese
8 oz. pork	3 eggs
1 chopped onion	2 oz. butter

Cut the aubergines in half lengthwise, scoop them out in the shape of boats, sprinkle with salt and leave to stand for an hour, hollowed out side down, to drain. Fry in hot olive oil, taking care not to burn them. Fry and chop the pork. In the same fat fry the onion until golden, add flour and the milk, little by little, stirring continuously. Season with salt. When boiling is established, add pork and cook slowly for 10 minutes, stirring all the time. Remove from heat, add half the cheese and the yolks of egg. Beat the whites until stiff and carefully fold into the mixture. Stuff the aubergines with this mixture, arrange in an oven-proof dish, sprinkle with cheese and melted butter and put in the oven to brown the top.

Marrow with Tomato   *Calabacines con tomate*

1 medium-sized marrow
4 oz. finely chopped onions
3–4 tablespoons olive oil
1 clove crushed garlic

1 tablespoon chopped parsley
1 lb. peeled, chopped tomatoes
salt

Cut off the ends of the marrow, peel thinly, wash, cut into pieces, cook in boiling salted water, taking care not to overcook, and drain. Fry the onions in oil. When they begin to colour, add garlic and parsley, stir, add marrow and fry together for a few minutes. Add tomatoes, season with salt, cover and cook gently until ready. Most of the recipes for cooking aubergines are equally suitable for marrows.

Onions with Cream Sauce   *Cebollitas a la crema*

2 lb. small pickling onions
2 oz. butter
1 teaspoon flour

seasoning
1 cup cream

Clean the onions, cook in boiling salted water, taking care not to overcook, and drain. Melt butter in a saucepan and add the onions. Sprinkle with flour, stir carefully with a spoon without breaking them, season to taste, cook over very low heat, stir in the cream gently, simmer for a few minutes and serve at once.

Stewed Onions and Potatoes   *Cebollitas y patatas estofadas*

2 tablespoons olive oil
1 medium-sized, chopped onion
1 bay leaf
½ gill sherry

1¼ lb. pickling onions
1¼ lb. new potatoes
salt

Heat olive oil in a pan and fry the onion until golden. Add bay leaf, sherry, onions and peeled potatoes. Season with salt, cover, and simmer until done, shaking the pan from time to time. If necessary, add a little water to prevent sticking.

Cabbage a la Victoria   *Col a la Victoria*

1 large cabbage
2 tablespoons olive oil
4 oz. diced fat salted pork
8 oz. diced potatoes

2 diced carrots
1 chopped onion
½ teaspoon salt

Separate the cabbage leaves, wash, boil them in salted water for 5 minutes and drain. Heat oil in a pan and fry the pork. When it is half cooked, add potatoes, carrots and onion. Cook lightly, add cabbage, season with salt, cover with water, bring to the boil and simmer under a lid until the cabbage is cooked.

Cabbage à la Vinaigrette   *Col a la vinagreta*

1 cabbage
2–3 tablespoons olive oil
2 or 3 cloves garlic

½ teaspoon paprika
salt
1 tablespoon vinegar

Cook the cabbage in boiling salted water for 5 minutes, drain, and chop coarsely. Heat oil in a pan and fry the garlic for a couple of minutes, remove and add paprika to the same oil. Stir, add cabbage and fry lightly. Season with salt. Pound the fried garlic in a mortar, dilute with vinegar and add to the cabbage. Blend well, cover the pan and cook gently for 20 minutes.

Cabbage with Potatoes   *Col con patatas*

1 large cabbage	4 cloves garlic
1¼ lb. potatoes	4 oz. diced fat salted pork
2 tablespoons olive oil	seasoning

Boil cabbage and potatoes together in salted water. Drain and put on a serving dish. Heat oil in a frying pan and fry the garlic together with the pork. Season. When the garlic is golden, take it out and pour the oil and the pork over the cabbage and potatoes. Serve very hot.

Cabbage Rolls   *Fardelillos de col*

2 chopped chicken livers	1 large cabbage
2 finely chopped onions	olive oil
seasoning	1 peeled, chopped tomato
2 tablespoons flour	½ cup water
½ pint milk	24 roasted chopped almonds

Make a thick *béchamel* sauce as for croquettes (p. 108) incorporating in it the chicken livers, one onion, seasoning, the flour and the milk. Leave this mixture to cool. Boil the large cabbage leaves in salted water for 5 minutes, taking great care not to break them. Drain. Put a spoonful of the mixture on each leaf, roll, coat with flour, and fry in oil. Heat two tablespoons oil in a pan and fry the second onion and the tomato. Add water and almonds. Bring to the boil, put in cabbage rolls, cover, and cook very gently for 20 minutes.

Spanish Cauliflower   *Coliflor a la española*

1 cauliflower	2 or 3 cloves chopped garlic
2 chopped hard-boiled eggs	1 tablespoon chopped parsley
1 cup olive oil	

Wash the cauliflower, divide into flowerets, boil in salted water, drain, put on a dish and sprinkle with chopped eggs. Heat oil in a pan, fry garlic and parsley, pour over the cauliflower and serve.

Cauliflower with Tomato Sauce   *Coliflor con salsa de tomate*

1 cauliflower	2 oz. butter
salt	1 cup tomato sauce (p. 71)
2 oz. grated cheese	

Boil the cauliflower in salted water, drain and put it in an oven-proof dish. Sprinkle with grated cheese and pieces of butter. Cover with very hot tomato sauce. Put it in the oven for a moment to heat through.

Braised Cauliflower   *Coliflor guisada*

1 large cauliflower	1 peeled, chopped tomato
1 tablespoon vinegar	½ cup water
2 tablespoons flour	½ teaspoon salt
olive oil	1½ oz. pounded roasted almonds
1 chopped onion	

Cut and wash the cauliflower, boil in salted water with vinegar for 8–10 minutes and drain. Divide the cauliflower into flowerets, roll in flour and fry in oil. Heat one tablespoon oil in a pan and fry the onion lightly, add tomato, fry together, pour in water, season with salt, add almonds and cauliflower, cover and simmer gently for a few minutes.

Fried Cauliflower   *Coliflor rebozada*

1 cauliflower	1 beaten egg
1 teaspoon salt	olive oil for frying
2 tablespoons flour	

Boil the cauliflower in salted water for 10 minutes, drain carefully, divide into flowerets, dip in flour and beaten egg and fry in hot olive oil until golden. Serve as a garnish for meat dishes.

Cauliflower Pudding   *Budín de coliflor*

1 cauliflower
1 lb. potatoes
salt
8 oz. pork
1½ oz. butter

1 finely chopped onion
4 eggs
1 tablespoon grated breadcrumbs
mayonnaise sauce (p. 74)

Cut the cauliflower and the potatoes into pieces and cook them together in boiling salted water, drain, and rub through a sieve while still hot. Fry the pork in half the butter, and chop it. Fry the onion lightly, add pork, cook for a few minutes, add potato and cauliflower purée. Beat the eggs and stir them into the mixture. Butter a mould, sprinkle with breadcrumbs and pour in the mixture. Cook in a *bain-marie* for about an hour. Turn it out and cover with mayonnaise sauce. This dish may be decorated according to the discretion of the cook: with strips of pimento and slices of carrot, or with sliced hard-boiled egg and slivers of truffle.

Cauliflower Pie   *Pastel de coliflor*

1 large cauliflower
1 tablespoon vinegar
6 beaten eggs
1 small cup cream
2 oz. butter

½ teaspoon salt
1 oz. flour
½ pint milk
2 oz. grated cheese
1 tablespoon chopped parsley

Trim and wash the cauliflower, boil in salted water with vinegar, drain and rub through a sieve. Add eggs, cream, half the butter and salt. Mix well, put into a buttered mould and cook in a *bain-marie* until set. Turn out on to a dish and cover with Mornay sauce (p. 75) made with the remainder of the butter, flour, milk, cheese and parsley.

Lettuce Pudding   *Budín de lechuga*

3 lettuces

béchamel sauce (p. 70)

4 beaten eggs

butter

breadcrumbs

1 bunch watercress

bread *croûtons*

English sauce (p. 74)

Boil lettuces in salted water for 3 minutes, drain and chop. Put *béchamel* sauce in a bowl, add lettuce and eggs, mix well and pour the mixture into an oval mould, previously buttered and sprinkled with breadcrumbs. Cook in a *bain-marie* in the oven for 50–60 minutes. Turn the mould out on to a dish, garnish with watercress and croûtons of fried bread. Serve English sauce in a sauce-boat.

Asparagus with Peas   *Espárragos con guisantes*

2 bunches asparagus

salt

1½ oz. butter

1 teaspoon sugar

pinch pepper

1 teaspoon flour

2¼ lb. peas

½ cup water

2 yolks of egg

2 tablespoons milk

bread *croûtons*

Cut off the asparagus tips and boil them in salted water for a few moments. Drain, put in a pan with the butter, pepper, sugar and flour. Stir, add shelled peas and water, season with salt, stir from time to time and simmer until the peas are tender. Remove from heat, add yolks diluted with milk, mix carefully and put on a dish. Garnish with slices of bread fried in butter.

Boiled Asparagus   *Espárragos hervidos*

Cut off the woody stalks of the asparagus, trim the tips to uniform length, peel the white part and wash. Boil in salted water for 20–30 minutes, drain and wrap them in a napkin until ready to serve. Put on a dish. Separately serve one of the following sauces: mayonnaise, vinaigrette, supreme, Mornay, etc. (see recipes).

Tomatoes au Gratin, Spanish Style   *Tomates gratinados*

8 tomatoes

½ teaspoon salt

½ teaspoon sugar

4 or 5 cloves garlic

4 or 5 sprigs parsley

1 oz. breadcrumbs

2 oz. grated cheese

3 tablespoons olive oil

Choose large red, firm tomatoes. Cut in half, put in an oven-proof dish and season with salt and a little sugar. Chop garlic and parsley, and mix them with breadcrumbs and the cheese. Cover the tomatoes with this mixture, sprinkle with olive oil and bake in the oven.

Tomato Soufflé   *Tomates suflés*

8 large tomatoes

salt

1½ oz. butter

1¼ oz. flour

½ pint milk

1½ oz. grated cheese

4 eggs

Cut off the tops of the tomatoes and scoop out the pulp. Season with salt and turn them upside down for a few minutes to let the liquid drain out. Then place them right way up in an oven-proof dish, put a little piece of butter in the bottom of each and cook in the oven for 10 minutes. Make a *béchamel* sauce (p. 70) using butter, flour and milk. Half way through the cooking, season with salt and add the cheese. The sauce should be thick and smooth. Separate yolks and whites of eggs. Remove sauce from heat, add yolks and mix well. Beat the whites until very stiff and fold carefully into the mixture. Fill tomatoes with this and put them in a slow oven until the mixture rises and is golden on top.

The wolf, surfeited of meat, becomes a friar

Vegetable Aspic *Aspic de verduras*

8 oz. potatoes	salt
4 oz. tender French beans	2 hard-boiled eggs
8 oz. shelled peas	1 sweet pimento
4 carrots	1 bouillon cube
2 turnips	3 leaves gelatine
watercress	supreme sauce (p. 76)

Clean, peel and dice the vegetables and cook with the peas in boiling salted water. Drain, and allow to cool. Cut a disc from the centre of one hard-boiled egg, and chop the rest. With the aid of a clean thimble cut some discs from the pimento and dice the rest. Bring a little water to the boil in a small saucepan, add bouillon cube and a little salt. Remove from heat, add one gelatine leaf and stir to dissolve completely.

Pour a little of the gelatine into a mould. When it begins to set, put the slice of egg in the centre, surround with peas, and round the edge put discs of pimento. Spoon over the rest of the gelatine (kept warm to prevent setting), taking care not to disarrange the pattern. Leave to set. (The aspic can be made the day before it is wanted. It takes 3 hours to set in a cool place; less in a refrigerator.) Make supreme sauce, add to it two leaves of gelatine dissolved in a little tepid water. Put the vegetables and the left-over eggs and pimento in a bowl, mix in the sauce, stirring carefully always in the same direction; fill the mould with this mixture, and leave to set. Before serving, dip the mould in hot water, turn out on to a round dish and garnish with watercress.

Vegetable Fritos *Fritos de verduras*

8 oz. potatoes	olive oil
1 pimento	1 lb. tomatoes
2 aubergines	½ teaspoon salt
8 oz. onions	1 teaspoon sugar

Cut the potatoes into uniform cubes, dice pimento and aubergines and slice the onions finely. Heat a generous amount of olive oil in a pan and fry the potatoes, pimento and aubergines. When half cooked, add onions, and cook until golden. Cook the tomatoes in half cup water, rub through a sieve and add to pan. Season with salt and sugar. Cover the pan, and leave to cook over a very low heat for about an hour.

Zarzuela of Vegetables   *Zarzuela de verduras*

1 oz. lard
4 oz. fat salted pork (diced)
1¼ lb. new potatoes
1¼ lb. pickling onions
1½ lb. shelled peas

8 oz. sliced carrots
½ cup water
salt
1½ oz. butter

Heat lard in a pan and fry the pork. Add potatoes and onions, peeled but left whole, peas and carrots. Pour in water, add salt to taste and cook gently until tender. Remove from heat, add butter and serve very hot.

Multicolour Pudding   *Budín multicolor*

1¼ lb. spinach
10 oz. carrots
1½ lb. potatoes
2 large lettuces
8 eggs
2–3 tablespoons olive oil
1 chopped onion

1 chopped sweet pimento
4 oz. chopped tomatoes
4 oz. breadcrumbs
½ cup milk
1 oz. butter
watercress

Boil the spinach, carrots, potatoes and lettuces, separately, in salted water, drain, keep separate and chop finely, except potatoes which should be rubbed through a sieve. Mix two beaten eggs with each cooked vegetable. Heat oil in a pan and fry onion, pimento and tomatoes, and divide them among the four vegetables. Soak breadcrumbs in milk, and mix two tablespoons with each vegetable. Butter a mould, sprinkle with breadcrumbs. Put in first spinach, then potatoes, carrots and lastly the lettuce. Cook in a *bain-marie* in the oven for 1 hour.

Turn out the pudding on to a dish and garnish with watercress. Serve with a sauce-boat of any suitable sauce such as: muselina, supreme, Victoria, etc. (see recipes).

Chick-peas with Spinach — *Garbanzos con espinacas*

1 lb. chick-peas	4 oz. chopped peeled tomatoes
1 teaspoon bicarbonate of soda	1 tablespoon paprika
salt	1¼ lb. spinach
5 tablespoons olive oil	1¼ oz. roasted almonds
1 slice bread	1 clove garlic
1 chopped onion	

Put the chick-peas to soak overnight in water with bicarbonate of soda. Rinse, put them in cold water, bring to the boil, cook until tender (at least an hour), adding salt to taste when almost ready, and drain. Heat three tablespoons oil in a saucepan and fry the bread until golden on both sides, remove, and in the same oil lightly fry the onions and tomatoes. Add the chick-peas.

Wash the spinach, shake out, sprinkle with salt and leave in a colander. Heat two tablespoons oil in a frying pan, add paprika, stir, and immediately add the spinach. Fry lightly and add it to the chick-peas. Pound together the almonds, the garlic and the fried bread and add them to the rest. Cook slowly together with the lid on for about 51 minutes.

*The wine by its colour, the bread by its smell
and everything else by its taste*

Chick-pea Stew   *Garbanzos guisados*

1¼ lb. chick-peas	4 oz. chopped onions
1 teaspoon bicarbonate of soda	4 oz. tomatoes
salt	1 clove garlic
2 oz. lard	1 hard-boiled egg
1 bread crust	

Soak the chick-peas overnight in water with bicarbonate of soda. Rinse, put them in cold water, bring to the boil. Boil gently but steadily until tender (at least an hour), adding salt to taste when they are almost ready. Drain but keep the liquid. Heat lard in a saucepan, fry bread crust, remove and, in the same fat, fry the onion until golden. Add peeled and chopped tomatoes. When cooked, add the chick-peas with a little of the liquid to make them juicy.

Pound the garlic in a mortar with the fried crust and the yolk of the hard-boiled egg. Dilute with two tablespoons water and add the mixture to the pan. Chop the white of egg and put this in with the rest, mix well, cover the pan, and simmer gently for 30 minutes.

Peas in Cream Sauce   *Guisantes a la crema*

After cooking and draining the peas, put them in a dish and cover with cream sauce (p. 70).

Fortune and olives are alike;
for sometimes a man has plenty, and sometimes none

Peas with Onions   *Guisantes con cebollitas*

1 oz. lard	*bouquet-garni*
2 oz. diced ham	salt
1¼ lb. pickling onions	1 level teaspoon sugar
2¼ lb. shelled peas	1 cup water

Heat lard in a saucepan and lightly fry the ham and the onions. Add peas and the *bouquet-garni*, season with salt and sugar, add water, cover and cook gently for 25 minutes, shaking the pan from time to time.

Peas a la Catalana   *Guisantes a la catalana*

2¼ lb. shelled peas	8 oz. sliced chicken giblets
salt	1 heaped tablespoon flour
2 tablespoons olive oil	4 hard-boiled eggs

Boil the peas in enough hot salted water to cover them. Drain, but keep the liquid for the sauce. Heat one tablespoon oil, lightly fry giblets and season with salt. Remove, add the rest of the oil and the flour to the pan and brown lightly. Just before serving, gradually add the liquid from the peas, cook for a few minutes and stir the sauce and the giblets into the peas. Garnish with halved hard-boiled eggs and serve.

Tossed Peas   *Guisantes salteados*

3 lb. peas	seasoning
1½ oz. butter	2 hard-boiled eggs
2 oz. diced ham	

Shell the peas, cook them in boiling salted water, uncovered to preserve their green colour, and drain. Fry the ham in butter, add the peas, season, stir well. Serve very hot, garnished with slices of hard-boiled egg.

Peas with Brussels Sprouts   *Guisantes y coles de Bruselas*

1½ lb. peas   1 teaspoon flour
1¼ lb. Brussels sprouts   pinch nutmeg
1 oz. lard   1½ oz. butter
1 chopped onion   bread *croûtons*
1 tablespoon chopped parsley

Cook the peas and the Brussels sprouts separately in boiling salted water; drain, but keep a little of the water in which the peas were cooked. Heat lard in a saucepan and lightly fry the onion and parsley. Add flour, cook for 2–3 minutes, pour a ladle of the water from the peas, season with nutmeg, add peas and sprouts, cover, and cook for 10 minutes. Remove from heat and blend in the butter, adding it in small pieces. Garnish with *croûtons* of fried bread.

Catalan Broad Beans   *Habas a la catalana*

9 lb. tender broad beans   4 oz. peeled and chopped tomatoes
2 oz. lard   1 sprig mint
olive oil   1 dessertspoon paprika
4 oz. diced fat salted pork   1 gill white wine
4 oz. sliced black sausage   salt
1 chopped onion   1 teaspoon sugar
3 cloves garlic

Shell the beans and keep in water. Heat an equal quantity of lard and olive oil in a saucepan and lightly fry the pork and the sausage. Add onion, garlic, tomatoes, mint, paprika and wine. Cook for a few minutes, add beans, season with salt to taste, add sugar. Shake the pan from time to time to mix all ingredients and ensure even cooking. Cover and cook gently until the beans are tender.

Broad Beans with Ham   *Habas con jamón*

9 lb. broad beans   2 oz. lard
1 tablespoon sugar   4 oz. diced ham

Shell beans and cook in boiling salted water with the sugar. Drain. Heat lard in a frying pan and fry the ham. Add the beans, fry together for 5 minutes and serve.

Dried Broad Beans   *Habas secas*

2 lb. dried broad beans   1 sprig mint
1 chopped onion   1 sprig parsley
1–2 cloves chopped garlic   12 small globe artichokes
3 tablespoons olive oil   pinch saffron
4 oz. peeled tomatoes   pinch caraway seeds
salt and pepper   2 tablespoons fried breadcrumbs
1 bay leaf   poached eggs

Soak the beans in cold water for 1½–2 hours. Rinse, put in a saucepan with enough cold water to cover and bring to the boil. Fry the onion and garlic in olive oil until golden. Add tomatoes. Drain the beans and return them to the saucepan. Add the contents of the frying pan, stir, pour enough water to cover, add bay leaf, mint, parsley and artichokes. Cover the pan tightly and simmer until the beans are tender and the liquid reduced by half. Add saffron, caraway, pepper and salt to taste, and fried breadcrumbs to thicken the sauce. Serve a poached egg on each helping of beans.

Spanish Haricot Beans   *Judías blancas a la española*

1¼ lb. white haricot beans   1 tablespoon flour
salt   ½ gill sherry
1½ oz. lard   1 bay leaf
1 chopped onion   parsley
2 peeled and chopped tomatoes

Put the haricot beans in cold water and bring to the boil, simmer for 1 hour, season with salt to taste and continue to cook for another hour. Heat the lard in a frying pan and lightly fry the onion. Add tomatoes, salt and flour. Cook for a few moments, add sherry and let it boil for a minute. Drain the beans, keeping a little water. Mix in the contents of the frying pan, add bay leaf, cook gently for 15 minutes, shaking the pan from time to time. Turn the beans out on to a dish and sprinkle with chopped parsley.

Haricot Beans with Pimentos and Tomatoes
Judías blancas con pimientos y tomates

1¼ lb. white haricot beans	salt
1 head garlic	2 sliced fresh pimentos
1 bay leaf	1 lb. tomatoes
3 tablespoons olive oil	

Wash the beans well, put in a pan of cold water with the garlic, bay leaf and one tablespoon olive oil. Bring to the boil, then simmer steadily for 2 hours. Do not add salt until the beans are nearly cooked. Heat two tablespoons olive oil in a frying pan and fry the pimentos. Season with salt, remove from pan. Cut the tomatoes in halves, fry lightly in fat left from pimentos and cover so that they remain juicy. Drain the beans and remove the garlic and bay leaf. Put the beans on a dish and arrange tomatoes and pimentos on top, and pour the oil in which they were cooked over the dish.

A vineyard, a girl, a pear tree and a bean garden are hard to keep

Haricot Beans with Sausages   *Judías blancas con salchichas*

1¼ lb. white haricot beans   salt
4 tablespoons olive oil   12 oz. sausages
4 oz. chopped onions   parsley
1 tablespoon flour

Put the beans in cold water, bring to the boil, simmer for 1 hour. Season with salt to taste, simmer for another hour and drain. Heat half the olive oil in a saucepan, put in onions and cover the pan so that they will cook without browning. Add flour, brown it lightly, add half cup water, season with salt, boil a few moments, add the beans, mix them well with the sauce and cook together for a few minutes. Fry the sausages in the rest of the oil. Put the beans on a dish and sprinkle with chopped parsley. Arrange the sausages around them and pour the oil in which they were fried over the beans.

French Beans   *Judías verdes*

2 lb. French beans   1 chopped onion
1½ oz. butter   *croûtons*
2 oz. diced ham

Clean and wash the beans well, and cook them in boiling salted water, then drain. Melt the butter in a saucepan and fry the ham lightly. Add onion, fry until golden, put in beans. Cook for a few minutes, then turn out on to a dish and garnish with small *croûtons* of bread fried in butter.

French Beans with Tomato Sauce
Judías verdes con salsa de tomate

2 lb. French beans   parsley
½ pint tomato sauce (p. 71)

Boil the beans and drain them; put them on a dish and cover with tomato sauce. Sprinkle with chopped parsley.

Braised French Beans   *Judías verdes guisadas*

2 lb. French beans   8 oz. peeled, chopped tomatoes
2 tablespoons olive oil   salt
1 chopped onion   1 tinned sweet pimento

Clean and wash the beans, and cook them in boiling salted water;
then drain. Heat olive oil in a saucepan and fry the onion. When
it becomes golden, add tomatoes, season with salt to taste, fry
5 minutes, put in beans, stir and cook gently for 12–15 minutes.
Dice and toss pimento in the frying pan for 2 minutes. Put the
beans on a serving dish. Garnish with pimento.

Stewed Lentils   *Lentejas guisadas*

1 lb. lentils   4 oz. diced fat salted pork
salt   1 chopped onion
2 tablespoons olive oil   4 oz. peeled, chopped tomatoes

Wash the lentils, put in a saucepan of cold water, bring to the boil
and simmer until done. Season with salt a little before taking
them off the fire. Drain. Heat olive oil in a saucepan and lightly
fry the pork. Add onion and tomatoes. Cook lightly together, add
lentils, stir well, cover the pan, cook gently for 20 minutes and
serve.

Pimentos with Fillet of Pork   *Pimientos con lomo de cerdo*

6 ripe pimentos   1 lb. sliced fillet pork
salt   olive oil

Seed the pimentos and season on the inside with salt. Season
slices of pork with salt and put inside the pimentos. Heat plenty
of olive oil in a large frying pan. When hot, fry the pimentos until
golden on all sides. Cover the pan and leave on a low heat until
the pimentos are soft.

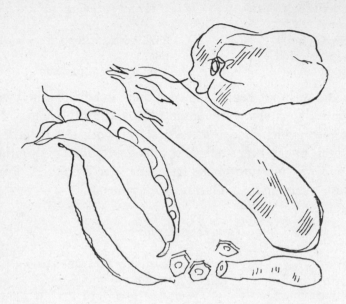

South American Pimentos   *Pimientos a la americana*

6 smooth, red pimentos
salt
8 oz. diced pork
2 oz. diced ham

1 chopped onion
8 oz. peeled, chopped tomatoes
1 lb. boiled rice
olive oil

Seed the pimentos, wash and sprinkle on the inside with salt. Season the pork with salt, fry lightly, remove and chop with ham. In the same frying pan lightly fry the onion and tomatoes, add pork and ham and cook together for 5–6 minutes. Partly fill the pimentos with the mixture. Finish filling the pimentos with cooked rice. Lay the pimentos upside down in an oven-proof dish, sprinkle generously with olive oil and cook in the oven.

Cream Potatoes, Spanish Style   *Patatas a la crema*

2¼ lb. potatoes
2 tablespoons olive oil
1 tablespoon flour
salt

2 cloves chopped garlic
chopped parsley
juice of ½ lemon
1 beaten egg

Peel and wash the potatoes and cut into round slices ½ inch thick. Heat olive oil in a saucepan, blend in flour and cook a moment, and immediately add potatoes. Cook well, then pour in just enough water to cover the potatoes, season with salt, add garlic and one tablespoon chopped parsley, leave to cook, stirring from time to time with great care so as not to break the potatoes. When cooked, remove from heat, add lemon juice and egg. Mix well but very carefully, turn out on to a dish and sprinkle with freshly chopped parsley.

Potatoes with All-i-oli   *Patatas con all-i-oli*

2¼ lb. potatoes
all-i-oli

1½ oz. butter
1 gill tomato sauce

Boil the potatoes, rub through a sieve and mix with *all-i-oli* (p. 69). Put the potatoes in an oven-proof dish, press down well, scatter pieces of butter on top, cover with tomato sauce (p. 71). Put the dish in the oven for 10 minutes and serve piping hot.

Provençal Potatoes   *Patatas a la provenzal*

1¼ lb. potatoes
2–3 tablespoons olive oil
1 lb. sliced onions

1 lb. peeled, sliced tomatoes
salt
1¼ oz. grated cheese

Peel the potatoes, cut into thin round slices, cook in boiling salted water for 15 minutes and drain. Heat oil in a frying pan, and lightly fry the onions, without allowing them to brown. Put one-third of the fried onions in an oven-proof dish, cover with a layer of tomatoes, season with salt to taste, put in potatoes, cover with half the remaining onion and the grated cheese. Put another layer of tomatoes and, finally, the rest of the onion. Sprinkle with olive oil and bake in the oven for 30 minutes.

Spanish Potatoes au Gratin   *Patatas al gratín*

2¼ lb. potatoes
1 teaspoon salt
½ teaspoon pepper
3 oz. butter

2 oz. grated Gruyère cheese
1 pint milk
2 eggs

Peel the potatoes, slice very finely, and season with salt and pepper. Butter a deep oven-proof dish, sprinkle with grated cheese, put in potatoes in layers with small pieces of butter between each layer, sprinkle the top with grated cheese. Boil the milk and let it cool a little. Mix in two well beaten eggs, pour the mixture over the potatoes, dot with pieces of butter, cover the dish and put in a hot oven for 30 minutes. Just before serving, remove lid and brown the top.

Potatoes au Gratin with Pork
Patatas gratinadas con carne de cerdo

3 lb. potatoes
2 oz. butter
1 gill milk
salt and pepper

8 oz. diced pork
2 oz. ham in thick slices
1 chopped onion
8 oz. peeled, chopped tomatoes

Peel and boil the potatoes, rub through a sieve, season to taste and mix in 1 oz. butter and the milk. Fry the pork, remove from pan and chop with the ham. In the same fat lightly fry the onion and tomatoes, add pork and ham and cook together for 5 minutes. Put half the potatoes in an oven-proof dish, press down well, spread the chopped mixture on top, cover with the rest of the potatoes, dot with pieces of butter and put in the oven until the top is golden.

Fried Potatoes with Pimento and Tomato
Patatas fritas con pimiento y tomate

2–3 pimentos
2 teaspoons salt
5 tablespoons olive oil

1 lb. peeled, sliced tomatoes
1 teaspoon sugar
2 lb. peeled, sliced potatoes

Cut up pimentos, season with salt to taste and fry in two tablespoons olive oil. Add tomatoes, season with salt and sugar, cover and cook slowly. Fry the potatoes separately in the rest of the oil, put them on a dish, arrange pimento and tomato on top and serve.

Buenavista Potatoes   *Patatas buenavista*

2 lb. new potatoes
1½ oz. butter
1 chopped onion

1 tablespoon chopped parsley
2 chopped hard-boiled eggs

Choose potatoes about the size of a walnut. Peel them, cook in boiling salted water and drain. Melt butter in a frying pan, fry the onion, without allowing it to brown, add potatoes and fry lightly. Turn them out on to a dish, sprinkle with a mixture of finely chopped parsley and eggs and serve very hot.

Potatoes with Red Sauce   *Patatas con salsa encarnada*

Boil potatoes in their skins in salted water, then peel and slice. When cold, put them on a dish and cover with red sauce (p. 72).

Potato Balls   *Ñoquis de patata*

2¼ lb. uniform sized potatoes   ½ teaspoon salt
2 oz. grated cheese   2 oz. butter
5 oz. flour   *béchamel* sauce (p. 70)
3 beaten eggs

1. Boil the potatoes in their skins. When cooked, peel them and rub through a sieve. Add cheese, 4 oz. flour and the eggs to the purée. Season with salt and mix well. Form mixture into balls, roll them in flour, drop into a pan of boiling salted water and cook for 3 minutes. Do not put in too many at a time. If necessary, boil them in two or three batches, as they must be cooked in plenty of water. Drain with a perforated spoon. Butter an oven-proof dish, put in the potato balls, sprinkle with a little melted butter, cover with *béchamel* sauce, put in a hot oven for 10 minutes and serve.

2. As above, but serve with *hollandaise* sauce (p. 73).

3. As above, but cover the potato balls with tomato sauce (p. 71), sprinkle with chopped parsley and put in the oven for a few moments.

Croquettes   *Croquetas de patata*

Croquettes generally is an excellent way of using up leftovers. They can be made from any chopped cooked meat, poultry, fish. liver, kidneys, etc., either plain or mixed with mashed potatoes, cooked rice or macaroni, with sufficient thick white or brown sauce to bind, with or without egg, according to richness desired. Chopped mushrooms, truffles, ham, shallots, chives, etc., as well as grated cheese, are often added to the basic elements. Cream may be added with a very rich mixture. A pinch of spices, such as mace or nutmeg, enhances the flavour. When the sauce is made and the cooked ingredients blended in, leave to cool completely. Take up a tablespoon of the mixture at a time, shape into desired form, coat in beaten egg and breadcrumbs, deep fry in sizzling hot olive oil until golden, drain thoroughly and serve at once, while the croquettes are crisp on the outside and creamy inside.

Potato Croquettes   *Croquetas de patata*

2 lb. potatoes	1 large finely chopped onion
salt and pepper	3 oz. grated cheese
1 raw yolk	1 beaten egg
2 oz. butter	breadcrumbs
flour	olive oil for frying

Boil potatoes in salted water, drain, rub through a sieve, blend in seasoning, yolk, 1 oz. butter and one tablespoon flour. While potatoes are cooking, fry the onion lightly, without allowing it to brown, in 1 oz. butter, add cheese, stir and remove from heat.

Divide potato into portions on a floured board, enclose a dessert-spoon of onion and cheese mixture in each portion and shape the croquettes. Roll in flour, dip in egg and freshly grated bread-crumbs, deep fry in oil until golden, as described above, drain and serve.

Potatoes with Fat Salted Pork   *Patatas con tocino*

4 oz. fat salted pork	2¼ lb. potatoes
2 tablespoons lard	salt
1 chopped onion	*bouquet-garni*
1 tablespoon flour	

Cut the pork into cubes and fry in lard. Brown lightly, add onion and fry lightly. Stir in flour and, when it begins to colour, put in the peeled and sliced potatoes. Turn them over once or twice, add hot water to cover, season with salt and put in *bouquet-garni*. Simmer gently until cooked. Discard *bouquet-garni* before serving.

Stuffed Potatoes   *Patatas rellenas*

8 fairly large potatoes	1¼ lb. chopped peeled tomatoes
8 oz. diced pork	olive oil for frying
1 tablespoon lard	1½ oz. butter
1 chopped onion	tomato sauce (p. 71)

Boil the potatoes in their skins in salted water, peel, leave to cool, cut out a circle and keep to use as a lid, then scoop out the pulp with a tablespoon. Fry the pork in lard, then chop finely. In the same fat, fry the onion and 4 oz. tomatoes, add pork, mix, fill the potatoes with this mixture and cover with the 'lid'. Heat oil and fry the potatoes on both sides. Butter an oven-proof dish, arrange the potatoes in it, cover with tomato sauce (made of the rest of the tomatoes) and put in a medium oven for 15 minutes.

Braised Potatoes and Peas   *Patatas y guisantes estofados*

2¼ lb. peas	1 teaspoon paprika
1¼ lb. potatoes	1 glass white wine
1 tablespoon lard	salt
1 chopped onion	1 teaspoon sugar
2 peeled and chopped tomatoes	½ cup water
1 sprig mint	

Shell the peas. Peel and dice potatoes. Melt lard in a saucepan and add the onion, tomatoes, mint, paprika and the wine. Stir, add peas and potatoes, season with salt to taste, add sugar, shake the pan, add water, cover with a lid and leave to cook on a moderate heat until done, shaking it from time to time.

Fried Potato Balls   *Fritos de patata*

2½ lbs. potatoes	1 tablespoon flour
Salt	1 white of egg
1 raw yolk	olive oil
1 tablespoon butter	

Boil potatoes in salted water, drain, mash or rub through a sieve, add yolk, a tablespoon butter, tablespoon flour, and stiffly beaten white of egg. Shape into balls and fry in hot olive oil. These potatoes may be served with all kinds of meat and it is an excellent way of using up left-over mashed potatoes.

Potato Pie   *Pastel de patata*

2¼ lb. potatoes   2 eggs
1½ oz. butter   2 tablespoons breadcrumbs
salt and pepper for seasoning   1 lb. loin of pork (fried and boned)

Boil potatoes in their skins in salted water, peel, rub through a sieve, add butter (keeping just enough to grease the mould), seasoning and the yolks of egg. Beat the whites until stiff, fold them into the potato mixture and stir until smooth. Butter a mould, sprinkle with breadcrumbs, fill with the potato mixture, put in the oven until it acquires a light golden colour, turn out on to a round dish, and surround with fried slices of pork. Serve very hot.

Potato and Spinach Patties   *Pastelillos de patata y espinaca*

2¼ lb. potatoes   1½ oz. butter
1 yolk   1 beaten egg
flour   olive oil
1¼ lb. spinach

Boil the potatoes in salted water, drain, rub through a sieve, stir in yolk, and, if consistency is too thin, add a little flour. Boil the spinach in salted water, drain, rinse with cold water, press out liquid, chop and toss in butter. Sprinkle a board with flour, and roll out potato mixture to a thickness of ¼ inch. Cut out with a round pastry-cutter, put a layer of spinach on top of each circle, cover with another circle of potato. Brush with beaten egg and fry the potato patties in very hot olive oil until golden on both sides.

Potato Soufflé   *Suflé de patata*

2¼ lb. potatoes	2 oz. grated cheese
2 oz. butter	seasoning
9 oz. minced fried pork	5 eggs

Peel potatoes, boil them in salted water, drain, rub through a sieve, add butter, pork, cheese, seasoning and yolks of egg. Stir well to obtain a very smooth mixture and fold in the stiffly beaten whites. Mix well. Pour the mixture into a greased soufflé dish and bake in a moderate oven until it has risen and become golden. Serve immediately or it will collapse.

Braised Potatoes   *Patatas guisadas*

4 tablespoons olive oil	2¼ lb. diced potatoes
1 chopped onion	1 or 2 cloves garlic
4 oz. peeled and chopped tomatoes	1 tablespoon chopped parsley
1 teaspoon paprika	salt

Heat oil in a saucepan and fry the onion lightly. Add tomatoes, fry for 5 minutes, add paprika, stir and put in potatoes. Fry them lightly for some minutes, pour in sufficient boiling water to cover and leave to simmer. Pound garlic in a mortar, add to the potatoes, together with parsley. Season with salt to taste and stir carefully from time to time until the potatoes are cooked.

Potatoes for Garnish   *Patatas para guarniciones*

1. Hazel-nut or *Noisette* Potatoes   *Patatas avellana*

(*a*) Choose large potatoes, peel, then with a special spoon scoop out balls the size of a hazel-nut. Fry them in olive oil until golden. Drain, and season with salt.

(*b*) After scooping potato balls out with a special spoon, cook them in boiling salted water for 5 minutes. Drain, toss lightly in butter, and sprinkle with chopped parsley.

2. Potato Straws *Patatas paja*

Choose round potatoes, peel and slice finely, then cut into fine straws. Fry in plenty of hot olive oil until golden, drain thoroughly, sprinkle with fine dry salt and serve at once.

3. Potato Puffs *Patatas suflés*

Choose long-shaped waxy potatoes. Peel, cut into rounds of $\frac{1}{5}$ inch thick and dry on a cloth. Heat plenty of olive oil in two deep frying pans. Put in the potatoes, a few at a time. As soon as they begin to colour, take them out and immediately plunge into the second pan of smoking hot oil. The potatoes will puff up. Remove, drain well, season with salt and serve immediately or they will become flat.

Fried Parsley for Garnish *Perejil frito para guarniciones*

Wash the parsley well, pick off stalks which are too long, squeeze dry in a cloth, put in a wire basket and plunge into the fat, after frying the article for which the parsley is intended. The pan should not be over the fire when putting in the parsley, and a few seconds' immersion in hot fat is sufficient. Use to decorate fried dishes.

Grilled Mushrooms *Setas a la parrilla*

Choose fresh and fairly large field mushrooms. Cut off stalks, carefully scrape off the earth on the top. In no case should they be washed. Grill the mushrooms first cavity downwards, then turn, season with salt and sprinkle with finely chopped parsley and garlic, and a few drops of olive oil. Do not allow to become too dry or the delicious flavour will be lost.

Baked Mushrooms　　　*Setas al horno*

Cut off mushroom stalks and wash well. Put plenty of olive oil in an oven-proof dish, arrange the mushrooms side by side close together, wedge chopped-up stalks between the caps, season with salt, and cook in the oven for 15 minutes. Sprinkle on top a mixture of finely chopped garlic, parsley and breadcrumbs, bake for further 10–15 minutes, basting from time to time with the oil in the dish.

Mushrooms with Croûtons　　　*Champiñones con fritos de pan*

1¼ lb. mushrooms
1¾ oz. butter
1 tablespoon flour
juice of ½ lemon

½ cup water
salt
1 yolk
5 oz. diced bread

Wash the mushrooms in plenty of water. Cut the large ones and leave the small ones whole. Melt half the butter in a saucepan, add flour, let it brown a little, stir in lemon juice and water, bring to the boil, add mushrooms, season with salt to taste, simmer gently for 12–15 minutes. Remove pan from heat, add yolk and blend in the rest of the butter, adding it in small pieces. Fry the bread, put on a dish, cover with mushrooms and serve.

EGGS

HUEVOS Y TORTILLAS

Spanish Eggs   *Huevos a la española*

6 hard-boiled eggs
béchamel sauce (p. 70)

2 oz. grated cheese
½ pint tomato sauce (p. 71)

Cut hard-boiled eggs in half, lengthwise, and remove the yolks. Make a *béchamel* sauce and add to it the grated cheese. Cover the bottom of a dish with this sauce, sieve the yolks on top and arrange the whites, filled with thick tomato sauce, in two lines down the centre of the dish.

Chinese Eggs   *Huevos chinescos*

6 hard-boiled eggs
1 lb. shelled peas
2 diced carrots
1 tinned sweet pimento

mayonnaise sauce (p. 74)
6 anchovy fillets
4 oz. stuffed olives

Shell eggs and trim off one end to enable the eggs to stand upright. Boil the peas and carrots in salted water and drain. Cut the pimento into strips. Pour mayonnaise sauce into a round dish, cover with peas and carrots, arrange the eggs upright in a circle, not too close together, decorate each egg with a strip of pimento and an anchovy fillet in a criss-cross pattern and pin a stuffed olive on top with a cocktail stick.

Cold Eggs   *Huevos fríos*

6 hard-boiled eggs
foie-gras
4 oz. butter
juice of ½ lemon
1 raw yolk

1 tablespoon tomato purée
olive oil
salt
sliced tinned sweet pimento

Cut the eggs across in half; remove yolks and fill the whites with *foie-gras* mixed with butter. Put the raw yolk in a mortar with lemon juice and tomato purée. Mix well together and add olive oil drop by drop, stirring fast all the time, until the sauce thickens slightly. Sieve the hard-boiled yolks, mix them with the sauce, season with salt to taste and turn out on to a dish. Arrange the stuffed whites on top and decorate with strips of pimento.

Stuffed Eggs   *Huevos rellenos*

7 eggs	1 cauliflower
2 tablespoons chopped parsley	2 oz. grated cheese
4 oz. butter	1½ oz. flour
½ teaspoon salt	½ pint milk

Hard-boil six eggs, shell and cut lengthwise. Take out the yolks and mash with parsley, half the butter and salt. Mix well, fill the whites with the mixture and sandwich the halves together to make 'whole' eggs. Divide cauliflower into flowerets and boil carefully. Do not overcook. Drain, put into a buttered oven-proof dish, sprinkle with grated cheese and place the eggs on top.

Make a cream sauce (p. 70) using the rest of the butter, flour and milk, add whatever is left of the filling, pour over the eggs, bake in the oven for 10 minutes and serve very hot.

Fried Eggs with *Chorizo*   *Huevos fritos con chorizo*

1 lb. potatoes	salt
olive oil	4 oz. *chorizo*
6 eggs	

Cut the potatoes into straws (p. 113) and fry until golden. Fry eggs in olive oil, season with salt. Arrange potato straws in the middle of a serving dish, surround with fried eggs. In the same oil in which the eggs were fried, fry slices of *chorizo*. Put one slice on top of each egg, sprinkle with oil and serve.

Soft-boiled Eggs with English Sauce
Huevos blandos con salsa inglesa

3 chicken livers	salt
½ oz. butter	6 eggs
1 glass sherry	English sauce (p. 74)
1 lb. sieved tomatoes	

Fry the chicken livers in one tablespoon butter, cut into strips, return to the pan, add sherry, simmer for 2 minutes, mix in sieved tomatoes, season with salt to taste and cook for 5 minutes. Prepare six soft-boiled eggs. Pour the tomato purée with the livers into a dish, arrange the eggs on top and cover with English sauce.

Eggs in the Nest   *Huevos al nido*

1½ lb. potatoes	cream sauce (p. 70)
olive oil	6 poached eggs
4 oz. ham	

Peel the potatoes, cut into straws and line a mould to form a nest. Dip it into very hot olive oil, deep enough to cover it, and fry until golden. Take the nest out of the mould, and make five more in the same way. Fry the ham and divide it between the nests. Put a poached egg into each nest and cover with cream sauce. Place the nests on a baking tin and put in a slow oven for a few minutes to heat them.

Egg Puff-paste Patties   *Huevos en pastelillos de hojaldre*

6 puff-pastry cases	6 poached eggs
6 slices *foie-gras*	*muselina* sauce (p. 75)

Line the bottom of each case with a slice of *foie-gras*, put a poached egg on top, cover with *muselina* sauce, put in the oven to heat through and serve.

Poached Eggs with Mussels   *Huevos escalfados con mejillones*

1 chopped onion
1½ oz. butter
1 lb. peeled and chopped tomatoes
2 tablespoons chopped parsley

18 cleaned and scrubbed mussels
6 slices bread
6 poached eggs

Fry the onion in butter until golden, add tomatoes and parsley, fry lightly for 1 minute, add mussels, cook together on a gentle heat for 15 minutes. Take the pan off the fire, remove mussel shells and keep the mussels on a plate. Fry bread in olive oil, arrange on a dish, put a poached egg on top of each piece of bread, cover with the sauce in which the mussels were cooked, garnish with mussels and serve.

Flamenca Eggs   *Huevos a la flamenca*

2 tablespoons lard
1 chopped onion
2 oz. chopped ham
12 oz. peeled, chopped tomatoes
8 oz. cooked, sliced French beans
8 oz. cooked peas

1 bunch cooked asparagus
2 diced, fried, sweet pimentos
1 lb. diced, fried potatoes
6 eggs
diced *chorizo*
2 tablespoons chopped parsley

Melt lard in a pan and fry the onion and ham. When they begin to colour, add tomatoes and fry for 5 minutes. Add beans, peas, asparagus tips, potatoes and pimentos. Cook gently for 10 minutes, transfer to an oven-proof dish, level out and break the eggs on top. Scatter *chorizo* on top of the whites and sprinkle the yolks with parsley. Put in the oven just until the whites are set. Serve immediately.

Eggs with Tomato Purée   *Huevos con puré de tomate*

8 oz. sliced onions
olive oil
salt

8 eggs
1 lb. peeled, sieved tomatoes
2 sweet pimentos

Fry the onions in oil, season with a little salt, cover the pan and cook on a gentle heat until soft, but do not brown. Turn out into an oven-proof dish, break the eggs on top, season with very little salt, cover with tomato purée and decorate with strips of pimento. Put in the oven for 10 minutes.

Eggs with Ham   *Huevos con jamón*

tomato sauce (p. 71)
6 oz. ham
6 raw yolks

parsley
olive oil

Pour tomato sauce into an oven-proof dish. Arrange squares of ham over the sauce and on top of each one put a yolk of egg sprinkled with finely-chopped parsley. Pour a little oil on the yolks and put the dish in the oven for 2–3 minutes.

Eggs with Prawn Sauce   *Huevos con salsa de gambas*

4 oz. large prawns (*gambas*)
2 oz. butter
1 oz. flour

½ pint milk
salt
6 eggs

Boil the prawns lightly, remove shells and chop up flesh. Make a thick *béchamel* sauce (p. 70), using $1\frac{1}{2}$ oz. butter, flour and milk, mix in the prawns, cook gently together and season with salt. Butter six individual oven-proof moulds, break a fresh egg into each one, fill the mould with the sauce, top with a little butter and put in the oven for 10 minutes. Serve in the same moulds.

Eggs with Tomatoes   *Huevos con tomates*

6 tomatoes   1½ oz. grated cheese
salt   5 oz. butter
6 eggs   1 lb. diced potatoes

Choose six ripe, firm tomatoes, big enough to hold an egg. Cut
off the top, scoop out the pulp, season with salt and put in the
oven on a buttered tin for 10 minutes. Remove, break an egg into
each one, season, sprinkle with cheese and top with a small piece
of butter. Return to the oven for 10 minutes. Fry the potatoes in
butter, put on a dish, arrange egg-filled tomatoes around and
serve.

Eggs in a Cave   *Huevos en cueva*

6 large potatoes   1 oz. butter
6 slices *foie-gras*   Colbert sauce (p. 70)
salt

Boil potatoes in their skins in salted water, peel, scoop out enough
pulp to make room for an egg, taking great care not to break the
potato. Put a little *foie-gras* into each potato, break an egg on top,
season with a little salt, top with a small knob of butter and put
in the oven until the whites are set. Serve with Colbert sauce.

Wonder Eggs   *Huevos maravilla*

12 oz. bread   4 oz. ham
4 eggs   olive oil
2 oz. grated cheese   watercress

Cut eight slices of bread ½ inch thick, without crust. Separate the
whites from the yolks. Mix the yolks with the cheese, spread this
mixture on top of each slice of bread and cover with a piece of

ham of the same size. Beat the whites of egg until very stiff and cover the slices with it. Heat plenty of olive oil in a frying pan and fry the slices, basting the whites with oil until golden. Garnish with watercress.

Egg Moulds   *Huevos moldeados*

2 oz. butter	6 slices bread
3 fried and chopped chicken livers	1 small tin *foie-gras*
6 eggs	cream sauce (p. 70)
salt	

Butter six small moulds, line each with chicken livers. Break an egg into each mould and season with salt. Bake in the oven in a *bain-marie* until the yolks are lightly set. Cut six round slices of bread a little larger than the moulds, spread with butter and put in the oven until golden. When cold, cover each with a layer of *foie-gras*. Arrange the slices of bread on a dish. Turn out the eggs, put the contents of one mould on each slice of bread. Cover with cream sauce and serve.

Spanish Snow Eggs   *Huevos nevados*

1¼ lb. spinach	1¼ oz. pine-kernels
1 lb. bread	olive oil
2 oz. butter	2 bunches watercress
6 eggs	

Wash the spinach well, boil in salted water, drain, rinse under cold water, drain well again and chop finely. Cut six slices of bread ½ inch thick, cut off crusts, butter one side and spread with a layer of spinach, leaving a hole in the middle. Separate yolks and whites. Slip a yolk into each hole in spinach. Beat the whites until very stiff, cover pieces of bread and decorate top with pine-kernels. Heat plenty of olive oil in a frying pan, put in the pieces of bread and, with a spoon, baste the oil over the whites until they turn golden. Serve on a bed of watercress.

Mushroom Soufflé   *Suflé de setas*

6 oz. mushrooms	2 oz. grated cheese
6 eggs	salt
1¼ pints milk	1½ oz. butter

Wash and chop mushrooms. Separate yolks and whites. Beat the yolks and the milk together, add cheese and mushrooms and fold in stiffly-whisked whites. Season with a little salt and mix well. Butter a soufflé dish, pour the mixture into it, put into a hot oven until it has risen and become golden. Serve immediately.

Baked Savoury Custard   *Flan de huevos*

12 yolks	8 oz. bread
6 whites of egg	2 beaten eggs
salt	olive oil for frying
1¼ pints milk	English sauce (p. 74)
2 oz. butter	

Beat well together the yolks and whites of egg, add a little salt and the milk, and whisk again. Butter an oblong mould and pour in the mixture. Put the mould in a *bain-marie* and bake in the oven. The custard will be ready when a cocktail stick inserted into it comes out dry. Turn the custard out on to a dish and cover with English sauce. Garnish with triangles of bread dipped in milk, then in beaten egg seasoned with salt and fried in olive oil until golden.

Baked Savoury Custard with Spinach
Flanes de huevo con espinacas

8 eggs	1¼ lb. spinach
½ teaspoon salt	2 oz. butter
1½ pints milk	1 oz. flour

Beat six eggs with salt and milk. Pour the mixture into small buttered moulds, filling them to just above half way, cook in a *bain-marie* in the oven until set. Prepare creamed spinach (p. 80), turn out the moulds on to this spinach foundation and serve.

Rolls with Egg   *Panecillos con huevo*

6 bread rolls	6 eggs
½ pint milk	4 oz. *sobrasada*
olive oil for deep frying	

Cut off tops of the rolls, to be used as 'lids', and carefully scoop out all soft part, leaving a crusty case. Boil the milk and let it get cold in a bowl. Dip each roll lightly in milk. Heat olive oil in a deep frying pan and fry the rolls, one by one, first cavity downwards, then turn and break an egg into each roll. Remove pan from heat (otherwise the bread will get too fried) and put small pieces of *sobrasada* on top of the egg. Return the pan to the fire and spoon hot oil over the egg until the white sets. Lightly fry the crust circles cut out for 'lids'. Remove roll from oil, cover with the 'lid'. Continue until all rolls are ready.

Egg Ring   *Roscón de huevos*

12 oz. large prawns
1 bunch asparagus
1¾ pints milk
6 eggs

¼ teaspoon salt
Victoria sauce (p. 76)
8 oz. ham

Boil the prawns in salted water, shell and cut the meat into pieces. Cook the asparagus. Boil the milk. Beat eggs as for an omelette, season with salt, incorporate the milk little by little, mix well and pour into a buttered ring-shaped mould. Cook in the oven in a *bain-marie* for 45 minutes. Make Victoria sauce, add prawns to it. Turn out the mould on to a round dish, fill the centre with the sauce, and dispose asparagus and pieces of rolled ham around it.

Gloria Rolls   *Panecillos Gloria*

6 rolls
½ pint milk
olive oil for deep frying
6 eggs

2 oz. butter
2 oz. grated cheese
salt
2 bunches watercress

Cut off tops of the rolls and keep for 'lids'. Carefully scoop out the soft part of the rolls leaving a crusty shell. Boil the milk, leave to cool completely in a bowl, dip the rolls lightly in it. Heat plenty of olive oil in a deep frying pan and fry the rolls, one by one, scooped out side downwards, then turn and, to ensure even cooking, spoon some oil over them. Make scrambled eggs, using eggs, butter, grated cheese and salt to taste. Lightly fry the 'lids' and drain. Fill rolls with the mixture, cover with 'lids', arrange on a layer of watercress and serve.

Rolled Omelette   *Tortilla doblada*

6 eggs	salt and black pepper
½ teaspoon water	1 oz. butter

Mix eggs in a bowl, add water and a pinch of salt and black pepper. Melt butter in a frying pan and when very hot pour in the eggs. As they begin to set, raise sides of omelette with a fork so that the uncooked part may flow under. When it is still quite runny on top, fold the omelette over and slide on to a heated dish. Bear in mind that the cooking takes only a couple of minutes and an omelette should never be kept waiting. Chopped parsley and garlic may be added to eggs during mixing.

Omelette a la Granadina   *Tortilla a la granadina*

3 chicken livers	1 glass white wine
1½ oz. butter	6 eggs
*fines herbes**	salt

Cook the chicken livers lightly in boiling salted water and slice finely. Heat 1 oz. butter in a frying pan, add the chicken livers, herbs and wine, and cook for 4 minutes. Beat the eggs, season with salt to taste. Heat butter in a frying pan, pour in the eggs, cook, stirring with a fork to prevent sticking until the mixture begins to solidify. Put the fried livers in the centre, gently fold over the omelette and serve.

Flat Omelette   *Tortilla redonda*

6 eggs	pinch salt
1 tablespoon lard	

Beat the eggs well and season with salt. Heat a little lard, or olive oil, in a frying pan, and when it is very hot pour in the eggs. As

---

* *fines herbes:* a mixture of equal parts of finely chopped parsley, tarragon, chives and chervil.

the bottom sets, allow a little more of the egg to cook by making a space round the edge of the pan with a knife, and letting the egg run into it. When nearly cooked through, put a large plate over the frying pan and turn it upside down to transfer the omelette on to the plate. Heat a little more lard, or olive oil, slide the omelette back into the pan to cook the other side.

Vegetable Omelette   *Tortilla a la jardinera*

4 oz. sliced French beans	1 small sliced pimento
4 oz. shelled peas	4 oz. peeled, chopped tomatoes
1½ oz. lard	salt
1 finely sliced onion	6 eggs

Boil the beans and peas separately in salted water. Heat lard (or olive oil, if preferred) in a frying pan and when it is hot, add the onion and pimento, cover and cook slowly. When cooked, add tomatoes, season with salt to taste and cook for 5 minutes. Beat the eggs, add beans, peas, and contents of the frying pan. Using this mixture, proceed to make a rolled or flat omelette (see recipes).

Balearic Omelette   *Tortilla balear*

8 oz. fresh sardines	6 eggs
pinch salt	1 tablespoon chopped parsley
juice of 1 lemon	1 clove chopped garlic
pinch paprika	2 tablespoons olive oil

Wash, scale and bone the sardines and leave them open. Season with salt and lemon juice, and sprinkle with paprika. Beat the eggs, add parsley, garlic and salt to taste. Heat oil in a large frying pan and when hot pour half the eggs into it. Immediately cover with sardines and pour the rest of the eggs on top. Cook slowly. When one side of the omelette is cooked turn it over and cook the other (see recipe for flat omelette). Serve at once.

Potato Omelette   *Tortilla de patata*

6 eggs   salt and pepper
1 lb. potatoes   oil for frying

Peel potatoes, slice very finely, fry in olive oil, covering the pan to
keep them soft. Beat the eggs, add potatoes and season to taste.
Heat some of the oil in which the potatoes were fried (only a
little is necessary for making an omelette), pour in the eggs and
make a flat omelette (p. 126) golden on both sides but soft in the
middle.

Omelette Stew   *Tortilla guisada*

6 eggs   1 chopped onion
4 oz. breadcrumbs   4 oz. peeled, chopped tomatoes
2 cloves chopped garlic   1 teaspoon flour
1 tablespoon chopped parsley   1 cup water
pinch salt   1 lb. shelled peas
3 tablespoons olive oil   1½ oz. pounded roasted almonds

Beat the eggs, add breadcrumbs and let them soak. Add garlic,
parsley and salt. Heat one tablespoon oil in a frying pan and make
two flat omelettes, one at a time, using half the eggs for each.
Heat two tablespoons oil in a saucepan and fry the onion lightly,
add tomatoes, cook for a few minutes, mix in the flour, stir well,
add water and a little salt. Bring to the boil, put in peas and
almonds. When they are half cooked, divide each omelette into
four and add to the pan. Reduce heat and shake the saucepan from
time to time to prevent sticking, but do not stir with a spoon as
it is easy to break the omelettes.

Omelette Filled with Béchamel   *Tortilla rellena de béchamel*

Make a thick *béchamel* sauce (p. 70). Heat a little olive oil in a
small frying pan, and when hot pour in one salted beaten egg;
make a rolled omelette, but before folding it over, put a tablespoon
of *béchamel* sauce in the centre, then fold the sides of the omelette
and remove from the pan with care. Continue in this way to make
the required number of omelettes.

Omelette Cake   *Pastel de tortillas*

9 eggs	8 oz. peeled and cooked tomatoes
1 large, finely sliced and fried potato	mayonnaise sauce (p. 74)
béchamel sauce (p. 70)	1 tinned sweet pimento
1 lb. cooked spinach	spring tomatoes (p. 33)

Make three flat omelettes (p. 126), one potato, one tomato and one
spinach, using three eggs in each. Make a thick *béchamel* sauce.
Put one omelette in the centre of a round dish, spread with a layer
of *béchamel*, making sure that none overflows down the sides.
Place another omelette over this, and follow with another layer
of *béchamel*. Finally, put the third omelette on top and cover with
a mayonnaise sauce. Decorate the centre with strips of pimento.
Garnish the cake with spring tomatoes.

PESCADOS, MOLUSCOS Y CRUSTÁCEOS

Eel, Country Style *Anguila a la paisana*

1½ lb. eel
salt
flour
olive oil
1 finely chopped onion

½ gill water
½ pint cream
1½ oz. butter
juice of 1 lemon

Rub the eel with salt to remove the glutinous substance on the skin. Many people skin the eel but the result is not so tasty. Remove the guts, wash well, and cut into pieces. Season with salt to taste, roll in flour, and fry in hot olive oil. Heat two to three tablespoons olive oil in a saucepan and fry the onion. When it becomes golden, add the pieces of eel and water, cover the pan, and cook gently until tender. Take the pieces of eel out of the pan and add cream, butter, lemon juice and salt to the pan juices. Return the eel to the pan and reheat without allowing the sauce to boil. Serve.

Eel with Sauce   *Anguila con salsa*

See recipe for Monk-fish with Sauce (p. 152).

Eel with Tartare Sauce   *Anguila con salsa tártara*

1½ lb. eel	olive oil
salt	1 lemon
flour	tartare sauce (p. 76)

Clean the eel by rubbing it with salt, remove the guts, cut into pieces, dip in flour and fry in hot olive oil. Arrange on a dish, surround with slices of lemon. Serve with tartare sauce.

Baby Eels   *Angulas*

1½ lb. small (baby) eels	tobacco
salt	2 chillis
olive oil	pinch pepper
3 cloves garlic	

Put the live eels in a bowl with water and a teaspoon of tobacco. Stir until they are dead and release saliva. Put them in a colander under a jet of water, and wash until the water is perfectly clear. Put the eels into salted boiling water a few at a time, stirring constantly. When the water begins to bubble again, remove from heat, drain the eels, and spread out on a cloth. Heat olive oil in a pan that can be brought to table and add garlic. Cut the chillis in half, remove seeds, and add to garlic. When the garlic browns lightly, take it and the chillis out of the pan, put in the eels, season with pepper, stir and immediately remove from heat. Serve in the same pan, piping hot. If the eels are fried too much, or are not served very hot, they will not be so tasty.

Herring Fritters   *Arenques abuñolados*

4 filleted herrings
½ pint milk
pinch pepper

batter (p. 262)
oil for frying
lemon

Wash the herring fillets, put in a jar, sprinkle with pepper, cover with milk and leave for 2 hours. Dip the herring fillets into batter, ensuring that both sides are covered, and fry in hot olive oil until nicely golden. Serve with slices of lemon.

Iberian Tunny   *Atún a la ibérica*

1½ lb. tunny in one piece
4 oz. fat salted pork
1 teaspoon salt
3 tablespoons flour
2 oz. lard

bread for *croûtons*
6 oz. finely sliced onions
1 gill white wine
1 small sprig thyme

Lard the tunny with fat salted pork cut into lardoons, season with salt, dredge with flour, fry lightly in lard and add wine. Bring to the boil, put in onions and thyme. Cover the pan with a well-fitting lid and cook on a very low heat for 50–60 minutes. Put the tunny on a dish, pour the sauce over it and garnish with fried *croûtons*.

Tunny Romana   *Atún a la romana*

1½ lb. tunny	1–2 beaten eggs
1 teaspoon salt	3–4 tablespoons flour
2 tablespoons olive oil	oil for frying
1 tablespoon lemon juice	fried artichokes (p. 81)

The most delicate part of a large tunny is the belly, which, sliced, resembles fillet of pork. Slice the tunny, cut off hard skin, season with salt, sprinkle with olive oil and lemon juice, leave for about an hour, then coat with egg and flour and fry in very hot olive oil. Arrange the tunny in a dish and surround with fried artichokes.

Tunny with Tomato Sauce   *Atún con salsa de tomate*

1½ lb. sliced tunny	oil for frying
salt	tomato sauce (p. 71)
flour	1 tablespoon chopped parsley

Season tunny with salt, dip in flour and fry in hot olive oil. Prepare tomato sauce, put in tunny, cook gently for 15–18 minutes, turn out on to a dish and sprinkle with parsley.

Estremadura Dried Cod   *Bacalao a la extremeña*

2 lb. dried cod	2¼ lb. spinach
3 large peeled, sliced potatoes	salt
3 tablespoons olive oil	

Soak the cod overnight, in enough water to cover, then change it from time to time. Drain the cod, dry carefully on a cloth and cut into pieces. Fry the potatoes in a covered pan to keep them soft. Line an oven-proof dish with the potatoes. In the same oil fry the cod lightly. Do not overcook. Arrange cod on top of potatoes. Cook the spinach in boiling salted water, drain, rinse under the cold tap, drain again, chop, toss in the oil in which the potatoes and cod were fried. Spread the spinach over the cod, bake in a hot oven for 12–15 minutes.

Basque Dried Cod (after Antonio Azcoaga)

Bacalao a la vizcaína

1¼ lb. dried cod	3 chillis
flour	2 slices fried and chopped bread
oil for deep frying	3 roasted and peeled sweet or
¾ lb. sliced onions	tinned pimentos
1¾ lb. peeled and chopped tomatoes	2 tablespoons grated breadcrumbs
1 clove garlic	1 tablespoon chopped parsley
1 tablespoon chopped onion	

Cut the cod into uniform pieces and soak in water overnight. Put in a pan with cold water, bring to the boil. Take the cod out just before the water begins to bubble. Drain, remove bones, taking care not to damage the fish, dip in flour and deep fry in smoking hot oil until golden. Drain on a cloth.

Fry the onions in 3 oz. olive oil until golden, add two-thirds of the tomatoes and fry slowly together. Soak the chillis in water and drain.

In another pan, fry the garlic and chopped onion. Add the rest of the tomatoes, the chillis and the fried bread. Cook together until the onion is tender, rub through a sieve, add to tomato and onion and mix well.

Cover the bottom of an oven-proof dish with a layer of the sauce, arrange pieces of cod on it, pour the rest of the sauce on top and cover with a layer of pimentos cut into thin strips (tinned pimento needs no cooking or peeling). Sprinkle with breadcrumbs mixed with parsley and put in the oven for 10 minutes to brown the top.

Baked Dried Cod　　　*Bacalao al horno*

1¼ lb. dried cod	salt
olive oil for frying	1 chopped onion
8 oz. cooked peas	2 cloves crushed garlic
1 chopped hard-boiled egg	12 oz. sieved tomatoes
2 diced sweet pimentos (tinned)	2 oz. roasted almonds

Soak the cod overnight, as described. Cut into pieces, fry in oil, arrange in an oven-proof dish, sprinkle peas, hard-boiled egg and pimentos on top and season with salt to taste. In the same oil in which the cod was fried lightly fry the onion. Before it becomes golden, add garlic and tomatoes. Pound the almonds, dilute with a tablespoon of water, add to the pan, bring to the boil and pour over the cod. Sprinkle with oil and put in a slow oven to heat through.

Dried Cod Pil-Pil   *Bacalao al pil-pil*

2¼ lb. thick-cut dried cod	2 cloves sliced garlic
½ pint olive oil	1 sliced chilli

Cut the cod into pieces 2 inches square. Soak in plenty of cold water for 24 hours, changing the water at least twice at the beginning. Drain, and scale the cod. Heat the oil in an earthenware dish and fry the garlic and chilli until golden. Allow the oil to cool, put in the cod skin-side up. Do not let it boil. Shake the dish gently and quickly over a low heat for 20 minutes, when the sauce should become white and acquire the consistency of mayonnaise. Serve in the same dish.

Dried Cod with Raisins and Pine-Kernels
Bacalao con pasas y piñones

1¼ lb. dried cod	4 oz. washed raisins
flour	3 oz. pine-kernels
olive oil for frying	½ cup water
1 chopped onion	pinch salt
4 oz. peeled, chopped tomatoes	bread

Cut cod into pieces 2 inches square and soak overnight. Flour the pieces of cod and fry in hot olive oil. Heat two tablespoons oil in a saucepan and lightly fry the onion. When it turns golden, add tomatoes, cook for 5 minutes, add raisins, pine-kernels and water and season with salt. Fry a slice of bread, chop it and add to pan together with the cod, cook gently for a few minutes and serve piping hot.

Dried Cod with Mayonnaise   *Bacalao con salsa mahonesa*

1¼ lb. dried cod
water
1 chopped onion
bouquet-garni
salt
garlic mayonnaise (p. 74)

8 oz. cooked French beans
2 sweet pimentos (grilled and peeled, or tinned)
4 hard-boiled eggs
2 gherkins

Soak the cod overnight, cut in slices ½ inch thick, put in a saucepan with just enough cold water to cover, add onion, *bouquet-garni* and salt to taste. Boil for 5 minutes, take off the fire, remove skin and bones with great care and leave to cool. When cold, arrange the cod in a dish, cover with garlic-flavoured mayonnaise sauce, allowing half clove garlic, decorate top with beans laid out in lattice pattern, mark the centre of each square with a disc of pimento and surround with slices of hard-boiled egg and gherkin.

Fried Dried Cod   *Bacalao rebozado*

1¼ lb. dried cod
2 beaten ggs
flour

olive oil for deep frying
salt
lemon

Soak dried cod overnight. Cut into pieces ½ inch thick, dip in beaten egg and flour, deep fry in olive oil until golden, drain on a cloth, sprinkle with fine salt and serve with slices of lemon.

Dried Cod Pudding   *Budín de bacalao*

2 lb. dried cod	4 eggs
3½ oz. butter	2 tablespoons flour
1 chopped onion	½ pint milk
1 lb. peeled, chopped tomatoes	

Soak the cod overnight. Put the cod into a saucepan of cold water, bring to the boil, carefully remove the skin and bones and chop the fish. Butter a mould and cover the bottom with buttered paper. Fry the onion lightly in 2 oz. butter, add tomatoes, finish frying, put into a bowl and mix in the cod. Beat two eggs and add to the mixture, blend well, add two more beaten eggs, mix and pour into the mould. Bake in a *bain-marie* in the oven until set. Turn out on to a dish, cover with *béchamel* sauce (p. 70) made with the rest of the butter, the flour and the milk.

Dried Cod Dumplings   *Buñuelos de bacalao*

4 oz. dried cod	1 teaspoon grated lemon rind
8 oz. flour	pinch salt
2 cloves chopped garlic	2 stiffly beaten whites of egg
1 tablespoon chopped parsley	olive oil for deep frying
2 yolks	

1. Chop the cod and soak overnight. Drain thoroughly, pressing out all water. Put the flour in a bowl, dilute with enough water to make a thick paste, add garlic, parsley, yolks, fish, lemon rind and salt. Blend well. Just before frying, fold in the stiffly beaten whites of egg. Heat plenty of olive oil and, when hot, drop the cod mixture into it a tablespoon at a time, not too close together to prevent sticking. Deep fry until golden on all sides, remove and drain well.

2. Soak the cod overnight. Boil it with two potatoes, drain, remove the skin and bones, mash with the potatoes and proceed in the same manner as in the previous recipe, but leave out the lemon peel and reduce the amount of flour by one tablespoon.

Dried Cod Croquettes   *Croquetas de bacalao*

8 oz. dried cod
1 chopped onion
1 oz. butter
2 cloves chopped garlic
1 tablespoon chopped parsley
2 oz. flour

1 pint milk
salt
2 beaten eggs
grated breadcrumbs
olive oil for deep frying

Chop the cod and soak overnight, drain and press out water. Fry onion lightly in butter, add garlic and parsley, stir, put in cod and fry lightly. Add flour and milk, little by little, simmer gently for 20 minutes, stirring all the time and season with salt to taste. If the mixture is too thick, add a little more milk; if too thin, stir in a little more flour. The mixture should be firm and the longer it is cooked, the smoother will be the texture. Spread it out on a dish to cool. The longer it is left, the easier it will be to shape the croquettes.

Taking a tablespoon at a time, roll first in flour, then in egg and breadcrumbs and shape with the hands. Fry a few at a time in plenty of hot olive oil, drain on a cloth and serve at once.

Dried Cod Soufflé   *Suflé de bacalao*

1 lb. dried cod
1 lb. potatoes
½ pint milk
1½ oz. butter

4 yolks
pinch salt
4 stiffly beaten whites

Soak the cod overnight. Peel the potatoes. Boil cod with potatoes. Remove skin and bones. Pound cod and potatoes together in a mortar, put in a bowl, add milk, butter and yolks and work together into a thin paste. Season with salt, fold in whites of egg, pour the mixture into a buttered soufflé dish and bake in the oven until golden on top. Serve immediately.

Barbel with Tartare Sauce   *Barbo con salsa tártara*

1½ lb. barbel
4 oz. olive oil
2 tablespoons chopped onion

1 tablespoon chopped parsley
seasoning
tartare sauce (p. 76)

Scale and clean the barbel thoroughly, marinate for 30 minutes in olive oil, chopped onion, seasoning and parsley, turning the fish from time to time. Grill and serve with tartare sauce.

Baked Sea-Bream   *Besugo al horno*

1 sea-bream
½ teaspoon salt
1 sliced lemon
1 sliced tinned sweet pimento
2 oz. lard
1 bay leaf

1 gill white
2 tablespoons grated breadcrumbs
2 cloves chopped garlic
1 tablespoon chopped parsley
3 tablespoons olive oil

Clean and scale the bream, leaving it whole, season with salt, make some cuts on both sides and insert a slice of lemon and a strip of pimento in each incision. Melt the lard in an oven-proof dish, put in the bream, add bay leaf, bake in the oven for 15 minutes, add wine and sprinkle with a mixture of breadcrumbs, garlic and parsley. Pour a dash of oil on top, cook in the oven until lightly golden, basting from time to time.

Roast Sea-Bream   *Besugo asado al horno*

1½ lb. sea-bream
2 oz. pork (or bacon) lardoons
½ teaspoon salt
lemon juice

2 tablespoons olive oil
2–3 hard-boiled eggs
supreme sauce (p. 76)

Clean and scale the bream, make incisions in both sides, insert a small lardoon in each, season with salt, put in a roasting pan, squeeze a dash of lemon juice, sprinkle a little olive oil over it and bake in a moderate oven for 30 minutes. Arrange it on a dish, and surround with the chosen salad, decorate with slices of hard-boiled egg and serve with supreme sauce.

Sea-Bream with Hollandaise Sauce

Besugo con salsa holandesa

2 sliced onions	pinch salt
2 sliced carrots	1½ lb. small, uniform sized potatoes
bouquet-garni	½ tablespoon chopped parsley
1 sea-bream	*hollandaise* sauce (p. 73)
1 gill white wine	

Put the onions, carrots and *bouquet-garni* in a fish-kettle, place the bream on the grid, cover with cold water, add wine and salt, cover with a lid, bring to the boil, reduce heat and simmer very gently for 15 minutes. Leave to cool in the cooking liquor. Peel the potatoes, boil in salted water and drain well. Arrange the bream on a dish, decorate with slices of carrots cooked with it, surround with potatoes and sprinkle with chopped parsley. Serve *hollandaise* sauce separately.

Sea-Bream with Green Sauce   *Castañola con salsa verde*

2 lb. sea-bream
salt
flour
olive oil for frying
1 chopped onion

1 large, peeled chopped tomato
½ cup water
2 cloves garlic
5 sprigs parsley
1 hard-boiled egg

Clean and scale the bream, fillet, cut into slices, season with salt, roll in flour and fry in hot olive oil. Using the same oil transferred to a saucepan, fry the onion. When it becomes golden, add tomato, stir in level teaspoon flour, gradually add water and season with salt to taste. Pound garlic in a mortar together with parsley and the yolk of hard-boiled egg, dilute with a little water and add to the pan. When the sauce begins to boil, put in the fish and cook on a gentle heat until it is ready.

Braised John Dory   *Dorada guisada*

1½ lb. John Dory
salt
flour
olive oil for frying
1 chopped onion
8 oz. peeled, chopped tomatoes

1¼ lb. *noisette* potatoes (p. 112)
12 oz. pickling onions
½ cup water
1 clove garlic
3–4 sprigs parsley
1 hard-boiled egg

Clean and scale the John Dory, fillet, cut into slices, season with salt, roll in flour and fry in hot olive oil. In a saucepan, using the same oil, brown the onion lightly, add tomatoes, fry lightly, add *noisette* potatoes and pickling onions, stir, pour in water and season with salt to taste. Cook for 10 minutes and put in fish. Pound garlic, parsley and the yolk of hard-boiled egg together in a mortar, dilute with a little water, add to pan, stir, cover, simmer gently for 15 minutes and serve.

Lamprey a la Marinera   *Lamprea a la marinera*

1½ lb. lamprey
4 tablespoons olive oil
2 sliced onions
1 gill white wine
2–3 cloves garlic
1 sprig parsley

1 bay leaf
salt
2 oz. diced mushrooms
1¼ oz. melted butter
1 teaspoon flour
croûtons

Clean the lamprey very well in three or four lots of water, remove the guts, cut into uniform pieces and put into a saucepan with olive oil, onions, wine, garlic, parsley and bay leaf. Season with salt and cook on a low heat with the lid on for 50–60 minutes. If necessary add a little water. Remove fish from pan, strain the sauce and return to pan. Add mushrooms, butter kneaded with flour, stir, put fish back in pan and simmer until done, without allowing the sauce to boil. Serve with *croûtons* of bread fried in butter.

Fillets of Sole au Gratin   *Filetes de lenguado gratinados*

2 lb. sole (filleted)*
2 oz. butter
salt
juice of 1 lemon
½ gill sherry
1 sliced onion
1 sliced carrot

1 bay leaf
1 sprig thyme
1½ pints water
1 oz. flour
2 oz. diced ham
2 oz. chopped mushrooms

Place the fillets of sole in a buttered oven-proof dish, season with salt to taste, sprinkle with lemon juice and sherry, cover with buttered greaseproof paper and put in the oven for 15 minutes.

Boil the bones, skin and head of the sole with onion, carrot, bay leaf, thyme, pinch of salt and water for 30 minutes; reduce liquid

* Remember to ask the fishmonger for the head, bones and skin.

by half and strain. Melt tablespoon butter in a pan, stir in flour, gradually add fish stock, then add the juices in which the fillets were cooked, the ham and the mushrooms, cook for 15 minutes, stirring continuously. Put the fillets in an oven-proof dish, cover with the sauce, dot with pieces of butter and put in the oven to brown the top.

Sole with Cream Sauce   *Lenguado a la crema*

1½ lb. filleted sole (keep bones, head and skin)
3 oz. butter
juice of 1 lemon
2 tablespoons brandy

12 oz. prawns
salt
1 oz. flour
2 raw yolks
½ pint cream

Place the fillets in an oven-proof dish with 1 oz. butter, lemon juice and brandy, cover with buttered greaseproof paper and put in the oven for 15 minutes. Boil the skin, bones and head in ½ pint water for 30 minutes. Add prawns, season with salt to taste and cook for further 5 minutes and strain.

Make *béchamel* sauce (p. 70) using 1 oz. butter, flour, strained fish stock and the juice in which the fillets were cooked. Remove from heat and blend in yolks and cream. Put the fillets in a buttered oven-proof dish, place a shelled prawn on top of each, cover with the sauce, dot with the rest of the butter and put in the oven to brown the top.

Bread, wine and raw garlic make a young man go briskly

Sole with Champignons   *Lenguado con champiñones*

1½ lb. filleted sole
4 oz. butter
juice of 1 lemon
1 gill white wine
salt

4 oz. button mushrooms
1 lb. tomatoes
pinch sugar
2 tablespoons grated breadcrumbs

Put the fillets of sole in an oven-proof dish with 1 oz. butter, lemon juice and wine. Season with salt to taste, cover with buttered greaseproof paper, and put in the oven for 20 minutes. Toss the mushrooms in 1 oz. butter and put around fish. Sieve the tomatoes into a pan, cook down to make a thick purée, season with salt, add sugar, simmer for a few moments, pour over the fish, sprinkle with breadcrumbs and the rest of the butter in tiny pieces, put the dish in the oven for 10 minutes and serve.

Costa Brava Bass   *Lubina a la Costa Brava*

2 lb. bass
salt
1½ oz. butter
juice of 1 lemon
1 gill white wine

Katherine sauce (p. 72)
1 truffle
2 bunches watercress
lobster in aspic (p. 175)

Clean and scale the bass, season with salt, put in an oven-proof dish with butter, lemon juice and wine and cook in the oven for 30 minutes, basting from time to time. Place the bass on a dish, cover with Katherine sauce, decorate with slivers of truffle, garnish with watercress down each side and arrange small moulds of lobster in aspic on top.

Bass with Hollandaise Sauce   *Lubina con salsa holandesa*

1¾ lb. bass
salt
1½ oz. butter
juice of 1 lemon
½ gill white wine

hollandaise sauce (p. 73)
1 hard-boiled egg
1 chopped truffle
2 bunches watercress
8 fish tartlets (p. 165)

Clean and scale the fish well, make a few incisions on both sides, season with salt, put in a buttered oven-proof dish, sprinkle with lemon juice and wine, cover with buttered greaseproof paper and bake in the oven for 30 minutes. Put the bass on a serving dish, cover with *hollandaise* sauce, decorate with slices of hard-boiled egg sprinkled with chopped truffle, garnish with watercress, arrange the fish tartlets on top and serve.

Catalan Hake au Gratin   *Merluza a la catalana gratinada*

1½ lb. hake
salt
4 oz. mushrooms
2 oz. olives
1 hard-boiled egg
1 sprig parsley

olive oil
1 small sliced onion
juice of ½ lemon
2 tablespoons breadcrumbs
2 oz. butter

Cut the hake into steaks and season with salt. Wash the mushrooms and chop together with olives, hard-boiled egg and parsley. Put sufficient olive oil to cover the bottom of an oven-proof dish, sprinkle with onion, put hake on top, sprinkle with lemon juice, cover with the chopped mixture, scatter breadcrumbs and small pieces of butter on top and bake in a moderate oven until golden.

Hake a la Marinera   *Merluza a la marinera*

1½ lb. hake
salt
4 oz. tomatoes
1 clove garlic

3 tablespoons olive oil
½ gill sherry
1 bay leaf
½ cup water

Wash the hake, cut into steaks and season with salt. Skin the tomatoes, remove seeds and pound with the garlic in a mortar. Heat olive oil in a saucepan. When it begins to smoke, add sherry and bay leaf, cover, boil for 2 minutes, add tomatoes and fry a few moments. Pour in water and add a pinch of salt. Bring to the boil, put in hake, boil hard for a few minutes and remove from heat.

This recipe was given by a fisherman who stressed the fact that the hake must be freshly caught. Otherwise, it is better to fry the fish before putting it in the sauce.

Baked Hake   *Merluza al horno*

1¾ lb. hake
salt
2 tablespoons olive oil
1 finely sliced onion
juice of ½ lemon
2 oz. butter

2 tablespoons flour
½ pint milk
4 oz. cooked peeled prawns
12 mussels
2 tablespoons grated breadcrumbs

Clean and bone the hake, season with salt. Put olive oil in an oven-proof dish, line with onion, place the opened out hake on top, sprinkle with lemon juice and cover with a sauce made in the following manner: Melt half the butter in a saucepan over a gentle heat. Stir in flour and gradually add milk, stirring continuously. Put the mussels in pan over heat and, as soon as the heat forces them to open, remove shells. Chop the prawns and mussels together, add to the sauce, cook for 5 minutes, pour over the hake, sprinkle with breadcrumbs and melted butter and bake in a moderate oven to brown the top.

Hake with Peas *Merluza con guisantes*

1½ lb. hake steaks	1 finely sliced onion
salt	4 oz. peeled, chopped tomatoes
flour	1 cup water
olive oil for frying	1 lb. shelled peas
1 sliced sweet pimento	½ teaspoon sugar

Clean the hake steaks, season with salt, roll in flour and fry in hot olive oil. Heat two tablespoons oil in a saucepan, fry the pimento, season with salt and remove from the pan. In the same oil, fry the onion and tomatoes, pour in water, add salt to taste, bring to the boil and put in peas. Cook for 5–6 minutes, add pimentos, sugar and hake. Cook gently together until the peas are ready and serve.

Baked Hake with Tomatoes *Merluza con tomate al horno*

1½ lb. hake steaks	8 oz. shelled peas
salt	12 mussels
olive oil	1 lb. peeled tomatoes
juice of 1 lemon	

Clean the hake steaks, season with salt, and put them with two tablespoons olive oil in an oven-proof dish. Sprinkle with lemon juice to taste and bake in the oven for 30 minutes. Cook the peas in boiling salted water and drain. Open the mussels by putting them over the heat and remove shells. Sieve the tomatoes over the hake, scatter the peas and mussels on top, sprinkle with a few drops of oil and return the dish to the oven for another 10 minutes.

Stuffed Hake   *Merluza rellena*

2 lb hake	1 oz. butter
2 oz. ham	salt
4 oz. mushrooms	juice of 1 lemon
1 hard-boiled egg	½ gill sherry
2 sprigs parsley	English sauce (p. 74)
8 medium-sized globe artichokes	8 large cooked, peeled prawns
8 oz. peas	

Clean the hake, cut off the head and remove the bones by slitting along the spine. Chop ham, mushrooms, egg and parsley together, rub through a sieve, stuff the hake with this mixture and close it to make it appear whole. Boil the artichokes (see recipe Boiled Artichokes). Boil the peas in salted water, drain, and stuff the artichokes with them. Put the hake in a well-buttered oven-proof dish, season with salt, sprinkle with lemon juice and sherry and bake in the oven for 20–25 minutes.

Transfer the hake to a serving dish, taking care not to break it, and cover with English sauce, incorporating in it the liquid in which the fish was cooked. Garnish with artichokes, alternating with the prawns, and serve.

Hake Croquettes   *Croquetas de merluza*

1 lb. hake	½ pint milk
salt	1 raw yolk
2 big peeled potatoes	1 beaten egg
1 chopped onion	grated breadcrumbs
1 oz. butter	oil for deep frying
1 oz. flour	

Put the hake in a small saucepan with enough cold water to cover it, add half teaspoon salt, simmer for 15 minutes and remove from heat. Cut the potatoes into pieces and cook in boiling salted water. While the fish and potatoes are cooking, fry the onion lightly in butter in a small saucepan. Add flour, stir, cook for a few minutes and gradually dilute this *roux* with milk. Cook gently for 15 minutes, stirring all the time to ensure smoothness, season with salt, remove from heat and stir in the yolk. Drain the fish, remove skin and bones and pound it in a mortar into a smooth paste. Drain the potatoes and rub through a sieve. Combine the sauce, the hake and the potatoes, mix well and leave to cool. Shape the croquettes, roll in flour, then in beaten egg and breadcrumbs and deep fry in hot olive oil until golden.

Tomato sauce (p. 71) may be served separately.

Mediterranean *Mérou*　　*Mero a la mediterránea*

1½ lb. *mérou*	1 bay leaf
flour	salt
olive oil for frying	1 lb. diced potatoes
1 chopped onion	2 cloves garlic
4 oz. peeled, chopped tomatoes	pinch saffron
1 small cup water	

Clean the *mérou*, cut into pieces, roll in flour and fry in hot olive oil. Brown the onion lightly in oil in a saucepan, add tomatoes, fry together for 2–3 minutes, add water and a bay leaf, season with salt to taste and put in potatoes.

Pound garlic in a mortar together with saffron, bind with a little oil and add to pan. When the potatoes are half cooked, put in the fish, cover and finish cooking over a low heat, shaking the pan from time to time to prevent sticking.

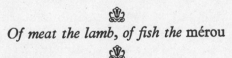

Of meat the lamb, of fish the mérou

Basque *Mérou*   *Mero a la vizcaína*

1½ lb. *mérou*
salt
juice of 1 lemon
olive oil
1 gill white wine
8 oz. finely sliced onions
2 cloves chopped garlic

1 tablespoon chopped parsley
1 lb. sieved tomatoes
1 soaked and pounded chilli
teaspoon sugar
2 tablespoons grated breadcrumbs
2 sweet pimentos (tinned)

Cut the fish in two or three pieces, put in an oven-proof dish, season with salt and lemon juice, sprinkle with a little olive oil, pour the wine over it, cover with buttered greaseproof paper and put in the oven for 20 minutes. Fry the onions in hot olive oil, brown lightly, add garlic and parsley, then put in tomatoes and simmer for 5 minutes. Add chilli, season with salt, sprinkle in sugar, pour in strained liquid in which the fish was cooked and simmer gently for 10 minutes. Place the *mérou* back in the oven-proof dish, cover with the sauce, sprinkle with breadcrumbs, decorate top with strips of pimento, moisten with a dash of olive oil and put in the oven for a few minutes.

Mérou with Mussels   *Mero con mejillones*

1½ lb. *mérou*
salt
flour
olive oil
1 chopped onion
½ teaspoon paprika

1 gill white wine
1 cup water
1 clove garlic
saffron
1 tablespoon chopped parsley
24 mussels

Slice the *mérou*, season with salt, roll in flour and fry in hot olive oil. Fry the onion lightly in a tablespoon of oil, add one teaspoon flour and the paprika. Simmer, add wine and water, season with salt to taste, bring to the boil and put in the fish. Pound garlic in a mortar with a pinch of saffron and the parsley, dilute with a little water, add it to the pan and cook gently for 10 minutes. Pour the contents of the saucepan into a dish. Bring the mussels to the boil, take them out of their shells, scatter over the fish and serve.

Catalan Monk-fish — *Rape a la catalana*

1½ lb. monk-fish
salt
flour
olive oil
1 finely sliced onion

3–4 cloves garlic
1 bay leaf
1 teaspoon vinegar
2 oz. grated cooking chocolate
croûtons

Cut the monk-fish into pieces, season with salt, roll in flour and fry in hot olive oil. Put the fish in a wide stewpot with onion, garlic, bay leaf, vinegar and chocolate. Pour in half cup water, cover with a well-fitting lid and cook slowly for 30 minutes.

Arrange the fish on a dish, strain the sauce over it, decorate with triangle-shaped *croûtons* of bread fried in butter or oil.

Malaga Monk-fish — *Rape a la malagueña*

1¼ lb. monk-fish
salt
flour
olive oil

1 finely chopped onion
4 oz. peeled, chopped tomatoes
1 lb. potatoes
1 sweet pimento (tinned)

Slice the monk-fish, season with salt, coat with flour and fry in hot olive oil in a small *paella* pan. Remove, and in the same oil fry the onion and tomatoes. Slice the potatoes in rounds and stir them in, adding just enough water to cook them. When they are half cooked, put in the fish. Cut pimento into strips, dip in olive oil and salt and lay on top of fish. Finish cooking very slowly. Serve in the same pan.

A *paella* pan is a frying pan with two handles in which the delicious '*paella*' (p. 64) is cooked, and from which the dish takes its name.

Quick Monk-fish   *Rape al minuto*

1¼–1½ lb. monk-fish steaks   olive oil
salt   3–4 cloves chopped garlic
juice of 1 lemon   2 tablespoons chopped parsley
flour   ½ teaspoon paprika

Clean monk-fish steaks, season with salt, sprinkle with lemon juice, coat with flour, fry in hot olive oil and keep on a hot dish.

Add a little more oil to the pan and quickly toss garlic and parsley. Add paprika and a pinch of salt, stir and sprinkle it over the fish. Serve immediately.

Monk-fish with Sauce   *Rape con salsa*

1½ lb. monk-fish steaks   1 clove garlic
salt   1 sprig parsley
flour   1¼ oz. roasted almonds
olive oil   1¼ oz. pine-kernels
1 slice bread   1 cup water
4 oz. peeled, chopped tomatoes

Clean the monk-fish steaks, season with salt, dip in flour and fry in hot olive oil. Heat three tablespoons olive oil in a saucepan, fry the bread and remove from pan. Fry the tomatoes in the same oil. Pound garlic, parsley, fried bread, almonds and pine-kernels in a mortar, add mixture to pan with water (enough to make a sauce), season with salt to taste, bring to the boil, put in the fish, cook slowly with the lid on for 30 minutes and serve.

Monk-fish with Scarlet Sauce   *Rape con salsa escarlata*

2 lb. monk-fish
salt

scarlet sauce (p. 73)
2 bunches watercress

Choose middle-cut of monk-fish, remove skin and bones and cut the fish in half along the spine. Put in a roasting pan. Season with salt, cover, bake in the oven without water or any other dressing, until done (it must remain white and dry). Allow to cool. When cold, cut into slices and arrange them in the centre of a dish to resemble a lobster's tail, cover with scarlet sauce, garnish with watercress and serve.

Turbot au Gratin   *Rodaballo al gratin*

2 lb. turbot (filleted and skinned)
salt
juice of 1 lemon
4 oz. butter
1 gill white wine
12 clams
4 oz. large prawns

8 oz. pickling onions
2 tablespoons flour
½ pint milk
4 oz. tinned or fresh button
    mushrooms
grated breadcrumbs

Clean the turbot fillets, season with salt and lemon juice, put in an oven-proof dish with 1 oz. butter and the wine, cover with buttered greaseproof paper and bake in the oven for 20 minutes.

Boil the clams and prawns for 5 minutes and remove shells, keeping the liquid for further use. Boil the onions whole in salted water and drain.

Melt 1 oz. butter in a saucepan, add flour and milk and make *béchamel* sauce (p. 70) incorporating the liquid in which the fish was cooked. Chop prawns and clams and add to sauce. If the sauce is too thick, pour in a little of the liquid in which the prawns and clams were cooked.

Arrange the fillets in a row in an oven-proof dish, put mushrooms and onions down the sides, cover all with the sauce, sprinkle with breadcrumbs and melted butter and put in the oven to brown the top.

Turbot with Mayonnaise   *Rodaballo con salsa mahonesa*

2 lb. turbot in four fillets
juice of ½ lemon
½ teaspoon salt
¼ teaspoon pepper
2 hard-boiled eggs

2 sprigs parsley
2 bunches watercress
8 oz. large cooked, peeled prawns
mayonnaise sauce (p. 74)

Clean the turbot fillets, put in a saucepan with just sufficient water to cover, add lemon juice, salt and pepper, bring to the boil, remove from heat and let the fish cool in the same water.

When cold, place the turbot fillets on a dish. Chop the parsley and hard-boiled eggs together and sprinkle over the fish. Arrange the watercress all around the dish, decorate with prawns. Serve mayonnaise sauce separately.

Turbot with Victoria Sauce   *Rodaballo con salsa Victoria*

1½–2 lb. turbot   breadcrumbs
salt   1¾ lb. boiled new potatoes
1 beaten egg   Victoria sauce (p. 76)
1 tablespoon olive oil   1 tablespoon chopped chervil

Clean the turbot, cut into steaks, season with salt, dip in egg beaten with a tablespoon of olive oil and coat with breadcrumbs. Heat and oil the grill tray and grill the turbot steaks under a moderate heat. Put the steaks on a dish, surround with new potatoes and cover with Victoria sauce. Sprinkle the potatoes with chopped chervil and serve.

Salmon with Mushrooms   *Salmón con champinones*

2 lb. piece salmon   4 oz. butter
salt   1 tablespoon flour
bouquet-garni   1 teaspoon sugar
1 chopped onion   1 tin (or 4 oz. fresh) mushrooms
1 gill white wine   1¾ lb. new potatoes
1 lb. tomatoes   1 tablespoon chopped parsley

Put the salmon in a pan with enough cold water to cover, season with salt, add *bouquet-garni*, onion and wine. Simmer gently for 20 minutes.

Peel and sieve tomatoes. Melt one and a half tablespoons butter in a saucepan and stir in the flour. Cook until the *roux* browns lightly, add tomato purée, a pinch of salt and sugar. Rinse the mushrooms, cut into pieces and add to pan. (If fresh mushrooms are used, they must be brought to the boil before cutting up.) Cook all together for 10 minutes.

Scrape potatoes and boil in salted water. Drain and fry in butter until golden. Arrange salmon in the centre of a dish, pour the sauce over it, sprinkle with chopped parsley, surround with potatoes and serve very hot.

Salmon with Crayfish Sauce   *Salmón con salsa de cangrejos*

2 lb. salmon steaks
6 crayfish
1 sliced onion
1 gill white wine
bouquet-garni
salt

1½ oz. butter
2 tablespoons flour
1 tablespoon crayfish butter (p. 77)
1 chopped truffle
3 hard-boiled eggs

Put the salmon steaks in a saucepan together with the crayfish, onion, wine, *bouquet-garni* and salt, cover with cold water, bring to the boil and simmer for 15 minutes.

Make *béchamel* sauce (p. 70) using butter, flour, and the liquid in which the fish was cooked. Add crayfish butter and truffle.

Arrange the salmon steaks on a dish, cover with the sauce and garnish alternately with crayfish and halved hard-boiled eggs.

Salmon or Tunny in Scallop Shells
Conchas de salmón o de atún

1 tin salmon or tunny
scarlet sauce (p. 73)
2 hard-boiled eggs

8 oz. cooked peas
2 sweet pimentos

Divide the fish, put a portion into each buttered shell, cover with scarlet sauce, place a slice of hard-boiled egg in the centre, surround with peas, decorate with discs of sweet pimento and serve.

NOTE. Tinned or fresh pimentos can be used. Fresh pimentos must first be grilled, peeled and seeded.

Red Mullet en Papillotes   *Salmonetes a la papillote*

1½ lb. red mullet
salt
1 tin (or 4 oz. fresh) mushrooms
1½ oz. butter

1 chopped onion
1 tablespoon chopped chervil
1 tablespoon chopped parsley

Clean the red mullets, scale and season with salt. Wash the mush-rooms well, drain and chop. Melt the butter in a small saucepan, add onion, chervil and parsley and fry lightly, without browning. Cut a piece of greaseproof paper for each mullet, oil one side, put a spoonful of the chopped mixture on it, lay fish on top, cover with another spoonful of mixture and wrap it in the paper. Put the fish in an oven-proof dish and bake for 30 minutes. Serve hot.

Grilled Red Mullet   *Salmonetes a la parrilla*

1½ lb. red mullet
pinch salt
3 tablespoons olive oil
juice of 1 lemon

1 tablespoon chopped parsley
potato straws (p. 113)
tomato (p. 71) or *romesco* sauce (p. 78)

Scale and clean the mullets, season with salt, sprinkle with olive oil and lemon juice and leave to marinate, then grill, arrange in a dish, sprinkle with chopped parsley and garnish with potato straws. Serve tomato sauce separately.

An even better sauce for grilled red mullet is *romesco*.

Baked Red Mullet   *Salmonetes al horno*

1½ lb. red mullet
1 teaspoon salt
2 oz. flour
1 cup olive oil
3 cloves chopped garlic

1 tablespoon chopped parsley
8 oz. peeled, chopped tomatoes
½ teaspoon sugar
2 tablespoons grated breadcrumbs

Clean and scale red mullets, season with salt, coat with flour and fry in hot olive oil. Arrange in an oven-proof dish. Heat two tablespoons oil in a frying pan and lightly fry garlic and parsley; add tomatoes, season with salt, add sugar, cook for 5 minutes and then cover the red mullet with this sauce. Sprinkle with bread-crumbs and a few drops of olive oil and bake in a hot oven for 10 minutes.

Fried Red Mullet   *Salmonetes fritos*

1½ lb. red mullet
pinch salt
juice of ½ lemon
1 cup olive oil
2 cloves chopped garlic

1 tablespoon chopped parsley
2 tablespoons flour
1 beaten egg
2 oz. grated breadcrumbs
1 lemon

Clean, scale and marinate the fish for 2 hours in salt, lemon juice, two tablespoons olive oil, garlic and parsley. Then dip in flour, egg and breadcrumbs and fry in hot olive oil. Drain, put on a dish, garnish with slices of lemon and serve.

Grilled Sardines   *Sardinas a la parrilla*

24 fresh sardines
salt
olive oil

2 tablespoons chopped parsley
2–3 cloves chopped garlic
green sauce (optional)

Clean fresh sardines, season with salt to taste, put a few drops of olive oil on each, grill, arrange on a dish and sprinkle with parsley, garlic and a few drops of oil. Fresh grilled sardines may also be served with green sauce (p. 76).

Fried Sardines   *Sardinas rebozadas*

24 fresh sardines
salt
flour

beaten egg
olive oil
1 lemon

Clean sardines, bone and, leaving them open, season with salt, dip in flour and beaten egg and deep fry in hot olive oil until golden. Drain well. Serve with slices of lemon.

Stuffed Sardines   *Sardinas rellenas*

1¼ lb. fresh sardines

chopped *fines herbes*

1 oz. grated cheese

1½ oz. butter

2 tablespoons grated breadcrumbs

1 tablespoon olive oil

Clean and bone sardines, leave them open. Mix chopped *fines herbes* (tablespoon each of tarragon, chives and parsley) with butter and cheese. Spread a spoonful of this mixture on one half of the fish, sandwich together to close the sardines, arrange on an oiled roasting pan, sprinkle with breadcrumbs and olive oil and bake in the oven until golden.

Suquet   *Suquet*

5 tablespoons olive oil

2 heads garlic (diced)

2 tablespoons flour

8 oz. peeled tomatoes

1 tablespoon chopped parsley

salt

pinch black pepper

1 lb. halibut

1 lb. turbot

1 lb. cod

Heat the oil and fry first the garlic, then the flour until golden. Add the tomatoes and parsley, season with salt and pepper and cook for a few minutes. Cut the fish (any firm fleshed fish is suitable for this dish) into slices, add to pan and cook for 15 minutes, shaking the pan frequently and adding a little water if the sauce is too thick.

If you bear your neighbour ill-will, put the goats into his olive garden

Fish Aspic *Aspic de pescado*

8 oz. hake
8 oz. prawns
salt
1 bay leaf
1 sliced onion
1 gill white wine
12 oz. diced potatoes

8 oz. shelled peas
2 sweet red pimentos (tinned)
1 hard-boiled egg
4 leaves gelatine
supreme sauce (p. 76)
olive oil

Cook the hake and the prawns in boiling salted water with bay leaf, onion and wine for 20 minutes. Drain and keep the stock for aspic jelly. Boil potatoes and peas. Drain.

Cut discs out of one pimento and cut up the other. Cut a disc of the centre of the hard-boiled egg and cut up the rest.

Soak two leaves of gelatine in one tablespoon water. Make supreme sauce (using ½ pint olive oil). Skin and bone the hake, add shelled prawns and chop in a bowl. Add potatoes, peas and pieces of pimento and egg, keeping the discs. Stir in the sauce and gelatine diluted with a tablespoon of hot water. Mix well, taking care to stir always in the same direction, so that the sauce does not separate.

Place the disc of hard-boiled egg in the centre of the bottom of an aspic mould, surround with discs of pimento, fill the mould with the fish and put in a cool place for 3 hours. (Less time required if the aspic is kept in a refrigerator.) Prepare aspic jelly by following the recipe for Lobster in Aspic (p. 175) using only the fish stock. Leave until set, turn out and chop the jelly.

Just before serving, dip the mould for a second in hot water, turn out on to a dish, garnish with chopped jelly and serve.

Fish Pudding   *Budín de pescado*

1½ lb. hake	1½ oz. grated cheese
salt	8 oz. sieved tomatoes
1 gill white wine	4 eggs
bouquet-garni	1 yolk
2 oz. butter	breadcrumbs
1 chopped onion	juice of ½ lemon
1 oz. flour	cooked peeled prawns (optional)
½ pint milk	cooked shelled clams (optional)

Put hake (monk-fish, sea-bream or any white fish is equally good) into boiling salted water, add wine and *bouquet-garni* and simmer for 25 minutes. Drain (keeping the stock), skin and bone the fish and pound into a paste. In a saucepan lightly fry the onion in one tablespoon butter, without allowing it to colour. Stir in flour, add the milk and an equal quantity of fish stock, little by little, to prevent the sauce becoming lumpy. Add cheese, a pinch of salt and tomatoes. Cook for 10 minutes, stirring continuously. Remove pan from heat, divide the contents in half. To one part add four yolks of egg, mix well, and stir in the fish paste. Beat the whites of egg stiffly and fold them into the mixture.

Butter an oval-shaped mould, sprinkle with breadcrumbs and pour in the mixture, taking care not to fill the dish to the top as the pudding will rise during cooking. Put in a *bain-marie*, bake in a moderate oven for 1 hour and keep hot.

Sauce for the pudding. Add a little fish stock to the other half of the sauce to thin it, pass through a sieve into a double saucepan, add yolk, lemon juice and the rest of the butter. It must be fairly thick and very smooth. Heat slowly and keep it hot until the moment of serving. Turn out the hot fish pudding on to a round dish, cover with the sauce and serve.

NOTE. Prawns or large clams may be used as garnish for the pudding. If clams are used, cover them with tomato purée.

Fish in Scallop Shells   *Conchas de pescado*

1. 1 lb. monk-fish   2 oz. flour
    8 oz. shrimps   1 pint milk
    1 sliced onion   4 oz. washed chopped mushrooms
    salt   ½ teaspoon pepper
    1 lb. peeled potatoes   2 tablespoons grated breadcrumbs
    3 oz. butter   1 egg

Boil the monk-fish and shrimps in just enough salted water to cover, with onion, for 20 minutes, drain, skin and bone the fish and peel the shrimps. Cut the flesh into small pieces.

Boil potatoes in salted water, drain, rub through a sieve, add 1 oz. butter and blend into the purée. Make *béchamel* sauce (p. 70), using 1½ oz. butter, the flour and the milk. Add monk-fish, shrimps and mushrooms, season with salt and pepper to taste and cook gently for 5 minutes. Remove from heat and add egg.

Fill the scallop shells with this mixture, sprinkle with breadcrumbs and the rest of the butter in small pieces. Pipe a border of potato purée around the edges through forcing bag with a fluted nozzle, put in the oven to brown the top and serve.

2. 8 oz. monk-fish   8 oz. prawns
    8 oz. hake   18 mussels
    salt   2 oz. butter
    1 sliced onion   1 oz. flour
    bouquet-garni   1 yolk (raw)
    1 gill white wine   1½ oz. grated cheese

Boil the monk-fish and hake in just enough salted water to cover, with onion, *bouquet-garni* and wine for 10 minutes, add prawns and mussels and simmer gently for 10 minutes. Drain, but keep the fish stock. Skin and bone the fish, peel prawns, shell mussels and cut them all into pieces.

Make *béchamel* sauce (p. 70) using 1 oz. butter, the flour and the strained fish stock, remove from heat and mix in the yolk.

Put an equal amount of fish, etc., into each scallop shell, cover with the sauce, sprinkle with grated cheese and the rest of the butter. Bake in the oven to brown the top.

Fish Pasties   *Empanadillas de pescado*

1. 8 oz. monk-fish   1½ oz. butter
    18 mussels   1 oz. flour
    salt   8 oz. cooked peas
    1 sliced onion   pastry for tarts (p. 262)
    1 sliced carrot   olive oil for deep frying
    1 bay leaf   fried parsley (p. 113)

Cook the monk-fish and mussels in boiling salted water with onion, carrot and bay leaf for 20 minutes and drain, keeping the liquid for later use. Remove the mussels from their shells and chop them up, together with the monk-fish.

Make a thick *béchamel* sauce (p. 70) using butter, flour and fish stock. Add fish and peas and cook together for 5 minutes.

Roll out the pastry, cut out with a round pastry cutter for pasties, put a tablespoon of filling on one side of the circle, fold over the other half, seal and crimp the edges.

Deep fry the pasties in hot olive oil, drain well, arrange on a napkin covered dish and garnish with fried parsley.

2. 12 clams   *béchamel* sauce (p. 70)
    6 anchovies   tart pastry (p. 262)
    3 hard-boiled eggs   olive oil for deep frying
    2 oz. butter

Open the clams by placing them over the heat. Bone the anchovies, wash well and soak in water for a while to de-salt. Shell the eggs, chop with the clams and anchovies, blend in butter, and proceed as described in the previous recipe, making the pasties smaller.

Fish Patties   *Pastelillos de pescado*

8 oz. large prawns	1½ oz. butter
1 large head of hake	1 oz. flour
1 onion	1 chopped truffle
1 bay leaf	puff-pastry (p. 261)
salt	1 beaten egg

Clean the prawns and the hake head, put them in a saucepan with just enough cold water to cover, add half an onion, a bay leaf and salt. Bring to the boil, simmer for 10 minutes, remove prawns and let the rest continue boiling fast for 30 minutes to reduce the liquid. Chop half onion finely, fry in butter in a saucepan, taking care not to let it colour, stir in flour, and slowly add the strained fish stock. (This *béchamel* sauce should be thick.) Peel and chop prawns. Pick out all flesh from the head of hake, chop finely and add to sauce, together with prawns and truffle. Season with salt and cook gently for 10 minutes, stirring continuously to ensure smoothness.

Roll out pastry, cut into rounds big enough to hold a tablespoon of mixture, arrange on a baking tray, brush with beaten egg, taking care not to go too near the edge (as this prevents pastry from rising), in the centre of each round of pastry put a tablespoon of the filling and bake in a hot oven until the pastry has risen and is golden.

Marinated Fish   *Pescado en escabeche*

Fresh sardines, tunny or bream may be treated in this way. Clean, season with salt, flour, fry the fish in hot olive oil, drain and put in a deep dish. Add more oil to the frying pan (sufficient to cover the fish afterwards) and fry a sliced onion, three or four cloves of garlic, a bay leaf, a sprig of thyme, a tablespoon of vinegar and a teaspoon of paprika. Season with salt. Pour over the fish, let it cool. When quite cold, cover the dish.

Fish prepared in this way will keep well for five or six days.

Fish Tartlets   *Tarteletas de pescado*

1 big hake head	8 oz. hake
1 sliced onion	2 oz. butter
1 bay leaf	1 oz. flour
1 sprig parsley	1 chopped truffle
1 gill white wine	2 yolks
salt	pastry for tarts (p. 262)
1¾ pints water	4 oz. cooked, peeled shrimps

Put head of hake, onion, bay leaf, parsley, wine and salt into water, bring to the boil, skim and simmer until liquid is reduced by ½ pint, then strain into another pan. Boil the hake, in one piece, in this stock for 10 minutes. Drain and cut into pieces. Keep the stock. Melt 1½ oz. butter in a saucepan and make a *béchamel* sauce (p. 70), with flour and the fish stock. Add truffle and hake, cook for 5 minutes, remove from heat and stir in yolks.

Butter tartlet tins and flour lightly. Roll out pastry to a thickness of ⅛ inch, cut out and line tartlet tins, trimming off excess pastry with a knife. Prick the bottom with a fork and fill with chick-peas or haricot beans to prevent pastry from rising. Bake blind in the oven until golden. Remove chick-peas or beans and return tins to oven for a moment to bake the inside. Remove tartlet cases, fill with the prepared filling, garnish the centre with a shrimp.

Zarzuela   *Zarzuela de pescado*

24 mussels	12 oz. sieved tomatoes
1 lb. squids	1 lb. diced and fried monk-fish
1 chopped onion	8 oz. prawns
2–3 tablespoons olive oil	salt and pepper
3 cloves chopped garlic	1 teaspoon brandy
1 tablespoon chopped parsley	

Scrub the mussels, put in a frying pan on the fire to open and remove the shells.

Cook the squids in a little olive oil very gently in a small covered pan and slice.

Fry the onion in olive oil lightly, add garlic and parsley, stir, add tomatoes, mussels, monk-fish, squids and prawns. Season with salt and pepper to taste, add brandy and simmer together with the lid on for 20 minutes, stirring from time to time.

Squids Romana   *Calamares a la romana*

Cut off the head and tentacles of the squids, taking care not to break the bag, remove fins, cut the bag into rings about ½ inch in width, put them in a bowl, sprinkle with olive oil and lemon juice and leave to macerate for an hour, turning from time to time. (Do not put any salt in until ready to fry as it hardens them.) Heat olive oil in a frying pan, salt squid rings, dip in flour and beaten egg and fry in smoking hot oil. Arrange on a dish and garnish with slices of lemon.

The head, tentacles and fins may be used in a rice dish.

Stuffed Squids (1)   *Calamares rellenos (1)*

1½ lb. squids	2–3 tablespoons olive oil
4 oz. minced pork	1 chopped onion
2 cloves finely chopped garlic	4 oz. peeled, chopped tomatoes
1 tablespoon chopped parsley	8 oz. sliced carrots
1 egg	½ cup water
salt	12 mussels au gratin (p. 168)

Clean and trim the squids, leaving the bags whole. Mince the head, the tentacles and the fins very finely. Add pork, garlic and parsley.

Mix well together, stir in an egg, season with salt to taste, stuff the squids with this mixture and sew up the opening.

Heat olive oil in a saucepan, fry the squids lightly, add onion and cook without allowing to brown. Add tomatoes and carrots, sti and pour in water. Season with salt and cook gently with the lid on, stirring from time to time, as the squids tend to stick to the pan. Arrange the stuffed squids on a dish, distribute the carrots over them and surround with mussels au gratin.

Stuffed Squids (2) *Calamares rellenos* (2)

1½ lb. squids	2 chopped onions
8 oz. peas	1 sliced sweet pimento
1 diced potato	8 oz. peeled chopped tomatoes
4 oz. French beans	salt
3 carrots	*noisette* potatoes (p. 112)
olive oil	1½ oz. pounded pine-kernels

Prepare the squids as in the previous recipe and fill with a stuffing made as follows:

Shell the peas and cook them in boiling salted water with one diced potato. In another pan, cook sliced beans and diced carrots and drain.

Lightly fry one of the onions in olive oil, add pimento and half the tomatoes; season with salt to taste, fry for a few moments, then add the vegetables and fry lightly for 2–3 minutes. Stuff the squids with this mixture and sew up.

Heat two to three tablespoons olive oil in a saucepan and fry the second chopped onion and the rest of the tomatoes. Put in the squids and fry lightly until golden. Pour in half cup water, bring to the boil, add *noisette* potatoes and pine-kernels, season with salt, cover and simmer until tender.

Fried Clams   *Almejas salteadas*

2 doz. clams   juice of ½ lemon
4 tablespoons olive oil   salt
2 cloves chopped garlic   pepper
1 tablespoon chopped parsley   ½ cup water

Wash the clams thoroughly. Heat olive oil in a saucepan and put in the clams. When they open, add garlic, parsley and lemon juice. Fry lightly, add water, season with salt and pepper to taste, simmer for 15 minutes and serve.

Mussels a la Marinera   *Mejillones a la marinera*

3 tablespoons olive oil   pinch sugar
4 oz. finely sliced onions   1 clove pounded garlic
8 oz. peeled chopped tomatoes   ½ tablespoon chopped parsley
½ teaspoon salt   3 pints well scrubbed mussels

Heat olive oil in a frying pan and fry the onion until golden. Add tomatoes, season with salt and sugar and add garlic and parsley. Put the mussels in the sauce and cook for 15–20 minutes, stirring gently from time to time.

Mussels au Gratin   *Mejillones gratinados*

3 pints mussels   1 tablespoon chopped parsley
2–3 tablespoons grated breadcrumbs   ½ teaspoon salt
2 cloves chopped garlic   2 tablespoons olive oil

Clean the mussels well, put in a frying pan on the fire to open, remove shells and place the mussels in a gratin dish.

Combine breadcrumbs, garlic, parsley and salt. Cover the mussels with the mixture, sprinkle with olive oil and put in the oven until they are golden.

This way of preparing mussels is excellent as garnish for fish.

Fried Mussels   *Mejillones rebozados*

3 pints mussels   flour
olive oil   salt
juice of 1 lemon   beaten egg

Clean the mussels well, put in a frying pan on the fire to open and remove shells. Put mussels in a bowl, sprinkle with eight tablespoons olive oil and lemon juice and leave to stand for an hour.

Dip the mussels in flour and beaten egg seasoned with salt. Heat olive oil in a frying pan. When it is very hot, fry the mussels, drain and serve.

Oysters au Gratin   *Ostras al gratín*

2 doz. oysters   *béchamel* sauce (p. 70)
salt   1 tablespoon mussel butter (p. 77)
1 tablespoon olive oil   2 tablespoons grated cheese
juice of ½ lemon   1 oz. butter

Open the oysters, put in an oven-proof dish, season with very little salt and sprinkle with olive oil and lemon juice. Put them in the oven for 10 minutes. Add mussel butter to *béchamel* sauce and pour over oysters. Sprinkle with grated cheese, scatter small pieces of butter and return to the oven to brown the top.

This recipe and the previous one are equally suitable for oysters, clams or mussels.

Octopus with Onion   *Pulpos con cebolla*

1½ lb. octopus   salt
4 tablespoons olive oil   pepper
2 large thinly sliced onions

Clean the octopus, cut into slices and put in a saucepan with olive oil. Cover and cook gently. When they begin to soften, add onions, season with salt and pepper to taste and simmer until the onions are soft.

The smaller the octopus the tastier the dish.

Octopus with Potatoes   *Pulpos con patatas*

1½ lb. octopus   salt
4 tablespoons olive oil   2 cloves garlic
8 oz. sliced onions   2 sprigs parsley
1 bay leaf   pinch saffron
1 lb. sliced potatoes

Clean the octopus and cut into pieces. Heat olive oil in a saucepan and lightly fry the onions. Add the octopus and a bay leaf, cover and cook very gently. When the octopus begins to soften, add potatoes, season with salt to taste, cover and simmer until done. Pound garlic in a mortar with parsley and saffron, blend with a little oil, mix with the octopus, stir and serve.

Stewed Cuttlefish   *Sepia estofada*

1½ lb. cuttlefish   1 bay leaf
4 tablespoons olive oil   2 tablespoons white wine
1 finely sliced onion   pinch salt
head of garlic

Clean the cuttlefish, cut it into pieces and put in a saucepan with olive oil, sliced onion, garlic, bay leaf and white wine. Do not add the salt until the fish is almost cooked, otherwise it will harden. Cook very gently; if it gets too dry add a little water.

Boiled Snails   *Caracoles cocidos*

2½ lb. snails   1 bay leaf
salt   1 sprig thyme
½ pint vinegar   1 sprig fennel
2 cloves garlic

The snails must be kept without food for at least 15 days before use. Wash the snails thoroughly in a bowl with a good pinch of salt and a glass of vinegar, stirring for a time to get rid of the slime and changing the water until it is completely clear. Leave the snails in fresh water until they emerge from their shells and inspect them one by one. If any fail to emerge from their shells, discard them, as this is a sign that they are dead.

Put the snails in a saucepan with cold water, garlic, bay leaf, thyme and fennel, bring to the boil, season with salt and simmer for 1 hour.

Drain and serve with vinaigrette sauce, or thin garlic mayonnaise (p. 74).

Stewed Snails   *Caracoles guisados*

2½ lb. snails	12 oz. peeled, chopped tomatoes
1 finely chopped onion	1 clove garlic
2–3 tablespoons olive oil	1 sprig parsley
4 oz. sliced *sobrasada*	salt and pepper
2 sweet sliced pimentos	

Clean and boil the snails as described in the previous recipe and drain. Fry onion lightly in olive oil in a saucepan. Before it begins to colour, add *sobrasada* (soft paprika sausage) and the pimento. Fry lightly and add tomatoes. Pound the garlic and the parsley in a mortar, dilute with a little water, stir into the contents of the saucepan, season with salt and pepper to taste, mix well and simmer until soft. Put in the snails and cook gently for 20 minutes.

Lightly Fried Snails   *Caracoles rehogados*

Clean and boil the snails according to the previous recipe and drain. Heat some olive oil in a frying pan, put in the snails, sprinkle with a little salt, pepper and flour, stirring from time to time, and cook over a gentle heat until a crust forms on the shells.

Fried Frogs' Legs   *Ranas rebozadas*

2 lb. frogs' legs	beaten egg
salt	grated breadcrumbs
juice of 1 lemon	olive oil for frying
flour	*croûtons*

Clean frogs' legs, skin and cut off feet. Soak in very cold water, changing it from time to time, for 2 hours, to make them white and plump before preparing them in any way.

Season the frogs' legs with salt and lemon juice, dip in flour, beaten egg and breadcrumbs. Fry in hot olive oil. Arrange on a dish and garnish with *croûtons*.

Frogs' Legs with Tomato Sauce   *Ranas con salsa de tomate*

2 lb. frogs' legs	tomato sauce (p. 71)
salt	1 tablespoon chopped parsley
lard	potato purée

Prepare the frogs' legs as described, season with salt and fry in pure lard. Make tomato sauce and simmer the frogs' legs in it for 10 minutes over a gentle heat. Put on a serving dish, sprinkle with chopped parsley and pipe with a border of potato purée.

Crayfish Martin   *Cangrejos de río Martin*

30 crayfish	salt and pepper
2 tablespoons butter	1 tablespoon flour
4 oz. chopped onions	2 tablespoons sherry
1 tablespoon chopped parsley	1½ oz. butter
2 tablespoons vinegar	

Wash and gut the crayfish. Heat butter in a saucepan and lightly fry the onions. Before they turn golden, add parsley. Add crayfish to onion and cook gently until they turn pink. Sprinkle with vinegar, season with salt and pepper to taste, cook very gently with the lid on for 15 minutes. Take out the crayfish and keep hot. Stir the flour into the sauce, cook a moment, pour in sherry and add butter, blending it in in small pieces. Stir well and pour the sauce over the crayfish.

Lobster and Chicken   *Langosta y pollo*

5 tablespoons olive oil
2 heads garlic
1 tablespoon chopped parsley
8 oz. peeled tomatoes

1½ oz. roasted almonds
2 tender roasting chickens
4–5 lb. live lobster
salt

Heat the oil and fry the peeled but whole cloves of garlic with the parsley until golden. Add tomatoes and cook for 5 minutes. Add almonds and put the whole mixture through a mincer into a pan. Joint the chicken and sprinkle with salt. Cut up the lobster. Cook chicken and lobster in the sauce for 30 minutes, adding a little water and salt, if necessary.

Lobster à la Villeroi   *Langosta a la Villeroi*

1 large *or*	breadcrumbs
2 medium-sized live lobsters	beaten egg
salt	olive oil for deep frying
Villeroi sauce (p. 70)	potato straws (p. 113)

Put a large saucepan on the fire with plenty of water and some salt. Bring to the boil, put in a live lobster, having tied up its claws. Boil fast for 20 minutes, remove from water, allow to cool. When cold, take off the shell and cut the meat into fine slices. Coat the slices of lobster with Villeroi sauce, roll in breadcrumbs, beaten egg and again in breadcrumbs. Deep fry in hot olive oil until golden on all sides. Drain well. Garnish with potato straws.

Lobster Costa Blanca   *Langosta Costa Blanca*

2¼ lb. live lobster	salt and pepper
olive oil	*bouquet-garni*
bread	2 cloves garlic
4 oz. chopped onions	pinch saffron
2–3 tablespoons sherry	1–2 sprigs parsley
1 lb. tomatoes	1½ oz. pine-kernels

Heat three to four tablespoons olive oil in a saucepan, fry a slice of bread until crisp, remove and keep. In the same oil lightly fry the onions. Add the lobster, cut into pieces, taking care to save the juices that escape while cutting it. Fry lightly for 5–6 minutes, pour in the sherry, cook gently for a few minutes, add tomatoes, season with salt and pepper to taste and add *bouquet-garni*.

Pound the garlic, fried bread, saffron, parsley and pine-kernels together in a mortar, add the juice collected when cutting the lobster and the pulp from the head, mix well, add to the saucepan, simmer with a lid on for 30–40 minutes.

Lobster Aspic   *Cubiletes de aspic de langosta*

2 pints water
1 teaspoon salt
1 sliced onion
1 gill white wine
1–1¼ lb. live lobster
1 large head of hake

1 egg
3 leaves gelatine
1 cooked sliced carrot
1 thinly sliced truffle
1 lb. cooked peas

Bring water to the boil with salt, onion and wine, put in lobster, cook for 20–25 minutes, then remove from the liquid and slice. In the same liquid cook the head of hake for 30 minutes, reducing the amount of liquid to 1½ pints, which is enough to make the aspic jelly. Strain the liquid into another saucepan, and put it back on the fire. Clarify with egg (see recipe for Consommé), strain through a damp cloth stretched over a sieve. If necessary, do this twice, using a clean cloth each time. Soak gelatine in cold water, then dissolve in just enough hot water and add to aspic liquor.

Fill a large flat basin with crushed ice and arrange the aspic moulds in it. Line each with a thin layer of aspic jelly. Before this sets, decorate with a slice of carrot and slivers of truffle, carefully spoon over another thin layer of jelly. When it begins to set, put a slice of lobster on it, add another layer of jelly, cover with a spoonful of peas and, finally, another layer of jelly to seal all ingredients.

To serve, dip the moulds into hot water, wipe and turn out the aspic jelly. Lobster in aspic can be made in a large mould, as well as in individual moulds.

Timbale of Lobster   *Timbal de langosta*

1 live lobster of 2¼ lb.	1 tablespoon crayfish butter (p. 77)
1½ lb. potatoes	2 tablespoons tomato purée
salt	breadcrumbs
4 oz. butter	radishes
1 oz. flour	stuffed olives
½ pint milk	

Cook the lobster and cut it in slices as described in the recipe for Lobster à la Villeroi.

Cook the potatoes in boiling salted water with their skins on, peel and cut into fine slices.

Make *béchamel* sauce (p. 70) using 1 oz. butter, flour and milk, blend in the crayfish butter and tomato purée.

Butter a mould, sprinkle with breadcrumbs and cover the bottom with a layer of potato, sprinkle with melted butter, cover with a layer of sauce, then of lobster. Continue in this way until the mould is full, sprinkling each layer of potato with melted butter. Cover with grated breadcrumbs and butter in tiny pieces and put in the oven to brown the top. Turn out on to a serving dish, decorate with radishes, cut to look like flowers, and stuffed olives.

Spanish Prawns   *Langostinos a la española*

4 tablespoons olive oil	2 cloves garlic
1 finely chopped onion	¼ cup water
4 sprigs chopped parsley	salt
1½ lb. raw peeled large prawns	

Heat oil in a saucepan and fry the onion until it becomes transparent. Add parsley, fry for 2 minutes, put in prawns and cook very gently until they turn pink. Pound the garlic in a mortar, dilute with water, stir, pour into the saucepan, season with salt to taste, boil fast for a moment, remove from heat and serve at once.

Prawns with Tartare Sauce   *Langostinos con salsa tártara*

1½ lb. large prawns
salt
1 bay leaf
1 sliced onion

1 gill white wine
1 lettuce
3 hard-boiled eggs
tartare sauce (p. 76)

Boil the prawns in a little salted water with a bay leaf, onion and
wine for 20 minutes, drain and peel. Serve cold on a foundation
of shredded lettuce, garnished with quarters of hard-boiled egg.
Serve tartare sauce separately.

Prawns with Rum   *Langostinos al ron*

olive oil
1 finely chopped onion
4 oz. peeled and chopped tomatoes
1 lb. raw peeled large prawns

salt
2 tablespoons rum
1 sliced onion
flour

Heat two to three tablespoons olive oil in a saucepan, lightly fry
the chopped onion, add tomatoes, cook for 2–3 minutes, add
prawns, season with salt and fry lightly for 10 minutes. Sprinkle
with rum and set alight. When it has burnt out, add two to three
tablespoons water, cover with a lid and simmer very gently for
15 minutes. Shake out the sliced onion into rings, dip in flour,
deep fry in smoking hot olive oil until golden and drain thoroughly.

Put the prawns on to a serving dish, decorate with onion rings
and serve.

CARNES

Veal, Country Style   *Ternera a la aldeana*

2 lb. joint of veal
salt
olive oil
1 gill white wine
1 halved onion

1 halved large tomato
1 halved carrot
2 cloves garlic
1 lb. new potatoes

Salt the veal. Heat two tablespoons olive oil in a deep roasting pan, brown the meat lightly all over, pour in wine, add onion, tomato, carrot and garlic, cover and cook in a moderate oven, for about 1 hour, basting from time to time. Scrape new potatoes and deep fry in hot olive oil until golden. Drain well and sprinkle with fine salt. Put the meat on a dish. Sieve the sauce, reheat and pour over the joint. Garnish with fried potatoes and serve.

Provencal Veal *Ternera a la provenzal*

1¾ lb. veal	6 medium-sized globe artichokes
salt	juice of ½ lemon
pinch paprika	1 teaspoon flour
3 tablespoons olive oil	1 lb. peas
8 oz. sliced onions	1½ oz. butter
1 sprig thyme	

Season the veal with salt and paprika. Brown lightly all over in olive oil, add onions and thyme, cover the pan and cook on a gentle heat until tender. Put the meat on a dish and pour the strained pan juices over it. Keep hot.

While the meat is cooking, prepare the artichokes in the following way: remove the hard outer leaves, cut the points off the rest, boil in salted water with lemon juice, flour and a teaspoon of oil until tender. Drain. Cook the peas, drain, toss a few moments in butter and fill the artichokes with them, putting them in between the leaves. Arrange the artichokes around the meat and serve.

Veal with Vinaigrette Sauce *Ternera a la Vinagreta*

1½ lb. boned veal	1 bay leaf
1 gill olive oil	1 teaspoon vinegar
8 oz. sliced onions	salt
1 head peeled garlic	1 lb. diced potatoes

Cut the veal into uniform pieces. Heat the oil in a saucepan, put in veal, onions, garlic, bay leaf and vinegar, season with salt, cover tightly and cook on a gentle heat for 30 minutes, shaking the pan from time to time to prevent sticking. Add potatoes, season with salt to taste, mix well, cook for 30 minutes or until the meat is tender. If it becomes dry, add a little water.

Veal Canigó   *Ternera Canigó*

1¼ lb. fillet of veal	1½ oz. butter
olive oil	salt
juice of 1 lemon	1 raw yolk
2 cloves sliced garlic	1 lb. potatoes
3–4 sprigs parsley	

Trim veal, put whole in a dish, sprinkle generously with olive oil, lemon juice, garlic and parsley. Leave the meat to steep in this dressing for at least 2 hours. Heat the butter with a little olive oil in a frying pan. Take the meat out of the dressing, season with salt and fry over a moderate heat to brown on the outside but keep inside underdone.

Pound half clove garlic and parsley from the dressing in a mortar, add the yolk and blend well, adding the juice of the dressing drop by drop, stirring continuously to make a thick mayonnaise sauce.

Put the meat on a dish. Gradually stir the fat from the frying pan into the contents of the mortar. Pour the sauce over the meat, garnish with potato straws (p. 113) and serve very hot.

Veal with Artichokes   *Ternera con alcachofas*

1¼ lb. boned veal	1 peeled, chopped tomato
salt	1 teaspoon flour
olive oil	12 tender globe artichokes
1 finely sliced onion	juice of 1 lemon

Slice the veal, season with salt, brown in hot olive oil and remove. Fry the onion and the tomato in oil in a saucepan, add flour, cook lightly, pour in half cup water, season with salt, bring to the boil, put in the meat and simmer with a lid on.

Remove hard outer leaves of the artichokes, cut off the tips, boil in salted water with lemon juice for 10 minutes, drain, cut in half, add to the meat and cook together until the meat is tender.

Veal with Chestnuts and Mushrooms

Ternera con castañas y setas

1½ lb. boned veal	1 chopped onion
salt	1 peeled, chopped tomato
flour	1 lb. chestnuts
olive oil	1 lb. mushrooms

Slice the veal, season with salt, roll in flour and fry in hot olive oil. Pour the oil in which the meat was fried into a saucepan, and lightly fry the onion and tomato. Pour in half cup water, season with a little salt to taste and add the meat.

Boil the chestnuts in their skins in salted water for 20 minutes, drain, peel and add to the meat. Clean the mushrooms, wash well and add to the rest; (if they are small, leave them whole; if not, cut into pieces). Cook together gently until the meat is tender.

Veal with Pickling Onions   *Ternera con cebollitas*

1½ lb. boned veal	1 chopped onion
salt	4 oz. peeled, chopped tomatoes
flour	1 tablespoon chopped parsley
2 tablespoons lard	1 lb. pickling onions

Slice the veal, season with salt, coat with flour and fry in hot lard (or olive oil). Pour the fat in which the meat was fried into a saucepan and lightly fry the onion, tomatoes and parsley. Add meat, half cup water, season with salt to taste, cover and cook gently for 30 minutes. Add pickling onions and simmer together for 20–25 minutes.

Veal with Plums   *Ternera con ciruelas*

2 lb. leg of veal
salt
2 oz. pure lard

1 sprig sage
2 tablespoons brandy
1 lb. plums

Sprinkle the meat with salt. Melt the lard in a saucepan, add sage and the meat. When the meat is browned all over, pour the brandy over it and cook slowly 1¼-1½ hours, adding a little water from time to time and turning the meat frequently to ensure even cooking. Simmer the plums in salted boiling water until soft, drain and add to the meat 20 minutes before serving. Place the meat in a dish, surround with plums and serve.

Veal with Mushrooms   *Ternera con champiñones*

1¾ lb. veal joint
salt
3–4 tablespoons olive oil
½ gill sherry
1 sliced onion

8 oz. quartered tomatoes
bouquet-garni
8 oz. button mushrooms
croûtons

Season the veal with salt. Heat olive oil in a saucepan and brown the veal on both sides. Pour the sherry over it, add onion, tomatoes, salt to taste and a *bouquet-garni*. Cover and cook very gently for about 1 hour, adding a little water, if necessary, during cooking. When the meat is cooked, remove from pan, strain the sauce and return everything to the saucepan. Reheat, add mushrooms and cook for 20 minutes.

Place the meat in the centre of a dish, cover with the sauce and garnish with *croûtons* of bread fried in butter or oil.

Veal with Peas   *Ternera con guisantes*

1¼ lb. veal fillets   1 finely chopped onion
salt   4 sprigs chopped parsley
flour   4 oz. peeled, chopped tomatoes
olive oil   1 lb. peas

Season the fillets of veal with salt, dip in flour and fry in hot olive
oil. Lightly fry the onion in oil in a saucepan, add parsley and
tomatoes, pour in a cup of water, bring to the boil, season with
salt and add the peas and the meat and cook for 15 minutes. If the
meat is not tender, the peas should only be added when the meat
is nearly cooked. Both peas and meat should be ready at the same
time.

Veal with Tomato Sauce   *Ternera con salsa de tomate*

1½ lb. fillet of veal   1 lb. sieved tomatoes
salt   1 teaspoon sugar
olive oil   1 lb. potatoes
2 cloves chopped garlic   1½ oz. butter
1 tablespoon chopped parsley

Slice the veal, season with salt, fry lightly in olive oil and remove.
In the same oil fry the garlic and parsley for 30 seconds, add
tomatoes, season with salt to taste, add sugar, boil for a moment,
add the meat, bring to the boil and remove from heat.

Boil potatoes in salted water, drain and rub through a sieve
into a saucepan. Reheat purée, stir in the butter and, if too thick,
a little milk or water in which the potatoes were boiled.

Arrange the meat on a dish, cover with the sauce and pipe a
border of potato purée, using a forcing bag with a fluted nozzle.

Veal with Tomatoes and Pimentos

Ternera con tomates y pimientos

1½–2 lb. veal fillets	3 sliced pimentos
salt	1 lb. tomatoes
2 oz. lard	pinch sugar

Season the fillets of veal with salt, fry in lard and remove. In the same lard, fry the pimentos, sprinkle with salt and remove from pan. Halve the tomatoes and season with salt and sugar. Fry them in the same pan, first upside down, then turn them over and fry the other side.

Put the meat in the centre of a dish, arrange the tomatoes and pimentos around it and serve.

Veal in Gravy   *Ternera en su jugo*

1¾ lb. veal joint	1 onion
salt	1 tomato
1 teaspoon paprika	1 carrot
2 tablespoons olive oil	1¼ lb. potatoes
2 tablespoons lard	1½ oz. butter
½ gill white wine	

Tie the joint with string and season with salt and paprika. Heat olive oil and lard in a saucepan and brown the meat lightly on all sides. Sprinkle it with wine. Cut onion, tomato and carrot in half, add to meat, cover and cook gently for 1 hour, turning the meat from time to time.

Boil the potatoes in salted water, drain, rub through a sieve to make a purée and incorporate butter. Cut the veal into slices, arrange on a dish, pour all the gravy collected during carving over the meat and pipe a border of potato purée, using a forcing bag with a wide nozzle.

Cold Veal   *Ternera fría*

1½ lb. fillet of veal	2 tablespoons sherry
2 oz. lard	12 peppercorns
1 bay leaf	salt
1 sprig thyme	scarlet sauce (p. 73)
1 clove	

Beat the veal lightly. Heat lard (or olive oil) in a saucepan and put in the meat, together with the bay leaf, thyme, clove, peppercorns, sherry and salt to taste. Pour in enough water to cover the meat, put the lid on and simmer over a gentle heat for 1½ hours until the meat is cooked. When cold, cut into slices and cover with scarlet sauce. The stock can be made into delicious soup.

Larded Veal   *Ternera mechada*

1½ lb. veal	1 chopped onion
2 oz. fat salted pork	8 oz. peeled, chopped tomatoes
salt	4 oz. sliced mushrooms
flour	1 lb. potatoes
2 oz. lard	2 oz. butter

Cut pork into strips, or lardoons. Lard the veal, i.e. insert the lardoons into it with a larding needle. Season with salt and sprinkle with flour. Heat the lard in a saucepan and put in the veal. Immediately add the onion, allow to colour lightly, add tomatoes, cook for 5 minutes, stir in teaspoon flour, add half cup water, check seasoning, simmer for 30–40 minutes, add mushrooms and continue to simmer 20-25 minutes until the meat is ready.

Peel the potatoes, scoop out to look like hazel nuts, boil in salted water, drain and fry in the butter until well golden. (See recipe for *noisette* potatoes (p. 112).) Arrange the meat on a dish, cover with the sauce and surround with the potatoes.

Stuffed Veal   *Ternera rellena*

4 oz pork	salt and pepper
2 oz. ham	1½ lb. breast of veal
2 oz. fat salted pork	½ gill sherry
2 chicken livers	1 sliced onion
1 truffle	1 sliced carrot
2 tablespoons grated breadcrumbs	1 chopped tomato
1 cup milk	1 dozen small tartlets (p. 262)
2 oz. lard	creamed spinach (p. 80)
1 beaten egg	

Mince the pork, ham and fat salted pork and keep aside. Chop the livers and truffle. Soak breadcrumbs in milk and squeeze out. Combine the minced ingredients, liver and truffle mixture, breadcrumbs and egg. Season with salt and pepper to taste and blend well to make the stuffing.

Bone the veal, beat the meat, put the stuffing in the middle, roll and secure with string. Season the meat with salt.

Heat the lard in a saucepan, brown the meat lightly on all sides, sprinkle with sherry, add onion, carrot and tomato, cover and simmer gently for 1¾–2 hours.

Take the meat out of the pan, remove string, arrange on a dish and pour the strained sauce over it. Garnish with tartlets filled with creamed spinach and serve.

Veal Escalopes with Mushroom Sauce
Bistecs con salsa de champiñones

1½ lb. fillet of veal	1½ oz. butter
1 chopped onion	1 tablespoon flour
1 peeled, chopped tomato	4 oz. sliced mushrooms
olive oil	bread
salt	lemon juice

Cut the veal into escalopes. Fry the onion and tomato lightly in two tablespoons oil in a small saucepan. Add one cup water, season with salt, simmer for 15 minutes and strain into a bowl. Melt the butter in a small saucepan and stir in the flour. When it is golden, add the strained pan juices, stirring all the time. Add mushrooms and simmer for 15 minutes.

Cut bread into slices of the same size as the escalopes and fry in hot olive oil. Keep hot on a dish. In the same oil briskly fry the veal, which must be very tender. Place an escalope on each piece of fried bread. Heat the sauce, remove from stove, add a dash of lemon juice, pour over the escalopes and serve.

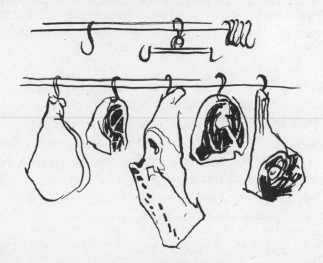

Veal Moderna   *Carne a la moderna*

1¼ lb. boned veal chops
1 teaspoon salt
½ teaspoon pepper
1 cup olive oil

1 clove garlic
5 shelled and peeled walnuts
3 de-salted anchovies
½ teaspoon vinegar

Put the chops on a plate, sprinkle with salt, pepper and a few drops of olive oil. Just before serving, grill them on a pre-heated grill, taking care not to overdo them. Put them on a heated dish and cover with the following sauce:

Pound the garlic, walnuts and anchovies in a mortar into a smooth paste, add vinegar, then, gradually, add olive oil, stirring all the time. Make enough dressing to cover the meat lightly.

Serve with potato straws (p. 113) or *croûtons*.

Round of Veal with Truffle Sauce
Redondo de ternera con salsa de trufa

1½ lb round of veal	2 oz. butter
3 oz. fat salted pork	1 teaspoon flour
salt	2 tablespoons sherry
6 slices bread	1 chopped truffle
olive oil	

Cut the veal into six thick round slices. Cut pork into strips. Lard each round slice of veal with strips of pork and season with salt. Cut the bread into slices of the same size as the veal and fry in hot olive oil. Fry the veal in butter and put each round on a slice of bread. Stir the flour into the butter in which the meat was fried, add sherry and truffle, cook lightly and pour it over the meat.

Serve with potato soufflé (p. 112).

Veal Roll   *Rollo de ternera*

1½ lb. rump or round of veal	2 oz. lard
1 thinly sliced potato	1 sprig savory
2 beaten eggs	1 gill white wine
2 oz. ham	1¼ lb. peas
1 sliced leek	1½ oz. butter
1 tablespoon chopped parsley	bread
salt	

Flatten the veal slightly with a beater. Fry the potatoes lightly, without allowing them to colour. Make a flat omelette with the eggs and potato. (The omelette should be thin and approximately the same size as the meat.) Put the omelette on the meat. Cut ham into strips. Cover omelette alternately with ham, leek and parsley. Roll up the meat, secure with string and season with salt.

Heat lard in a saucepan and put in the meat with savory. Brown lightly on all sides, sprinkle with wine, cover the pan and cook gently for 1-1¼ hours, adding a few drops of water from time to time. Boil the peas in salted water, drain and toss in butter.

When cooked, slice the meat, arrange in the centre of a dish to resemble one whole piece, garnish with peas and surround with small pieces of fried bread.

Fillet of Veal with Vegetables
Solomillo de ternera a la jardinera

1¼ lb. fillet of veal	½ pint stock
4 oz. fat salted pork	4 oz. sliced mushrooms
2–3 tablespoons lard	6 globe artichokes
2 oz. butter	1 lb. cooked peas
1 tablespoon flour	

Trim the meat, lard with strips of pork,* season with salt, tie with string, put in a pan with lard (or olive oil) and roast in the oven for 50 minutes.

Melt half the butter, stir in flour, cook until golden, gradually dilute with stock (or water), cook for 5 minutes, add mushrooms and simmer to cook the mushrooms and thicken the sauce.

Boil the artichokes as described (p. 81), fill with peas tossed in the rest of the butter.

Put the meat on a dish, cut into slices, arrange to resemble whole piece, pour mushroom sauce over it and surround with stuffed artichokes.

* For description of larding see recipe for larded Veal (p. 185).

Fillet of Veal with Spinach Fritters

Solomillo de ternera con fritos de espinacas

1½ lb. fillet veal	2 oz. butter
salt	1 small tin *foie-gras*
olive oil	spinach fritters (p. 80)
bread	

Choose fillet from the middle cut and cut into six slices. Season with salt, brush with olive oil, put on the grid of a roasting pan and cook in a moderate oven for 20 minutes, keeping a little under-done on the inside. Fry six thin slices of bread in hot olive oil, butter them and spread a layer of *foie-gras*.

Place the bread on a hot dish, put a slice of fillet on each piece, top with small pieces of butter, garnish with spinach fritters and serve at once.

Fillet of Veal with Egg Tartlets

Solomillo de ternera con tarteletas

1½ lb. fillet of veal	½ gill sherry
salt	12 small tartlet cases
3 tablespoons olive oil	(p. 262)
juice of ½ lemon	egg sauce (p. 72)

Put the veal in a saucepan, sprinkle with salt, olive oil, lemon juice and sherry and leave in this dressing for 3 hours, turning it from time to time to impregnate thoroughly. Put the saucepan on the fire and let the meat cook in the dressing for 30 minutes on a moderate heat. Cut into slices and arrange on a dish in its original shape. Pour the pan juices over it, surround with small tartlets filled with thick egg sauce.

Fried Fillet of Veal   *Lonjas de solomillo salteadas*

1¼ lb. fillet veal
1 oz. butter
1 tablespoon olive oil
salt and pepper

1 tablespoon chopped parsley
juice of ½ lemon
puff pastry patties
Villeroi sauce (p. 70)

Cut veal into slices and fry in butter and olive oil 4–5 minutes on each side. Season with salt and pepper to taste, arrange on a hot dish and sprinkle with chopped parsley. Add lemon juice to the butter in which the meat was fried, heat and pour over the veal. Serve with puff pastry patties filled with Villeroi sauce.

Veal Rolls (1)   *Rollos de ternera* (1)

1¼ lb. fillet veal
2 sliced hard-boiled eggs
2 oz. ham
1 sliced leek

flour
olive oil
1 finely chopped onion
½ pint veal stock

Cut the fillet into thin slices and beat them out well. In the centre of each place a slice of hard-boiled egg, a small slice of ham and a small piece of leek. Roll up, tie with thread, dip in flour and fry in hot olive oil. Fry the onion in a saucepan, add the rolls, pour in stock (or water) and simmer gently for ½ hour until cooked. Serve with a vegetable such as peas, cauliflower, artichokes, etc.

Veal Rolls (2)   *Rollos de ternera* (2)

1½ lb. fillet veal
salt
8 oz. sliced ham
4 oz. diced olives
3 sliced leeks
2–3 tablespoons lard

1 sliced onion
1 teaspoon flour
½ cup stock
noisette potatoes (p. 112)
1¼ oz. roasted almonds
1 hard-boiled yolk

Cut the veal into slices, beat them to a uniform thinness, season with salt, on top of each fillet put a slice of ham, teaspoon olives and a slice of leek, roll up and tie with thread.

Heat lard in a saucepan, fry the rolls lightly and remove from the pan. In the same fat fry the onion. When it begins to colour, add flour, stir in stock (or water), add salt to taste, put in rolls, braise slowly for 20 minutes. Add *noisette* potatoes. Pound the almonds in a mortar with the yolk, dilute with two tablespoons water, add to the saucepan, leave to cook gently for 10-15 minutes until ready. Remove thread before serving.

Veal Rolls (3)   *Rollos de ternera* (3)

1½ lb. top side veal	flour
salt	olive oil
4 oz. lean bacon	1 chopped carrot
2 chicken livers	1 peeled, chopped tomato
1 chopped onion	½ cup stock or water
2 tablespoons breadcrumbs	1 lb. Brussels sprouts
1 beaten egg	

Cut the meat into thin slices, beat and season with salt. Mince the bacon and livers, add a teaspoon onion, mix with breadcrumbs, season with salt to taste and bind with egg.

Put a little of the mixture on each slice of veal, roll up, tie with thread, dip in flour and fry in hot olive oil. Remove from pan.

Using the same oil, lightly fry the onion and carrot in a saucepan, add tomato, pour in stock or water, season with salt to taste and put in the rolls and simmer for 20 minutes. Boil the Brussels sprouts, drain, dredge with flour, fry, add to the saucepan and simmer together on a gentle heat for 10 minutes until ready.

Balearic Veal Rolls

Fardelillos baleares

1½ lb. fillet veal   salt
4 oz. sliced fat salted pork   paprika
8 oz. sliced *sobrasada*   1 gill white wine
flour   bread
2–3 tablespoons olive oil   1 egg
2 cloves garlic   3 tablespoons milk
pinch powdered mixed herbs

Cut the fillet into very thin slices, beat them out to an oval shape, put a slice of pork and a round of *sobrasada* on top of each fillet, roll up, tie with thread, dredge with flour and fry in hot olive oil in a saucepan. Pound the garlic with herbs and add to the pan. Season with salt and paprika to taste. Sprinkle with wine and continue to simmer for 30 minutes, adding a little water from time to time.

Arrange the rolls on a dish, remove the thread, cover with their sauce and keep hot. Cut bread into small slices. Beat egg with milk, dip bread into the mixture, fry in olive oil until golden and use to garnish veal rolls.

Meat Balls with Peas

Albóndigas con guisantes

8 oz. veal   salt
8 oz. pork   flour
2 oz. fat salted pork   olive oil
1 finely chopped onion   1 peeled, chopped tomato
1 tablespoon sieved breadcrumbs   1½ gills water
2 eggs   1 lb. peas

Mince the veal, pork, fat salted pork (or bacon) and teaspoon onion, mix, add breadcrumbs and eggs, season with salt to taste, shape into balls, roll in flour and fry in hot olive oil. Pour the oil in which the meat balls were fried into a saucepan and lightly fry the onion; when it begins to colour, add tomato, and fry together for 5 minutes, add water, season with salt, bring to the boil, add peas and meat balls, cover and leave to cook over a moderate heat for 10–12 minutes.

Meat Balls with Tomato Sauce
Albóndigas con salsa de tomate

8 oz. veal
2 oz. fat salted pork
8 oz. calf's liver
1 clove garlic
1 sprig parsley
2 tablespoons breadcrumbs

2 eggs
salt
flour
olive oil
tomato sauce (p. 71).

Mince the veal, pork, liver, garlic and parsley. Blend well. Add freshly grated sieved breadcrumbs, beat in the eggs, season with salt and mix well. Shape the mixture into balls, roll in flour and fry in hot olive oil. Add meat balls to tomato sauce, cook gently for 25–30 minutes and serve.

Veal Pudding   *Budín de ternera*

1 lb. veal
2 oz. butter
1 slice bread
½ glass milk
1 oz. grated cheese
1 peeled, seeded and chopped
   pimento

4 oz. peeled, chopped tomatoes
4 beaten eggs
salt
pinch nutmeg
1–2 tablespoons breadcrumbs
béchamel (p. 70) or tomato sauce
   (p. 71)

Trim the veal and mince it. Melt the butter in a saucepan (keeping a little for greasing a mould), fry the veal lightly and put in a bowl. Cut crusts off bread, soak in milk and squeeze out. Add cheese, bread, pimento, tomatoes and eggs to the veal forcemeat, season with salt and nutmeg and mix well. Butter a mould, sprinkle it with breadcrumbs, pour in the mixture and put it in the oven for an hour. Turn it out of the mould on to a dish and cover with béchamel sauce or tomato sauce (see recipes).

Fried Calf's Head   *Cabeza de ternera con fritada*

2 lb. calf's head	1 peeled, seeded and sliced pimento
court-bouillon	1 lb. peeled, chopped tomatoes
salt	salt
olive oil	1 teaspoon sugar
6 oz. finely sliced onions	

Preliminary preparation: Cut the head into pieces, bone, soak in plenty of cold water for 5–6 hours, until all blood has drained out. It is also advisable to blanch the head and parboil in *court-bouillon* made as follows: Mix two tablespoons flour with cold water into paste, strain into pan big enough to contain head, etc., with 4 pints water, two teaspoons salt, two tablespoons vinegar, one onion studded with two cloves and a *bouquet-garni*. Wrap the head in muslin cloth and cook in boiling *court-bouillon* for 45–50 minutes. Drain the pieces of head.

Season with salt, fry in hot olive oil, remove, and in the pan lightly fry the onion, add pimento and tomatoes, season with salt to taste, sprinkle in sugar, stir, add the pieces of head, cover the pan and simmer gently for 15 minutes, until done.

Calf's Head Fritters   *Cabeza de ternera frita*

Cook the calf's head, bone and cut up as described in the previous recipe. Marinate the pieces in olive oil, lemon juice and chopped parsley. Make a batter for frying (p. 262), season the pieces of calf's head with salt, dip in batter and fry in hot olive oil until golden. Drain well. Serve with tomato sauce (p. 71.)

Catalan Tripe   *Callos a la catalana*

2 lb. tripe
4 oz. finely chopped onions
4 oz. finely chopped tomatoes
olive oil
1 gill white wine

1 cup water
1 lb. sliced potatoes
1 clove garlic
1 sprig parsley
salt

Wash the tripe well, boil until tender and cut into pieces. Heat the oil in a saucepan and lightly fry the onions and tomatoes together in a saucepan, add tripe and cook gently for a few minutes, sprinkle with wine, pour in water, cover and simmer gently for 1 hour. Add potatoes. Pound garlic and parsley together in a mortar, add to pan. Season with salt to taste and cook for another hour.

Tripe with Sauce   *Callos con salsa*

2 lb. tripe
1 chopped onion
olive oil
4 oz. peeled, chopped tomatoes

salt
½ cup water
1 clove garlic
1½ oz. roasted almonds

Wash the tripe and cut into pieces. Fry the onion in olive oil in a saucepan. When it begins to colour, add tomatoes, cook gently for 5 minutes, add tripe, season with salt, fry lightly and pour in water. Pound the garlic and the almonds in a mortar, add to the pan, cover and simmer for 2 hours.

Calf's Liver with Cream Sauce   *Hígado de ternera a la crema*

bread
1¼ lb. calf's liver
8 oz. fat salted pork
olive oil
1 tablespoon flour
¼ cup stock or water

½ tablespoon chopped parsley
salt
1½ oz. butter
1 raw yolk
juice of ½ lemon
bunch watercress

Cut the same number of slices of bread, liver and pork. Fry in oil separately, remove and keep hot. Into the same fat, blend in the flour, add stock or water and parsley, season with salt, simmer gently for 10 minutes, remove from heat, stir in butter, yolk and lemon juice. Keep hot but do not allow to boil. Arrange the slices of fried bread on a hot dish, place a slice of pork, then a slice of liver on top of each, cover with the sauce, garnish with watercress and serve.

Calf's Liver Rolls   *Rollos de hígado de ternera*

1½ lb. calf's liver	1 sprig parsley
salt	flour
4 oz. lean bacon	4 oz. lard
2 oz. ham	1 lb. tomatoes
1 small onion	1 teaspoon sugar
1 hard-boiled egg	

Cut the liver into thin, wide slices and season with salt. Fry the bacon and chop it together with ham, onion, egg and parsley. Blend well to make a smooth forcemeat. Put a spoonful of the forcemeat on each slice of liver, roll it up, tie with thread, flour and fry the rolls in lard.

Sieve the tomatoes into the pan in which the rolls were fried, season with salt, add sugar, cook lightly for 5 minutes, put in the rolls for a moment or two (liver needs little cooking, otherwise it will harden) and serve.

Calf's Tongue with Vegetables
Lengua de ternera a la hortelana

1 calf's tongue	1 cup water
2 oz. lard	8 oz. peas
1 chopped onion	12 oz. potatoes
1 peeled, chopped tomato	4 diced carrots
1 tablespoon chopped parsley	2 diced turnips
salt	

Put the tongue in a bowl, scald with boiling water, skin and wash it. Melt the lard in a saucepan, lightly fry the onion, tomato and parsley, put in tongue, season with salt, cook gently for a few minutes, pour in water and continue cooking slowly for 1½-2 hours. When half cooked, add peas, potatoes scooped out to look like hazel nuts (see recipe for *noisette* potatoes, p. 112), carrots and turnips. Season with salt to taste and cook gently, adding more water if necessary. Cut the tongue into slices, put in the centre of a dish and surround with the vegetables and their juice.

Stewed Calf's Tongue   *Lengua de ternera estofada*

1 calf's tongue	1 head peeled garlic
3–4 tablespoons olive oil	1 bay leaf
salt	1 sprig thyme
1 gill white wine	1 lb. peas
4 oz. sliced onions	

Put the tongue in a pan of cold water, bring to the boil, drain, skin, slice and put in a saucepan with olive oil. Season with salt, add wine, onion, garlic, bay leaf and thyme, cover and cook slowly, shaking the pan from time to time to prevent sticking. When the tongue is nearly cooked (about 1 hour), add peas and finish cooking together.

Andalusian Calf's Foot   *Manos de ternera a la andaluza*

8 oz. chick-peas	4 oz. chopped onions
bicarbonate of soda	4 oz. peeled, chopped tomatoes
salt	1 gill white wine
1 calf's foot	1 clove garlic
3–4 tablespoons olive oil	2 seeded pimentos
1 slice bread	½ *chorizo*

Soak the chick-peas overnight in cold water with a pinch of bicarbonate of soda. Boil in salted water for 2-2½ hours and drain.

Boil the calf's foot for 2½-3 hours, remove the big bones and cut the meat into pieces. Strain the stock and keep for further use.

Heat olive oil in a saucepan, fry a slice of bread and remove it. In the same oil lightly fry the onions. Add tomatoes, fry together, pour in the wine and a cup of stock. Pound the garlic and fried bread together in a mortar. Soak the pimentos in hot water, add to mortar, pound into paste with bread and garlic mixture, dilute with a little stock and pour into the pan. Add chick-peas and calf's foot. Slice the *chorizo*, fry and add to pan. Cook gently until ready. Serve very hot.

Larded Calf's Kidneys   *Riñones de ternera mechados*

2 calf's kidneys
vinegar
4 oz. fat salted pork
flour
2 oz. lard
2 cloves garlic

2–3 sprigs parsley
12 oz. peeled, chopped tomatoes
juice of ½ lemon
½ gill sherry
salt and pepper
croûtons

Soak the kidneys in cold water with a dash of vinegar, remove membranes and wash in several waters. Cut the pork into strips or lardoons and stud the kidneys with these, using a larding needle, then cut into slices, dredge with flour and fry lightly in lard. Chop the garlic and parsley, fry together with tomatoes, sprinkle with lemon juice and sherry, season with salt and pepper to taste and cook gently. Strain this sauce over the kidneys and garnish with *croûtons* of bread fried in butter.

Kidneys must not be over-cooked, or they will harden.

Calf's Kidneys with Mushrooms
Riñones de ternera con champiñones

2 calf's kidneys
2 tablespoons olive oil
4 oz. diced fat salted pork
salt and pepper

1 gill white wine
4 oz. small button mushrooms
1½ oz. butter
potato straws (p. 113)

Soak, trim and wash the kidneys as described in the previous recipe and cut into thin slices. Heat olive oil in a saucepan, lightly brown the pork, add the kidneys, season with salt and pepper to taste, cook on a high flame for 2 minutes, stirring constantly, and pour in the wine. Fry the mushrooms lightly in butter, add to the kidneys, stir and serve with potato straws.

Calf's Brains with Potatoes   *Seso de ternera con patatas*

1 calf's brain	3 oz. butter
juice of ½ lemon	flour
salt	1 beaten egg
1¼ lb. potatoes	2 tablespoons olive oil
1 lb. peas	cream sauce (p. 70)
1 raw yolk	

Soak the brains in cold water for 1 hour. Remove skin and all traces of blood, wash thoroughly, put in cold water in a saucepan with lemon juice and salt, bring to the boil, skim, reduce heat, simmer for 10 minutes, drain and leave to cool.

Boil the potatoes and peas separately in salted water, drain and rub through a sieve together. Blend into this purée the yolk and half the butter, stir well and keep hot. Slice the brains, coat with flour and beaten egg and fry in hot olive oil.

Make a border of the purée on a round dish, put the brains in the centre and cover with cream sauce.

Calf's Brains with Mayonnaise   *Seso de ternera con mahonesa*

1 calf's brain	1 tinned sweet pimento
1 teaspoon salt	1 bunch watercress
1 teaspoon vinegar	2 hard-boiled eggs
mayonnaise (p. 74)	

Wash the calf's brain well, put in a saucepan with cold water, salt and vinegar, bring to the boil, cook for 10 minutes, drain, put on

a dish, cover with thick mayonnaise and decorate with discs
of tinned sweet pimento. Arrange watercress round the brains,
scatter slices of hard-boiled egg on top and serve.

Shepherd's Beef   *Vaca a la pastora*

1¾ lb. rump   1 onion
4 oz. fat salted pork   1 clove
1 bay leaf   salt
1 carrot

Lard the piece of beef with strips of pork, put in a saucepan with
enough water to cover the meat half-way, add bay leaf, carrot and
onion with a clove stuck in it, season with salt and simmer for
3–4 hours, until the water has evaporated, turning the meat from
time to time. Slice the meat and serve with green vegetables,
boiled and tossed in butter.

Stewed Beef   *Vaca estofada*

1¾ lb. top of rump   1 gill white wine
½ cup olive oil   1 lb. small peeled potatoes
1 sliced onion   1 lb. pickling onions
1 head peeled garlic   2 oz. diced fat salted pork
1 bay leaf   4 oz. sliced pork sausage
1 sprig thyme   1 cup stock or water
salt

Cut the meat into 1½-inch pieces. Heat olive oil in a saucepan, put
in the meat, onion, garlic, bay leaf and thyme, season with salt,
pour in wine, shake well, cover and simmer gently for 30 minutes.
Add potatoes and onions. Fry pork and sausage lightly, add to pan,
pour in stock or water and cook all together for 15–20 minutes.

Sirloin with Cauliflower Pudding   *Rosbif con budín de coliflor*

1½ lb. sirloin	2 tablespoons olive oil
2 oz. ham	juice of ½ lemon
1 finely sliced truffle	2 tablespoons sherry
salt	cauliflower pudding (p. 91)
4 oz. fat salted pork	

Cut ham into strips. Insert these strips and slivers of truffle into the joint. Season with salt. Cut pork in two slices of the same shape as the sirloin, put one on top and the other underneath the joint, tie with string and put in a saucepan with olive oil, lemon juice and sherry. Cover and simmer gently for 40–45 minutes. Remove meat and slice. Put cauliflower pudding in the centre of a round dish, surround with slices of meat, sprinkle with its sauce and serve.

Mutton Chops with Spinach
Chuletas de carnero con espinacas

6 chops	creamed spinach (p. 80)
salt	12 small *croûtons*
olive oil	

Season the chops with salt, brush with olive oil and grill on a hot grill. Put creamed spinach on a dish, arrange the chops around it, garnish with *croûtons* of bread fried in butter, sticking them upright in the spinach. Serve very hot.

Leg of Mutton in Sauce   *Pierna de carnero en salsa*

3½–4 lb. leg of mutton	1 gill olive oil
salt	1 chopped onion
1 gill white wine	1 slice bread
1 bay leaf	2 cloves garlic
1 sprig thyme	1½ oz. roasted almonds
1 tablespoon chopped parsley	

Put the leg of mutton in a saucepan, season with salt, add wine, bay leaf, thyme, parsley and olive oil. Macerate for 2 hours, then put the pan on the fire and lightly brown the meat on all sides. Add onion, and when it begins to colour, pour half cup water, season with salt to taste, cover and simmer gently for 45 minutes. Fry a slice of bread and two cloves garlic, pound in a mortar together with the almonds into a smooth paste, dilute with two to three tablespoons water, add to the saucepan and continue to simmer gently for 1½ hours until the meat is ready.

Stewed Leg of Mutton   *Pierna de carnero guisada*

1 leg mutton
4 oz. fat salted pork
salt
2 tablespoons lard
2 onions

1 head garlic
1 peeled, chopped tomato
2 sprigs parsley
1½ oz. roasted almonds
1 slice fried bread

Bone the leg of mutton, lard it with strips of pork, bind, season with salt and put in a saucepan with lard, a whole onion and a peeled head of garlic. Brown the meat lightly, cover and cook gently for 1½ hours; then remove the meat and cut into thick slices. Remove onion and garlic and, in the same fat, lightly fry a chopped onion and tomato, pour in half cup water and season with a little salt. Pound together in a mortar one clove garlic, parsley, bread and the almonds into a smooth paste, dilute with a little water, pour into the saucepan, return the meat to the pan, and leave them to cook gently for another hour.

Brain Pancakes Gloria   *Crêpes Gloria*

1 sheep's brain
salt
2 chicken livers
1 truffle
1½ oz. butter
1 tablespoon flour

1 small glass milk
pancake batter (p. 250)
1 egg
½ tablespoon olive oil
2 bunches watercress

Wash the brains, remove all membranes, boil for 3 minutes in salted water and drain. Fry the chicken livers and chop them together with the brains and truffle. Melt butter in a small saucepan, stir in flour, gradually add milk, season with salt and cook for 10 minutes, stirring constantly to ensure smoothness. Add the chopped mixture and cook together for 5 minutes. Make the pancakes as described, put a tablespoon of the brain mixture on each, roll up the pancakes, coat with beaten egg (mixed with a few drops of olive oil and a tablespoon of milk or water) and fry until golden. Drain well, arrange on a dish, garnish with watercress and serve.

Lamb Cutlets a la Navarra   *Chuletas de cordero a la navarra*

1½ lb. lamb cutlets	4 oz. finely chopped onions
salt	1 lb. peeled, chopped tomatoes
2 oz. lard	1 teaspoon sugar
olive oil	6 oz. *chorizo*
2 oz. diced ham	

Season the cutlets with salt, fry in lard and olive oil (in equal parts) until golden and put in an oven-proof dish. In the same fat lightly fry the ham and onion, add tomatoes, season with salt to taste and sprinkle in sugar. Bring to the boil, pour this sauce over the cutlets and put in the oven for 10 minutes. Then cover with thin slices of *chorizo*, return the dish to a hot oven for 5 minutes and serve very hot.

Lamb Cutlets   *Chuletas de cordero*

1¾ lb. lamb cutlets	2 tablespoons sherry
salt	1 tablespoon chopped chervil
2 oz. butter	1 tablespoon chopped parsley
sifted breadcrumbs	watercress

Season the cutlets with salt, dip in melted butter, coat with bread-crumbs, grill under a hot grill and keep on a dish. Heat the rest of the butter in a small saucepan, pour in sherry, bring to the boil, add the chervil and parsley, cook lightly for a few moments, pour over the cutlets, garnish with watercress and serve immediately.

Shoulder of Lamb with Vegetables
Espalda de cordero a la jardinera

1 shoulder lamb	1 chopped turnip
salt	1 tablespoon chopped parsley
4 oz. fat salted pork	1 tablespoon chopped chervil
2 oz. lard	1 tablespoon chopped celery
⅛ gill dry sherry	1½ oz. butter
1 chopped onion	1 teaspoon flour
2 chopped carrots	3 aubergines

Bone the shoulder and flatten on the table. Season with a little salt. Cut the pork into strips. Cover the shoulder with pieces of pork, roll it up carefully, tie with string and season the outside with a little salt. Melt the lard in a saucepan and brown the meat lightly on all sides. Sprinkle with sherry, add onion, carrots, turnip and the herbs, cook lightly for a few minutes, add cup water, cover, and simmer gently for 2 hours.

Remove the meat and discard string. Strain the pan juices. Melt the butter, stir in flour, gradually dilute with the pan juices. Put the meat back into the pan, pour in the sauce and simmer for 10 minutes. Put the meat on a dish, cover with the sauce and serve with fried aubergine (p. 85).

If we should have money for bread, meat and onions, our neighbours will lend us a saucepan

Shoulder of Lamb, Country Style

Espalda de cordero a la casera

1 shoulder of lamb	1 lb. diced potatoes
salt and pepper	1 lb. pickling onions
4 oz. lard	1½ oz. butter
1 bay leaf	1 tablespoon chopped parsley
1 sprig thyme	

Bone the shoulder, season the inside with salt and a little pepper, roll, tie with string and salt the outside. Melt the lard in a casserole, add bay leaf, thyme and the meat. Brown the meat on all sides, cover the pan tightly and cook gently for 1 hour. Add potatoes and onions, sprinkle with butter and finish cooking in the oven for another hour, until the meat is done. Put the meat on a dish, surround it with potatoes and onions and sprinkle with chopped parsley.

Stuffed Shoulder of Lamb

Espalda de cordero rellena

1 shoulder lamb	1 gill white wine
salt	1 finely chopped onion
8 oz. sausage meat	2 peeled, chopped tomatoes
1 finely chopped leek	8 globe artichokes
3–4 tablespoons olive oil	2 oz. diced ham

Bone the shoulder of lamb, lay flat on the table, season with salt, spread the sausage meat and chopped leek over it, roll up, tie with string. Heat oil in a saucepan and brown the meat lightly on all sides. Sprinkle with wine, add onion and tomatoes, cover and simmer gently for 2 hours. If necessary, add a little water from time to time.

Trim the artichokes, boil in salted water and drain. Fry the ham and distribute among the artichokes. Arrange the meat on a dish, cover with its gravy and garnish with the artichokes.

Leg of Lamb with Peas and New Potatoes
Pierna de cordero con guisantes y patatitas

1 leg of lamb	2 tablespoons brandy
salt	1 lb. peas
4 oz. lard	2 lb. new potatoes
1 sprig savory	

Rub the meat with salt and brown lightly in lard with a sprig of savory. Sprinkle with brandy, cover the casserole and put in a moderate oven for 1½-2 hours, turning the meat from time to time to ensure even cooking. When done, remove the meat. In the same casserole cook the peas and potatoes on top of the stove. Season with salt, add a little water if necessary, cover and cook gently for 15 minutes. Put the meat in again for a few minutes to heat through. Put the leg on a dish and surround with potatoes and peas.

This is the classic dish for Easter Day.

Pork with Aubergines   *Carne de cerdo con berenjenas*

3 large aubergines	olive oil
1½ lb. pork	1 chopped onion
salt	1 peeled, chopped tomato
flour	1½ oz. roasted almonds

Wash the aubergines, cut into rounds, put in a colander, season with a little salt and leave for 1 hour. Cut the pork into slices, season with salt, dip in flour and fry in smoking hot olive oil. Lightly fry the onion and tomato in a saucepan, pour in half cup water, season with salt to taste, bring to the boil, put in the meat, cover and simmer gently for 1 hour.

Fry the aubergines and add to the meat. Pound the almonds in a mortar, put into the pan, cook all together for a few minutes and serve.

Pork with Brussels Sprouts
Carne de cerdo con coles de Bruselas

1½ lb. pork fillet
salt
olive oil
1 finely chopped onion

1 peeled, chopped tomato
1½ oz. roasted almonds
1 lb. Brussels sprouts
flour

Slice the pork, season with salt and fry in hot olive oil. Using the same oil transferred to a saucepan, lightly fry the onion and tomato, pour in half cup water and season with salt to taste. Pound the almonds in a mortar, add them and the meat to the saucepan, cover and cook gently for ¾ hour. Clean the sprouts, boil in salted water, taking care not to overcook, drain, roll in flour and fry them. Five minutes before the meat is cooked, add them to the pan and finish cooking together on a low heat.

Put the meat on a dish, garnish with sprouts, pour the sauce over it and serve.

Pork with Tomato Sauce   *Carne de cerdo con salsa de tomate*

Follow the recipe for Veal with Tomato Sauce (p. 183).

Fillet of Pork with White Sauce   *Lomo de cerdo a la crema*

1½ lb. fillet pork
salt
2 tablespoons olive oil
juice of ½ lemon
1 oz. butter

1 finely chopped onion
1 oz. flour
½ pint milk
1 raw yolk

Cut the pork into slices, put in a dish, season with salt and sprinkle with olive oil and two teaspoons lemon juice. Melt the butter in a small saucepan and lightly fry the onion. Blend in flour and make a *béchamel* sauce (p. 70), gradually incorporating the milk.

Season with salt, remove from heat, add yolk and heighten with a teaspoon of lemon juice.

Grill the fillets under a hot grill, arrange on a dish overlapping them slightly and cover with the sauce. Serve with fried artichokes or aubergine fritters (see recipes).

Saragossa Fillet of Pork *Lomo de cerdo a la zaragozana*

1¼ lb. fillet pork	1 chopped onion
salt	4 oz. peeled, chopped tomatoes
flour	½ cup water
2 oz. diced ham	1 sliced hard-boiled egg
olive oil	4 oz. small black olives
2 tablespoons white wine	

Rub the pork with salt and dust with flour. Fry the ham in olive oil in a saucepan and remove. In the same oil, brown the pork lightly and add wine and onion. As soon as the onion begins to colour, add tomatoes and water, cover the pan and simmer gently for 30 minutes, until the meat is half cooked. Add egg, olives and the fried ham. When the meat is ready, slice it and serve with its sauce.

Fillet of Pork Atlantis *Lomo de cerdo atlántida*

1½ lb. fillet pork	6 large tomatoes
salt	2 tablespoons olive oil
1 lb. mashed potatoes	8 oz. bacon rashers
2 oz. butter	2 bunches watercress
1½ lb. cooked peas	

Cut the pork into slices, season with salt and grill. Add half the butter to the potato purée, mix well, and keep hot. Toss the peas in the rest of the butter. Cut off the tops of the tomatoes, scoop out pulp, season them with salt and fry lightly in oil, first scooped out side down, then turn and cook the other side.

Put a portion of potato purée on each rasher, roll it, securing with a cocktail stick, and grill. Fill the tomatoes with peas, arrange on a dish, surround with slices of pork, then make another circle of bacon rolls, having removed the cocktail sticks, alternating with small bunches of watercress.

Home Style Cold Meat Roll   *Fiambre casero*

1½ lb. fillet pork
8 oz. ham
4 oz. freshly grated breadcrumbs
2 chopped hard-boiled eggs
1 raw egg

1 thinly sliced truffle
1 diced gherkin
salt and pepper
1 onion
1 bay leaf

Mince or chop the pork and the ham finely and put in a bowl. Add breadcrumbs, eggs (both cooked and raw), truffle and gherkin. Season with salt and pepper, stir well and shape into a roll like a large sausage. Wrap the roll in a muslin cloth, secure with thread to keep the shape and boil in a shallow pan, with onion, bay leaf and a little salt, for an hour. Remove from pan, allow to cool under a weight, unwrap, cut into slices and serve.

Fillet of Pork with Haricot Beans   *Lomo de cerdo con judías*

1½ lb. haricot beans
1½ lb. fillet pork

salt
2 oz. lard

Soak the beans overnight, rinse, boil for 2 hours in salted water, drain and leave until cold. Slice the pork, season with salt, fry in 1 oz. lard and remove from frying pan. Add the rest of the lard and fry the haricot beans until golden. Put the pork on top to heat through and serve. This is a very tasty Catalan dish.

Fillet of Pork with Milk   *Lomo de cerdo con leche*

1½ lb. fillet pork
2 oz. pounded roasted almonds
salt
1½ oz. lard

½ gill sherry
1 finely chopped onion
½ pint milk
croûtons

Slice the fillet without cutting right through, so that it resembles a book, season with salt in between the 'pages' and spread with a layer of almonds. Secure with string and season with a little salt on the outside. Melt the lard in a saucepan, brown the pork lightly on all sides, add sherry and onion, cook lightly, add milk, cover and simmer gently for 45–50 minutes. Shake the pan and turn the meat from time to time to prevent sticking. When cooked, remove string and serve the pork in the sauce, garnished with *croûtons* of bread fried in butter or oil.

Fillet of Pork with Mushrooms — *Lomo de cerdo con setas*

1½ lb. sliced fillet pork
salt
3–4 tablespoons olive oil

1 lb. small button mushrooms
2 or 3 cloves chopped garlic
1 tablespoon chopped parsley

Season the pork with salt, fry in very hot olive oil in a saucepan and remove from pan. In the same oil fry the mushrooms, cover and simmer gently for 25-30 minutes. Add garlic and parsley, cook for 1 minute, add sliced pork and cook briskly for a moment, stirring vigorously. Arrange the meat in a line down the centre of a dish, garnish with mushrooms and serve.

Pork with Turnip Tops — *Lacón con grelos*

2 lb. shoulder of pork
salt
pepper
1 clove chopped garlic

1 finely sliced onion
1 tablespoon oil or lard
1 peeled, chopped tomato
1 lb. turnip tops

Bone and cut the pork into small pieces and season with salt and pepper. Fry the garlic and onion in oil or lard until golden. Add tomato and cook together for a few minutes. Put in the pork, add turnip tops. Pour in a little water and simmer for 20-30 minutes, until the meat and vegetables are cooked and most of the liquid evaporated.

Stuffed Fillet of Pork   *Lomo de cerdo relleno*

1½ lb. fillet pork	1 beaten egg
2 chicken livers	1 chopped gherkin
2 oz. fat salted pork	1 chopped onion
2 oz ham	1 tablespoon chopped chives
1 truffle	1 tablespoon chopped parsley
2 oz. freshly grated breadcrumbs	1 tablespoon chopped chervil
½ gill sherry	

Slice the fillet of pork lengthwise without cutting right through, making three long fillets, and season with salt. Chop the chicken livers, salted pork, ham and truffle together, put in a bowl, add breadcrumbs, sherry, egg and gherkin, season with salt to taste and mix well. Put layers of this stuffing between the fillets, press them together and tie with string. Put the pork into a pan with enough water to cover, add onion, chives, parsley and chervil, cover and simmer gently for 1½ hours. Serve cold.

Pork and Butter Beans   *Fabada asturiana*

4 lb. butter beans	4 oz. sliced lean pork
1 quartered onion	8 oz. sliced *chorizo*
½ cup olive oil	8 oz. sliced blood sausage
4 oz. sliced fat pork	pinch saffron
8 oz. sliced rib of pork	salt

Soak the beans for 1½–2 hours. Put in a pan with enough cold water to cover, bring to the boil three times, adding a little cold water each time. Add onion and olive oil. Bring to the boil, put in the rest of the ingredients, except saffron. Pound saffron in a mortar with a pinch of salt, dilute with a little water and add to beans. Cover the pan tightly, simmer for 2½–3 hours, making sure that the beans are always covered with liquid. Season with salt when the beans are tender.

Fillet of Pork with Truffles   *Lomo de cerdo trufado*

4 oz. lean bacon
1 small tin truffles
1½ lb. fillet pork
salt

4 tablespoons olive oil
½ gill sherry
1 sprig savory

Cut the bacon and the truffles into strips and insert these into the fillet of pork. Season with salt, brown lightly in olive oil on all sides, add sherry and savory, cover and simmer very gently for 45-50 minutes. When ready, cut the meat into slices, arrange in the centre of a dish and serve with fried potatoes.

Pork Rolls   *Rollos de lomo de cerdo*

½ oz. dried mushrooms
1½ lb. fillet pork
salt
2 sliced tinned pimentos
flour

olive oil
1 finely chopped onion
1 peeled, chopped tomato
1 cup stock or water

Soak the mushrooms in cold water, rinse, drain and remove stalks. Cut the pork into slices, beat them flat, season with salt, put a strip of pimento in the centre of each, roll up, tie with strong thread, coat with flour and fry in hot olive oil.

Fry the onion in a saucepan. When it begins to colour, add tomato, cook lightly, stir in a heaped teaspoon of flour, dilute with stock or water. Season with salt, add mushrooms, bring to the boil, put in the rolled fillets, cover and simmer on very low heat for 15-20 minutes.

Pork Cheese   *Queso de cerdo*

8 oz. pork
4 oz. streaky bacon
4 oz. fat salted pork
8 oz. pig's liver
3 tablespoons flour

1 egg
salt and pepper
1 piece pig's caul
2 bay leaves

Mince the pork, bacon and fat salted pork. Chop the liver and mix it with the other ingredients in a bowl. Add flour and egg, season with salt and pepper to taste and mix well. Put the pig's caul on a plate with warm water to soften it, then use to line a mould, keeping a little to cover the contents of the mould when it is filled with the mixture. Put in the mixture, lay the bay leaves on top and cover with the caul. Put the mould in the oven in a *bain-marie* for 1½ hours. When cooked, take the mould out, cover it, press with a weight on top and leave until the following day. Before turning out, dip the mould for a second into hot water.

Pork Pâté   *Pastel de lomo de cerdo*

1¼ lb. fillet pork	1 raw yolk
salt	2 oz. butter
3 oz. olive oil	1 truffle
1 chopped onion	cream sauce (p. 70)
1 peeled, chopped tomato	1 bunch watercress
1 chopped carrot	stuffed olives
1½ lb. diced potatoes	

Rub the fillet of pork with salt. Heat olive oil in a saucepan, put in pork, add onion, tomato and carrot, cover and cook on a low heat for 1½ hours, turning the meat from time to time. When ready, take the meat out of the pan and keep on a plate.

Boil the potatoes in salted water, drain, rub through a sieve, stir in the yolk and blend in 1½ oz. butter. (If the potato purée is too thick, thin down with a little milk.)

Cut the meat and the truffle in fine slices. Butter a mould, line with pork slices, sprinkle with slivers of truffle, follow with a layer of potato purée and continue in this manner until all ingredients are used up, ending with a layer of potato. Bake in the oven until golden on top, turn out on to a round dish, cover with cream sauce, garnish with watercress, decorate with stuffed olives and serve.

Apples Stuffed with Pork   *Manzanas rellenas de cerdo*

6 large sweet apples   olive oil
8 oz. pork   flour
1½ oz. fat salted pork (or bacon)   1 finely chopped onion
½ clove garlic   1 peeled, chopped tomato
2–3 oz. freshly grated breadcrumbs   ½ pint water
1 egg   1½ oz. pounded roasted almonds
salt

Core the apples carefully, wash and season with salt. Chop the meat together with the fat salted pork and garlic. Add breadcrumbs, egg and salt to taste. Blend well. Fill the apples with this mixture, using surplus stuffing to shape into balls.

Heat some olive oil in a frying pan and fry the apples, first upside down then turn and cook the other side. Roll the balls in flour and fry.

Fry the onion in a saucepan until golden, add tomato, pour in water, season with salt and mix in the almonds. Put in the apples and the balls, cook gently, turning to cook all sides evenly. Great care must be taken not to break the apples in turning them.

Cold Fillet of Pork   *Fiambre de lomo de cerdo*

1¼ lb. fillet pork   2 oz. lard
4 oz. shredded ham   ½ gill sherry
4 oz. sliced fat salted pork   1 chopped onion
1 sliced hard-boiled egg   1 chopped carrot
1 sliced tinned pimento   1 chopped tomato
1 finely sliced truffle   watercress
salt

Make two deep cuts lengthwise in the fillet of pork, stuff with strips of ham, fat salted pork, hard-boiled egg, pimento and truffle, press together, tie with strong thread and season with salt.

Heat lard (or olive oil) in a saucepan, brown the meat lightly on all sides, sprinkle with sherry, add onion, carrot and tomato, cover and simmer for 2 hours, turning the meat from time to time. When the meat is ready, take it out of the sauce and keep it for the following day.

This meat is eaten cold. Before serving, cut into slices, arrange on a dish and garnish with watercress.

Pig's Trotters with Turnips   *Manos de cerdo con nabos*

1¾ pints of water
2 pig's trotters
salt
6 oz. onions
1 carrot
fines-herbes
1 bay leaf

1 gill white wine
1 clove
olive oil
1 tomato
8 small diced turnips
1½ oz. roasted almonds

Clean and blanch the trotters, cut them lengthwise in half, put in a saucepan with water, salt, one small onion, carrot, *fines-herbes*, bay leaf, wine and clove, bring to the boil, reduce heat and simmer for 3 hours. Heat olive oil in a saucepan, lightly fry the rest of the onions, finely chopped, and the peeled and chopped tomato. Put in the turnips, cook lightly, add half cup of the stock from the trotters. Remove the largest bones from the trotters. Add the trotters to the vegetables. Pound the almonds in a mortar, add to pan, cover and cook gently for 15-20 minutes, until ready, shaking the pan from time to time to prevent sticking.

Pig's Kidneys Sauté   *Riñones de cerdo salteados*

3 pig's kidneys
vinegar
2 oz. lard
1 heaped teaspoon flour
1 gill white wine

1–2 cloves chopped garlic
1 tablespoon chopped parsley
salt and pepper
croûtons

Wash the kidneys and soak in cold water with a dash of vinegar for 15 minutes. Drain, dry, remove skin and membranes. Cut them into slices ½ inch thick and fry in lard over a lively heat, turning two or three times. Stir in the flour, cook for a few moments, pour in the wine, add garlic and parsley, stirring all the time, season with salt and pepper to taste and continue to cook over a lively heat for 2 or 3 minutes until the kidneys are soft.

Serve with *croûtons* of bread fried in butter.

Pig's Blood and Liver with Onion

Sangre e hígado de cerdo con cebolla

1 lb. pig's liver	½ teaspoon salt
1 lb. pig's blood	¼ teaspoon pepper
2 oz. lard	6 slices fried bread
12 oz. finely sliced onions	

Cut the liver and blood into pieces, season with salt, fry first the liver, then the blood, in lard and remove from pan. In the same fat fry the onions, season with salt and pepper, cover and cook gently without browning, stirring from time to time. When the onion becomes soft, add the blood and the liver, stir, heat through and serve with slices of fried bread.

Pig's Brains   *Sesos de cerdo*

2 pig's brains	batter (p. 262)
salt	olive oil
2 tablespoons lemon juice	fried artichokes (p. 81)

Clean the brains well, removing skin, blood, etc. Put in a saucepan with enough salted water to cover, add lemon juice, boil for 5 minutes, drain, leave to cool and cut into thin slices. Dip in batter and fry in hot olive oil until golden. Serve with fried artichokes.

Fowl & Game

AVES Y CAZA

Pigeons a la Española · *Pichones a la española*

2 cleaned, quartered pigeons
salt and pepper
1 oz. butter or lard
4 oz. finely sliced onions

1 lb. sieved tomatoes
pinch sugar
1 bay leaf
1 sprig thyme

Season pigeons with salt and pepper, fry in butter (or lard) in a saucepan until golden. Remove, and in the same fat cook the onions with the lid on over a very gentle heat, so that the onions become very soft without colouring. Add tomatoes and season with salt to taste, add sugar, bay leaf, thyme and the pigeons. Cover and cook very slowly until the pigeons are tender (40–50 minutes). This method of cooking is intended for young pigeons.

Pigeons Montañesa   *Pichones a la montañesa*

2 cleaned, quartered pigeons   *bouquet-garni*
salt   batter for frying (p. 262)
2 oz. lard   *croûtons*
½ gill sherry

Season the pigeon quarters with salt. Heat the lard in a saucepan,
cook the pigeons lightly, add the sherry and *bouquet-garni,* cover
and cook gently until done. Remove the pieces of pigeons, dip in
batter and fry until golden. Put each piece of pigeon on a croûton
of the same size and serve with fried potatoes (p. 110).

Pigeons with Katherine Sauce   *Pichones con salsa Katherine*

2 cleaned pigeons   1 lb. diced boiled potatoes
salt and pepper   2 hard-boiled eggs
2 oz. butter   Katherine sauce (p. 72)

Split the pigeons in half along the breastbone, season with salt
and pepper, brush with melted butter and grill. Arrange on a dish,
surround with potatoes and sprinkle the potatoes with chopped
hard-boiled egg. Serve Katherine sauce separately.

Pigeons with Peas   *Pichones con guisantes*

2 cleaned pigeons   1 finely chopped onion
salt   ½ cup water
2–3 tablespoons olive oil   1 tablespoon mint leaves
1 gill white wine   1 lb. shelled peas

Cut the pigeons into quarters and season with salt. Heat olive
oil in a saucepan and fry pigeon quarters until golden. Sprinkle
with wine, leave to simmer for 2–3 minutes and remove. Fry the
onion in the same oil. As soon as it begins to colour, add water
and mint leaves. Bring to the boil, season with a little salt, put in
the peas and the pigeons, add a little more water, if necessary,
cover the pan and cook gently until the peas are ready.

Stuffed Pigeons　　　*Pichones rellenos*

2 cleaned pigeons	4 oz. finely chopped ham
salt and pepper	4 oz. chopped mushrooms
2 oz. butter	chopped *fines-herbes*

Split the pigeons and season with salt and a little pepper, brush with melted butter and grill on the inside. Combine ham, mushrooms and *fines-herbes*, cook lightly in butter, spread some of this mixture on the grilled side and close the pigeons, sandwiching together to make them appear whole. Finish grilling on both sides. Serve with potato soufflé (p. 112).

Catalan Chicken　　　*Pollo a la catalana*

1 young chicken	4 oz. finely sliced onions
2 oz. lard	1 fresh sliced pimento
salt	1 lb. peeled, chopped tomatoes
2 tablespoons sherry	½ teaspoon sugar

Cut chicken into pieces. Melt the lard in a saucepan, put in the chicken, season with salt and fry over a moderate heat until golden. Add sherry, stir, and remove chicken from the pan. In the same fat, lightly fry the onions, without browning. Add pimento, cook lightly, put in tomatoes, season with salt to taste and add sugar. Return chicken to pan, cover and simmer over a very gentle heat for 20 minutes.

Chicken Chilindrón　　　*Pollos a la chilindrón*

1 or 2 tender chickens	12 oz. thinly sliced lean ham
olive oil	1 chopped onion
1 clove garlic	6 red peeled, chopped pimentos
salt	6 peeled, chopped tomatoes
pepper	

Joint the chicken. Heat plenty of olive oil in a saucepan and fry
the garlic. Salt and pepper the pieces of chicken and fry until
golden on both sides. Add ham and onion. Stir, cook together for
a few minutes, add pimentos and tomatoes. Simmer gently until
the chicken is tender and all liquid given out by the vegetables
reduced.

Chicken Vinaigrette   *Pollo a la vinagreta*

1 young cleaned chicken
salt
2 tablespoons olive oil
8 oz. finely sliced onions

1 small head of garlic
1 bay leaf
1 teaspoon vinegar

Cut the chicken into pieces, season with salt, put in a saucepan
with olive oil, onions, garlic, bay leaf and vinegar, cover and cook
gently, shaking the pan from time to time, until the chicken is
ready (20–25 minutes).

Grilled Chicken   *Pollo al minuto*

1 tender young chicken
salt
juice of ¼ lemon

1 tablespoon olive oil
butter

Clean chicken and cut into quarters. Season with salt and sprinkle
with lemon juice and olive oil. Wrap each piece of chicken in a
piece of buttered greaseproof paper, moisten the paper with water
on the outside and grill under a hot grill. Remove the paper and
serve with a salad.

Braised Chicken   *Pollo asado*

1 young cleaned chicken
2 oz. butter
2 tablespoons olive oil
1 sliced onion

1 sliced carrot
2 tablespoons sherry
1 cup hot water
fried cauliflower (p. 90)

Put the chicken whole into a saucepan with the butter, olive oil, onion and carrot. Cover with a well fitting lid, cook for 10 minutes, pour in the sherry and water and simmer very gently for 1½ hours. Put the chicken on a dish, strain the sauce over it, garnish with fried cauliflower and serve.

Chicken with Pickling Onions   *Pollo con cebollitas*

1 young chicken
salt
2 tablespoons olive oil
4 oz. diced fat salted pork

½ gill dry sherry
bouquet-garni
1 lb. pickling onions
flour

Clean the chicken and cut it into pieces. Season with salt. Heat olive oil in a saucepan and lightly fry the pork, then fry the chicken until golden. Sprinkle with sherry, add *bouquet-garni* and cook gently for 20 minutes. Roll onions in flour, fry them, add to chicken with a little water and simmer for 20 minutes. Put the chicken in the centre of a dish, pour the sauce over it and surround with the onions.

Chicken and Lobster   *Pollo y langosta*

See recipe Lobster and Chicken (p. 173).

Spanish Casserole Chicken   *Pollo en cocotte*

1 trussed chicken	4 oz. peeled, chopped tomatoes
salt	1 finely sliced truffle
4 oz. lard	1¼ lb. potatoes
1 tablespoon brandy	8 oz. stoned olives
4 oz. chopped onions	4 oz. butter

Rub the chicken with salt, inside and outside. Put it in a saucepan with the lard and cook until golden. Transfer the chicken and the juice into a casserole dish. Sprinkle with brandy, add onions, tomatoes and truffle, pour in half cup water, cover and cook in the oven until done.

Scoop out the potatoes to look like hazelnuts (p. 112), boil in salted water, drain, fry in butter until golden and remove from pan. Fry the olives. Arrange the potatoes and the olives around the chicken in the casserole dish and serve.

Chicken in Aspic   *Aspic de pollo*

1 drawn chicken	4 oz. ham
salt	2 hard-boiled eggs
2 tablespoons lard	2 truffles
½ gill sherry	4 oz. sliced mushrooms
½ cup water	pastry for tartlets (p. 262)
1 sliced onion	mayonnaise (p. 74)
1 sliced carrot	1 sweet pimento
1 raw egg	1 bunch watercress
3 leaves gelatine	

Cut the chicken into pieces, season with salt and fry in lard until lightly golden. Pour in sherry and half cup water, cover and simmer very gently. The chicken must be cooked but not browned.

Aspic Jelly: Cook the giblets, including feet, neck, gizzard and wing tips with onion and carrot in 2¾ pints water. Season with salt and simmer gently until the liquid is reduced by half. Strain the stock, and return to the fire, bring to the boil, drop in a stiffly beaten white of egg and the shell, to clarify. Let it boil up once or twice, then strain through a cloth soaked in cold water and wrung out. Soak gelatine in cold water until soft, dilute with a little hot water and add to the stock.

Dice the ham and slice the eggs. Fry the chicken liver and cut it up. Slice the truffle. Bring mushrooms to the boil, drain and chop.

Bone the chicken. Decorate the bottom of a mould with a slice of egg and strips of truffle. Add a layer of small pieces of chicken, and another of all the other prepared ingredients. Repeat these layers until the mould is almost full, pour in the jelly slowly and carefully without disturbing the layers. Leave to set. Dip the mould into hot water and turn out on to a dish.

Serve with small savoury tartlets filled with a mixed vegetable salad, dressed with mayonnaise, decorate the top with a disk of sweet pimento and garnish with watercress.

Chicken with Samfaina Sauce   *Pollo en samfaina*

1 jointed chicken   *samfaina* sauce (p. 78)
olive oil

Fry the chicken lightly in olive oil, put in a casserole dish, cover with *samfaina* sauce and finish cooking in the oven.

Pudding Rosaura   *Budín Rosaura*

2 chicken livers   pinch grated nutmeg
salt   4 eggs
4 oz. ham   breadcrumbs
2 oz. butter   potato straws (p. 113)
3 tablespoons flour   Colbert sauce (p. 70)
1 pint milk

Fry the chicken livers in butter, season with salt and chop together with the ham to make a paste. Make a *béchamel* sauce (p. 70) using 1½ oz. butter, the flour and the milk, season with nutmeg and mix with liver and ham paste. Beat the eggs and add to the rest, mixing well together. Butter a mould, sprinkle with grated breadcrumbs, pour in the mixture and bake in the oven until done.

Turn the pudding out on to a dish and garnish with potato straws. Serve Colbert sauce separately.

Baked Chicken Custard   *Flan de pollo*

2 breasts of chicken	½ pint boiled milk
salt	pinch grated nutmeg
olive oil	¾ oz. butter
4 eggs	cream sauce (p. 70)

Rub the breasts of chicken with salt, brush with olive oil, grill them, then skin and bone and chop the flesh very finely. Beat the eggs, mix with milk, add chicken, season with a little salt and nutmeg. Butter a mould, pour in the mixture, bake in the oven in a *bain-marie* until it sets. Turn out on to a dish and cover with cream sauce.

Chicken Jelly   *Gelatina de gallina*

¼ of a chicken	1 turnip
8 oz. lean veal	1 leek
½ calf's foot	salt
1 carrot	1 pint water

Cut the chicken and veal into small pieces. Bone the calf's foot and cut up the flesh. Put all these ingredients into a pan, add carrot, turnip, leek, a little salt and water. Seal the lid hermetically and cook in a *bain-marie* for 4 hours without uncovering. If the water evaporates in the bottom pan, keep adding boiling water.

Cool, strain into a bowl, first through a sieve, then through a cloth soaked in cold water and wrung out. Leave to set, then cover and store. This jelly is very good for convalescents.

Ramekins Carmencita　　*Platitos de pollo Carmencita*

2 chicken breasts
1 sliced onion
1 sliced carrot
salt
3 oz. butter

2½ oz. flour
1 yolk
2 oz. diced ham
1¾ oz. grated cheese

Boil the chicken with onion, carrot and salt in 2½ pints water, reduce the quantity of liquid by half. Strain the stock. Dice the chicken.

Make *béchamel* sauce (p. 70), using 2 oz. butter, the flour and the stock, remove from heat, blend in yolk, add chicken and ham, mix well and fill six small buttered china oven-proof dishes. Sprinkle with grated cheese, top with small pieces of butter and put in the oven to brown the top lightly.

Chicken Soufflé　　*Suflé de gallina*

3 breasts of chicken
1 sliced onion
1 sliced turnip
1 sliced carrot

salt
2 oz. butter
2½ oz. flour
6 eggs

Put the chicken with onion, turnip and carrot into 2¾ pints boiling water, season with salt and simmer over a moderate heat until the liquid is reduced by half. Strain the stock and chop chicken finely. Make a thick *béchamel* sauce (p. 70), using the butter, flour and stock, cook for 10 minutes, add chicken, cook for another 10 minutes, remove from heat and stir in six yolks. Beat the whites until very stiff and carefully fold into the soufflé mixture. Pour the mixture into a buttered soufflé dish, bake in the oven until it rises and serve immediately on taking it out of the oven, as it collapses at once.

Dulcinea Tartlets   *Tarteletas dulcinea*

2 breasts of chicken	1½ oz. butter
1 sliced onion	1¼ oz. flour
1 sliced carrot	1 raw yolk
salt	pastry for tartlets (p. 262)
1 truffle	

Put the chicken breasts, onion and carrot into 1¾ pints water, season with salt, bring to the boil and simmer until the liquid is reduced by half. Strain the stock and chop up the chicken finely together with the truffle. Make *béchamel* sauce (p. 70), using the butter, flour and stock, cook for 10 minutes, add chicken and truffle, cook together for 10 minutes, remove from heat and blend in the yolk.

Make the tartlets as described and fill them with the mixture.

Chicken Pepitoria   *Gallina en pepitoria*

1 boiling chicken	1 teaspoon flour
salt	1 gill white wine
4 oz. lard	1 sprig thyme
4 oz. finely chopped onions	1¼ oz. roasted almonds
2 cloves chopped garlic	1 hard-boiled egg yolk
1 tablespoon chopped parsley	

Clean the chicken, joint, season with salt, put in a saucepan, fry in lard until golden and remove. In the same fat fry the onions until golden, add garlic and parsley, cook gently for a moment, stir in the flour, gradually pour in the wine, add thyme, bring to the boil and return the chicken to pan. Pour in a cup of water, season with salt to taste, cover and cook gently until the chicken is soft. Pound the almonds and the yolk in a mortar and stir into the pan 20 minutes before serving.

Galantine of Chicken   *Galantina de gallina*

1 singed, plucked boiling fowl
12 oz. minced pork
12 oz. minced veal
salt and pepper
3 tablespoons freshly grated bread-
    crumbs
1 gill milk
2 tablespoons brandy
2 beaten eggs

8 oz. sliced fat salted pork
8 oz. sliced ham
2 thinly sliced truffles
1 sliced onion
1 sliced carrot
1 bay leaf
1 whole egg
3 leaves gelatine

Remove feet and pinions. Slit the chicken along the back and with a small sharp knife bone it without tearing the flesh. To make this operation easier, follow the joints of the chicken, working inwards towards the carcase, shaving off the flesh as close to the bone as possible. Remove bones from legs, thighs and wings, without damaging the skin. Lay the chicken on a board, cut away the breast fillets and the fleshy parts of the joints and slice. Cut liver into thin slices. Spread the boned chicken flat on the board and season with salt and pepper.

Soak breadcrumbs in milk and squeeze out. Mix pork, veal, breadcrumbs, brandy and the beaten eggs, season with salt and blend well. Spread a layer of this mixture on top of the open chicken, cover with sliced chicken, alternating with slices of fat salted pork, ham, truffle and the chicken liver, until the stuffing is used up. Sew up the chicken, press into shape, wrap tightly in a cloth, tying it at the ends and put into a saucepan with enough water to cover, together with the bones and giblets, onion, carrot and bay leaf. Simmer for 2 hours. Remove the bird and leave to cool. Take it out of the cloth and leave for 4–5 hours with a weight on top.

Jelly: Strain the stock and cook down to reduce the liquid, clarify with egg (see recipe for consommé, p. 36) and strain through a damp cloth. Stir in gelatine leaves, softened with a little warm water. Pour into a mould to set.

To serve, gently remove stitches and place the galantine on a serving dish. Turn out the jelly, chop or cut into fancy shapes and place the galantine of chicken on top.

Left-Overs of Cooked Meat or Chicken
Aprovechamiento de carne o gallina hervidas

Slice two or three onions very finely, brown lightly in olive oil, season with a little salt and pepper, add meat or chicken (or both), cut into small pieces. Cook lightly, add a dash of vinegar, stir and serve hot.

Stuffed Capon   *Capón relleno*

1 capon	1½ oz. roasted almonds
6 oz. lard	1½ oz. pine-kernels
8 oz. diced fillet pork	1 thinly sliced truffle
8 oz. sliced pork sausages	salt
8 oz. boiled prunes	1 sprig savory
2 oz. blanched raisins	½ gill sherry

Clean and singe the capon, cut off the feet and neck, being careful to keep some skin at the neck end to sew up, when the capon is stuffed. Heat 2 oz. lard in a saucepan, lightly fry the pork and the sausages, together with prunes, raisins, almonds, pine-kernels and truffle, cook for 10 minutes, season with salt to taste, stuff both ends of the bird with the mixture and sew it up. Rub capon with salt, grease with lard, put in an oven-proof dish with the rest of the lard and a sprig of savory and roast gently in the oven until golden. Pour the sherry over the capon, cover with a sheet of greased paper, which must be kept moist with drops of water sprinkled on top from time to time, and finish cooking in the oven.

This dish may also be cooked in a covered saucepan on top of the stove.

Roast Turkey, Spanish Style　　　*Pavo asado*

1 oven-ready turkey	2 tablespoons sherry
salt	1 sprig savory
lard	

Rub the turkey with salt inside and outside, grease the inside with lard, put in a roasting pan with a lid, cover generously with lard, sprinkle with sherry, put a sprig of savory on top, cover the pan and roast in a moderate oven, basting from time to time.

Put the turkey on a dish with potato soufflé (p. 112) and serve the pan juices separately, and very hot.

Stuffed Roast Turkey   *Pavo asado y relleno*

See recipe for Stuffed Capon (p. 229).

Stuffed Turkey with Cream Sauce   *Pavo relleno a la crema*

1 oven-ready turkey	2 beaten eggs
salt	pinch powdered thyme
1¼ oz. dried mushrooms	12 oz. lard
3 tablespoons freshly grated bread- crumbs	2 tablespoons brandy cream sauce (p. 70)
1 gill milk	1¼ oz. butter
8 oz. sausage meat	¼ pint cream
8 oz. chopped fillet pork	watercress
4 oz. chopped ham	

Rub the turkey with salt inside and outside. Soak the mushrooms in water, drain and chop. Soak breadcrumbs in milk and squeeze out. Combine sausage meat, pork, ham, mushrooms, breadcrumbs, eggs and thyme. Blend well, stuff the turkey at both ends with this mixture and sew it up. Truss the bird with a long needle and strong thread through the legs, binding the wings to the back. Grease the turkey with lard and put the rest of it in a covered roasting pan with the bird. Sprinkle with brandy, cover with a piece of damp greaseproof paper and the lid and roast in the oven for 2–3 hours, depending on size. Baste from time to time and keep the paper damp by moistening with a few drops of water on top. Make cream sauce, remove from heat, add butter and cream, mix well and pour into a sauce-boat. This sauce should not be too thick.

Put the turkey on a dish, remove trussing string, pour two to three tablespoons of the pan juices over the bird, surround with watercress and serve with cream sauce.

Truffled Turkey with Orange Sauce

Pavo trufado con salsa de naranja

1 pig's tongue	1 sprig thyme
1 oven-ready turkey	1 chopped onion
8 oz. truffles	1 stick celery
salt and pepper	1 grated peel of orange
½ pint cream	juice of ½ orange
12 oz. lard	1 tablespoon mint leaves
1 sliced onion	2 raw yolks
1 sliced carrot	2 tablespoons top of milk
1 bay leaf	1¼ oz. butter

Scald the tongue, peel, clean and dice. Blanch and dice the gizzard and liver. Cut truffles into fine strips. Put these ingredients into a bowl, season with salt and pepper to taste, add cream and mix well. Grease the inside of the turkey with lard, season with salt, stuff with the mixture, sew up and truss.

Put the rest of the lard into a covered roasting pan, put in the bird, sliced onion, carrot, bay leaf and thyme, cover and roast in the oven until it is cooked, basting from time to time with the pan juices.

Orange Sauce: Cook the feet, giblets, neck, chopped onion and celery in 1¼ pints water. Season with salt. Boil down to reduce liquid to ¾ pint. Strain, put back on the fire, add orange peel, mint and orange juice. Bring to the boil. Dilute the yolks with top of milk. Remove sauce from heat. Stir in yolks, add butter, stirring constantly. Reheat gently, but on no account allow the sauce to boil. Strain.

Put the turkey on a serving dish, remove string and garnish with salad of your choice. Serve sauce separately.

Turkey Pâté   *Pastel de pavo*

1 good-sized cabbage	1 lb. tomatoes
cooked diced turkey	breadcrumbs
sliced lean and fat ham	1 oz. butter
1 tablespoon lard	*muselina* sauce (p. 75)

This is an excellent way of using up turkey leftovers. Separate the cabbage leaves and boil in salted water. Drain carefully. Fry ham lightly in lard, remove, sieve tomatoes into the same pan. Simmer to cook down liquid and thicken tomato purée.

Grease a mould with lard, sprinkle with breadcrumbs, line the bottom with slices of ham, then with two cabbage leaves, cover with a layer of tomato purée, follow with diced turkey and continue in this sequence until the mould is filled, ending with a layer of cabbage. Top with small pieces of butter and put the mould in a moderate oven for 30 minutes.

Turn the mould out on to a dish and cover with *muselina* sauce.

Braised Duck   *Pato asado*

1 duck	1 medium sliced onion
2 tablespoons lard	1 sliced carrot
salt	1 peeled, chopped tomato
2 tablespoons sherry	1 bay leaf

Joint the duck, put in a saucepan with lard, season with salt, and when it begins to turn golden, sprinkle with sherry. Add onion, carrot, tomato and bay leaf, cover pan and cook gently until tender.* Serve with a salad.

* The cooking time varies from 40 minutes to 1½ hours, depending on size and age of bird.

Duck with Mushrooms   *Pato con setas*

1 oven-ready duck
salt
1 tablespoon lard
1 sprig savory
2 tablespoons brandy

8 oz. mushrooms
3 tablespoons olive oil
flour
1 tablespoon butter

Rub the duck with salt both inside and outside. Put it in a saucepan with lard and savory, and brown lightly. Sprinkle with brandy, cover the pan, and leave on a gentle heat until cooked,* turning the duck from time to time. Clean the mushrooms, fry in olive oil, dredge with flour. Add butter to the oil and return mushrooms to the pan. Cook for 5 minutes. Put the duck on a dish and surround it with mushrooms.

Duck with Almonds   *Pato con almendras*

1 young duck
4 oz. lard
1 sliced onion
3 cloves garlic

salt
4 oz. peeled, chopped tomatoes
12 roasted almonds
½ cup water

Wash the duck, dry well with a cloth and joint it. Heat the lard in a saucepan, fry the duck liver, remove and in the same fat fry the onion and garlic until golden. Take them out of the pan and put in the duck. Season with salt, brown lightly and add tomatoes. Pound the almonds, liver, onion and garlic in a mortar into a smooth paste, dilute with water and pour it into the saucepan. Season with salt to taste and simmer gently until the duck is ready.*

* See note on p. 233.

Giblets with Tomato Purée   *Menudillos con puré de tomate*

2 sets giblets   1 tablespoon chopped parsley
salt   8 oz. sieved tomatoes
2 tablespoons lard   1 teaspoon sugar
2 cloves chopped garlic   *croûtons*

Wash and slice the giblets, season with salt and fry in lard. Add garlic and parsley, fry for 2–3 minutes, stir in tomatoes, season with salt to taste, sprinkle with sugar and simmer gently for 20 minutes. Serve with *croûtons* of bread fried in butter or oil.

Giblets with Sauce   *Menudillos con salsa*

2 sets giblets   2 sprigs parsley
salt   1 slice fried bread
1–2 tablespoons lard   2 oz. roasted almonds
2 cloves garlic   ½ cup water

Wash and slice the giblets, season with salt and fry in lard. Pound garlic, parsley, fried bread and almonds in a mortar, dilute with water and add it to the giblets. Cook together gently for 30 minutes.

Giblet Pudding   *Budín de menudillos*

4 sets giblets   4 beaten eggs
salt   1 tablespoon butter
2 oz. lard   2 tablespoons breadcrumbs
béchamel sauce (p. 70)   English sauce (p. 74)

Clean the giblets, chop, season with salt and fry in lard. Make *béchamel* sauce, add the giblets to it, remove pan from heat, stir in eggs and mix well. Butter a mould, sprinkle with breadcrumbs, pour the sauce with giblets into it and cook in a *bain-marie* until set. Turn the pudding out on to a dish, cover with English sauce and serve.

Partridge Vinaigretté   *Perdices a la vinagreta*

2 partridges	1 bay leaf
1 small cup olive oil	1 tablespoon vinegar
4 oz. sliced onions	salt
1 small head garlic	bread *croûtons*

Joint the partridges, put in a saucepan together with olive oil, onions, garlic (peeled but whole), bay leaf and vinegar. Season with salt, cover the pan with greaseproof paper, put a small earthenware dish with water on top and cook gently, shaking the pan from time to time to prevent sticking. Put the partridges on a dish, strain the sauce over them and surround with *croûtons* of bread fried in butter or oil.

Partridges with Cabbage   *Perdices con col*

1 medium-sized cabbage	1 chopped onion
flour	4 oz. peeled, chopped tomatoes
lard	salt
2 partridges	1½ oz. roasted almonds
1 tablespoon brandy	

Trim the cabbage leaves, cut away tough stems, season with salt, boil carefully in salted water for 10 minutes, drain and leave to cool. Roll up each leaf, coat in flour and fry in lard until golden.

Clean the partridges and cut each into four pieces. Heat two to three tablespoons lard in a saucepan, fry the pieces of partridge until golden, sprinkle with brandy, cover, simmer for 10 minutes, then remove, and in the same fat lightly fry the onion, add tomatoes, fry together, pour in half cup water and season with salt to taste. Fry the partridge livers lightly, drain, pound with almonds in a mortar and add to pan. Return the partridges and the cabbage rolls to the pan, cover and simmer for 1–1¼ hours until ready,* adding a little water, if necessary.

* See note on p. 233.

Stewed Partridges   *Perdices estofadas*

2 jointed partridges
1 gill olive oil
2 oz. diced fat salted pork
4 cloves peeled garlic
1 bay leaf

1 gill white wine
2 oz. grated cooking chocolate
1 lb. pickling onions (or shallots)
salt

Heat olive oil in a saucepan, put in partridges, together with the pork, garlic, bay leaf and the wine. Cover and cook gently for 45 minutes, shaking the pan from time to time to prevent sticking. Add chocolate and pickling onions, season with salt to taste, and simmer 40–45 minutes. Arrange partridges on a dish, surround with onions and pour the sauce over them.

Quails Maître d'Hôtel   *Codornices a la maître d'hôtel*

6 quails
1 teaspoon salt
½ teaspoon pepper
2 tablespoons olive oil
juice of ½ lemon
2–3 cloves chopped garlic

1 tablespoon chopped parsley
1 lb. potatoes
1 egg yolk
2 oz. butter
6 medium-sized tomatoes
maître d'hôtel sauce (p. 75)

Clean the quails well, open them along the back, flatten slightly, season with salt and pepper, sprinkle with olive oil, lemon juice, garlic and parsley and leave to macerate for 1 hour.

Boil potatoes in salted water, drain, rub through a sieve, blend in the yolk and one tablespoon butter. Cut the tops off the tomatoes, carefully scoop out all pulp, season inside with a little salt, leave to drain upside down. Put a little butter inside each tomato, put them in the oven for a few minutes, stuff with the potato purée, using a forcing bag with a fluted nozzle, and put back in the oven to brown the top lightly. Grill the partridges on a hot grill, arrange on a dish, cover with *maître d'hôtel* sauce and surround with tomatoes. Serve very hot.

Quail Salmis   *Salmís de codornices*

6 quails	*bouquet-garni*
salt	1½ oz. butter
3 tablespoons lard	1 tablespoon flour
1 gill white wine	4 oz. sliced mushrooms
1 chopped onion	6 slices fried bread

Clean the quails well, dry with a cloth and season with salt. Heat lard in a saucepan, fry quails until golden, sprinkle with wine, turn once or twice, pour in half cup water, cook gently for 30 minutes and remove from pan. In the same fat fry the giblets, discarding the gizzards. Add the onion, let it fry a little, pour in half cup water, season with salt, add *bouquet-garni*, simmer for 30 minutes, strain and keep the liquid. Pound the rest, rub through a sieve and mix with the liquid to make a sauce.

Melt the butter in a saucepan, cook the flour until golden, stir in the sauce gradually. Add mushrooms. If the sauce is too thick, add a little water. Cook for 15 minutes, then return the quails to the pan, spoon the sauce over them, draw the pan to the side of the burner and keep hot but do not allow to boil.

Arrange slices of fried bread (*croûtons*) on a dish, place a quail on each, cover with the sauce and serve at once. More *croûtons* can be added as a garnish.

Lark Tartlets   *Alondras en tarteletas*

4 chicken livers	8 tartlet cases (p. 262)
1½ oz. butter	8 larks
4 oz. sliced mushrooms	8 oz. fat salted pork
1 tablespoon chopped *fines herbes*	lard
1 slice bread	1 tablespoon brandy
¼ pint milk	1 lb. sieved tomatoes
salt	2 bunches watercress

Clean the chicken livers, cut them up and fry in the butter together with mushrooms, *fines herbes* and a slice of bread, soaked in milk and squeezed out. Season with salt, stir, and cook lightly. This mixture will be used to line the tartlets.

Bake tartlet cases big enough to hold one lark each.

Clean the larks inside and outside, season with salt, wrap each in a slice of pork and tie with a thread (which is removed when the bird is cooked). Cook in lard until golden, sprinkle with the brandy, cover the pan and leave on a gentle heat until cooked. Line the tartlets with the prepared mixture, put a lark on top and cover with a tablespoon of thick tomato purée. Arrange the watercress on a dish and place the tarts on top of it.

This recipe may be used for other small birds, matching the size of the tartlet case to the size of the bird.

Rabbit Stew   *Conejo estofado*

2 oz. lard	1 chopped carrot
4 oz. diced fat salted pork	1 clove chopped garlic
1 lb. pickling onions (or shallots)	1 tablespoon chopped parsley
1 jointed rabbit	½ gill white wine
salt	1 teaspoon flour
1 chopped onion	½ cup water

Heat the lard in a saucepan, put in the pork and pickling onions, brown lightly, remove. Season rabbit with salt and fry until golden in the fat in which the pork and onions were cooked.

Remove, and in the same fat fry the chopped onion, carrot, garlic and parsley. Pour in the wine, blend in the flour, cook lightly for a moment, add water, check seasoning, and return the rabbit to the pan. Cover and simmer gently until done (50–60 minutes). Ten minutes before serving, add the pickling onions and pork.

Catalan Rabbit   *Conejo a la catalana*

Follow recipe for Catalan Chicken (p. 220).

Huntsman's Rabbit   *Conejo a la cazadora*

3 tablespoons olive oil
1 slice bread
1 sliced onion
3 cloves garlic

4 sprigs parsley
1 young jointed rabbit
salt
½ cup water

Heat olive oil in a pan and fry a slice of bread. Take it out of the pan, fry onion, garlic and parsley, remove and pound them together with the slice of fried bread in a mortar. Season the rabbit with salt and fry lightly in the same oil. Add the pounded mixture and water. Check seasoning, cover and cook on a moderate heat until the rabbit is ready (about 1 hour).

Rabbit, Country Style   *Conejo a la labradora*

1 young rabbit
salt
4 tablespoons olive oil
½ gill white wine
1 small bay leaf
1 small sprig thyme

1 lb. shelled peas
1 lb. shelled broad beans
1 diced carrot
1 diced turnip
1 chopped onion
8 oz. diced potatoes

Clean and joint the rabbit, season with salt and brown lightly in olive oil in a saucepan. Add wine, bay leaf and thyme. Cook gently for 30 minutes, add peas, beans, carrot, turnip, onion and potatoes. Cook together for 3–4 minutes, add water (barely enough to cover), season with salt and simmer gently until done. (Cooking time—about 1 hour.)

Quick Rabbit   *Conejo al minuto*

1 young jointed rabbit
salt
flour
4 oz. lard

1 tablespoon chopped parsley
4 oz. chopped onions
2 tablespoons brandy
½ cup water

Season the rabbit with salt, coat with flour and fry in lard. Remove and in the same fat fry parsley and onions. When they begin to turn golden, return the rabbit to pan, sprinkle with brandy, cook a few minutes, add water, season with salt, and cook on a lively heat for 30 minutes, stirring from time to time to prevent sticking.

Wine, oil and friend are best for being old

Grilled Rabbit with All-i-oli

Conejo asado a la parrilla

1 jointed rabbit	*Garnish:* lettuce
salt	tomatoes
olive oil	pimento
all-i-oli (p. 69)	olives

Season rabbit with salt and brush with olive oil. Heat the grill and grill the rabbit under a gentle heat, otherwise it will burn on the outside while the inside will remain raw. When grilled, arrange on a serving dish, cover with *all-i-oli* and garnish with a salad consisting of lettuce, tomato, fresh pimento and olives.

Rabbit with Plums   *Conejo con ciruelas*

Follow the recipe for Veal with Plums (p. 182).

Rabbit with Almonds   *Conejo con almendras*

1 young rabbit	salt
olive oil	1 rusk
1 chopped onion	1½ oz. roasted almonds
1 peeled, chopped tomato	

Clean and joint the rabbit, season with salt and fry it and its liver in hot olive oil in a saucepan until golden. Take out the rabbit, and in the same oil lightly fry the onion and tomato. Pour in half cup water and season with salt to taste. Soak the rusk in a little water. Pound the almonds in a mortar, add the fried liver, pound together into a smooth paste, add rusk, mix, dilute with a little water, put the mixture in the pan, add rabbit, cover and cook gently until ready (45–60 minutes).

Wild Rabbit Basque Style   *Conejo de monte a la vizcaína*

1 wild rabbit
1 gill olive oil
2 oz. lard
3 or 4 cloves chopped garlic
1½ tablespoons chopped parsley
1 bay leaf

1 clove
1 gill white wine
1 oz. grated cooking chocolate
½ cup water
salt

Clean and joint the rabbit. Heat olive oil and lard in a saucepan and put in the rabbit together with garlic, parsley, bay leaf, clove, wine, grated chocolate and water. Season with salt, stir, cover and leave to cook on a moderate heat for 40–45 minutes, shaking the pan from time to time to prevent sticking.

When cooked, arrange the pieces of rabbit on a dish and strain the sauce over them.

Fried Rabbit   *Conejo rebozado*

1 young rabbit
1 gill white wine
juice of ½ lemon
1 bay leaf
2 cloves halved garlic

flour
2 beaten eggs
lard
potato straws (p. 113)

Clean the rabbit, cut into pieces of uniform size, put in a bowl with wine, lemon juice, bay leaf and garlic and leave for 3 or 4 hours, or better still, overnight. Coat with flour and beaten egg and fry in lard on a moderate heat until golden.

Serve with potato straws.

Eat to live and drink to eat

Stewed Hare Spanish Style   *Liebre estofada*

1 hare	*bouquet-garni*
6 oz. sliced onions	2 oz. grated cooking chocolate
1 head garlic	1 gill red wine
½ pint olive oil	salt

Clean and joint the hare, wash, dry and put in a saucepan together with onions, garlic, olive oil, *bouquet-garni*, chocolate and wine. Season with salt to taste, cover and cook gently on a moderate heat for 2–2½ hours until the hare is tender, shaking the pan from time to time to prevent sticking.

Sweets, Cakes, Pastries & Jams

SWEETS AND DESSERTS

POSTRES

Melon Surprise   *Melón sorpresa*

1 ripe melon
fruit salad

castor sugar
kirsch

Choose a ripe melon, cut off the top, to be used later as a cover, discard seeds, scoop out the flesh and dice, leaving the outside shell undamaged.

Mix diced melon with prepared fruit salad in a bowl, sprinkle with sugar and kirsch to taste, stir carefully, fill the melon with the mixed fruits, replace the top, chill and serve.

Melons and women are difficult to judge

Dessert Mariona   *Postre Mariona*

1 sponge cake   kirsch for flavouring
fruit salad   custard cream (p. 252)

Cut cake into layers horizontally. Prepare kirsch-flavoured fruit salad, using fruit of your choice. Put a layer of sponge cake in a fruit bowl, then a layer of fruit. Continue in alternate layers, cover with custard cream and decorate with hulled strawberries, stoned cherries, or halved apricots if available.

Cup Montblanc   *Copas Montblanc*

1 pint milk   1 tablespoon cornflour
piece lemon peel   8 oz. strawberry jam
2 raw yolks   1 pint whipped cream
3 oz. castor sugar   2 oz. glacé cherries

Make a custard using the milk, lemon peel, yolks, sugar and cornflour (p. 252) and leave to cool. Put a tablespoon of strawberry jam into each individual sundae dish, then a good layer of custard, fill with whipped cream, put a glacé cherry on top, chill and serve.

Cup Nuria   *Copas Nuria*

6 eggs   peach or apricot jam
6 tablespoons castor sugar   1 oz. grated chocolate

Separate the yolks from the whites. Cream the yolks with the sugar into a smooth paste. Divide the mixture between six champagne glasses and spread with a layer of peach or apricot jam. Beat the whites into a stiff foam, add a little syrup (made by boiling some sugar moistened with very little water and cooled), whisk again, put into an icing bag and pipe a spiral on top of the jam. Sprinkle with chocolate and serve very cold.

Rice Jaimito *Arroz Jaimito*

8 oz. rice
2 pints milk
4 oz. sugar
small pinch salt

peel of ½ lemon
1 cinnamon stick
2 eggs
8 oz. jam

Boil the rice in enough water to cover for 5 minutes, drain, rinse with cold water, put back in pan, pour boiling milk over it, add salt, sugar, lemon peel and cinnamon and simmer gently until the rice is cooked. Remove from heat. Separate yolks and whites. Beat the yolks and stir into the rice. Spread the rice on a shallow dish, cover with a layer of jam according to taste (apricot, peach, cherry, strawberry, etc.). Whisk the whites with a tablespoon of sugar until stiff and with a forcing bag pipe a border round the rice.

Rice Pudding and Apples *Arroz con leche y manzanas*

8 oz. rice
2 pints milk
4 oz. sugar
3 yolks

6 apples
syrup
8 oz. jam
3 whites of egg

Cook the rice as described in previous recipe, remove from heat, stir in three yolks. Peel and core the apples and cook them in a thin syrup (made with sugar and water boiled together), taking great care to keep them whole. Spread the rice in an oven-proof dish, make six holes and place the apples in them. Reduce the syrup by boiling down until it thickens, pour over the rice and fill the apples with any jam, according to taste. Beat the egg whites until very stiff, top the apples with it and bake in the oven until the whites of egg are golden.

Rum Torrijas   *Torrijas al ron*

Cut square slices of bread ½ inch thick, cut off crusts and soak in
yolks of egg diluted with rum for 20 minutes. Dip in beaten egg,
fry in hot olive oil until golden, drain. Leave to cool, sprinkle with
fine sugar, glaze with a glazing iron and serve.

Jam Torrijas   *Torrijas con mermelada*

8 slices bread	3 tablespoons milk
apricot or peach jam	½ teaspoon grated lemon peel
3 eggs	olive oil
sugar	

Cut the crusts off the slices of bread, spread one side with apricot
or peach jam and sandwich together. Beat eggs with one tablespoon sugar, milk and lemon peel. Coat both sides of each sandwich with this mixture and leave on a plate for 15–20 minutes.
Heat olive oil, fry the sandwiches until golden, sprinkle with
sugar and serve.

Celestial Torrijas   *Torrijas de cielo*

Cut stale bread into slices, butter, spread with a layer of jam,
cover with whites of egg, whisked with icing sugar until very stiff,
and put in a slow oven until golden.

This is a very good way of using up whites of egg.

Torrijas Santa Teresa   *Torrijas de Santa Teresa*

Cut the ends off a French loaf and slice it. Fill a deep plate with
milk, sweetened with a teaspoon of sugar and flavoured with
grated lemon peel. Moisten the slices lightly in milk, place them

side by side on a plate and leave for 30 minutes. Beat two or three eggs, depending on how many *torrijas* are required, add a small pinch ground cinnamon, coat the slices with the egg and fry in hot olive oil until golden. Spread fried slices with honey and serve.

Torrijas Purita   *Torrijas Purita*

Cut crusts off a small sandwich loaf, slice it into ¾-inch slices, make a hole in the centre of each slice to a depth of ½ inch and fill with English cream (p. 254), mixed with a little cream. Put in the oven until golden, then cover with thick jam, sprinkle with sugar and put back in the oven to caramelize the sugar.

Rum Omelette   *Tortilla al ron*

8 eggs	4–6 oz. sugar
2–3 slices sponge cake	1 tablespoon butter
rum	

Separate the eggs and beat the whites until very stiff. Soak sponge cake lightly in rum, crumble and mix with the yolks. Add sugar to taste. Fold in the whites of egg and make rolled omelettes with butter, as described. When ready sprinkle with sugar and rum, set alight and serve immediately.

Omelette Soufflé   *Tortilla suflé*

8 separated eggs	1 tablespoon grated orange peel
9 tablespoons sugar	1 tablespoon butter

Cream yolks with eight tablespoons sugar and orange peel and mix well. Beat the whites until stiff, add a tablespoon sugar and beat again until very stiff (on this depends the success of the dish). Fold the whites into the yolk mixture, pour into a buttered soufflé dish, bake in the oven for 20 minutes and serve immediately.

Pancakes (1)   *Crêpes* (1)

10 oz. flour	2 oz. butter
1 pint boiled milk	custard cream (p. 252)
3 beaten eggs	sugar
pinch salt	

Sieve the flour into a bowl, gradually stir in milk, add eggs and salt. Brush a small frying pan with melted butter, and when it is hot pour in a tablespoon of batter, tilting the pan to spread the batter evenly. Fry until golden on one side, turn, and fry the other side. Continue in this way until all the batter is used up, keeping the pancakes overlapping on a cloth. Spread the pancakes with custard cream, fold, sprinkle with sugar and glaze with a glazing iron.

Pancakes (2)   *Crêpes* (2)

10 oz. flour	2 oz. butter
1 pint boiled milk	jam
2 eggs	sugar
zest of ½ orange	rum

Make the batter as in the preceding recipe, incorporating orange zest. Fry the pancakes as described, then spread with jam, roll up, sprinkle with sugar and rum, set alight and serve immediately.

Pancakes (3)   *Crêpes* (3)

10 oz. flour	sugar
1 pint boiled milk	2 oz. butter
3 eggs	powdered cinnamon
grated rind of ½ lemon	

Stir the milk into the flour, mix in three yolks, lemon rind and a tablespoon of sugar. Beat the whites of egg until very stiff and fold into the batter just before making the pancakes. Fry the pancakes as described. As they are taken out of the frying pan, sprinkle both sides with sugar and a little cinnamon on top and serve.

Snowy Mountain   *Monte nevado*

1 sponge cake	3 oz. sugar
rum	6 whites of egg
6 yolks	1 tablespoon water and sugar syrup

Cut the cake into slices and use to line the bottom of a soufflé dish. Sprinkle with rum. Cream the yolks with sugar, blend well and spread a layer of the mixture over sponge slices. Put another layer of sponge, sprinkle with rum and cover with yolks. Whisk the whites very stiff, add syrup, whisk again, pour over the contents of the soufflé dish and bake in a moderate oven until it is golden on top.

Pilar Fingers   *Barritas del Pilar*

10 oz. sugar	8 oz. roasted ground almonds
juice of ½ lemon	2 oz. very small aniseed balls

Melt the sugar in a small saucepan, add lemon juice and almonds, cook gently, stirring with a wooden spoon until the sugar turns a dark caramel colour, remove from heat, pour out on to a lightly buttered marble slab or a greased tin, roll out to a thickness of ½ inch, sprinkle with the aniseed balls and, before it cools, cut into fingers 1 inch wide and 4 inches long. Greasing the knife with butter makes the cutting easier.

Stuffed Dates   *Dátiles rellenos*

1. Cut the dates on one side, remove stone, fill with a halved walnut (or almond, or any other nut), close and roll in icing sugar.

2. Cut the dates on one side, remove stone, fill with egg or coconut *yema* (p. 259) and dip in caramel (sugar and water boiled together until the sugar becomes a dark caramel colour). Dates filled with *yema* should be left open, so that plenty of *yema* can be used.

Custard Cream   *Crema*

2 pints milk
peel of ½ lemon
1 cinnamon stick
6 yolks of egg

10 oz. sugar
¼ teaspoon salt
1½–2 oz. cornflour

Boil the milk with lemon peel and a small piece of cinnamon, strain and keep aside a small cup for mixing with the cornflour. Put the yolks of egg into a pan, add 8 oz. sugar, stir until smooth, add milk slowly, season with a tiny pinch of salt and cook on a moderate heat, stirring continuously and always in the same direction. Mix cornflour with milk kept for this purpose and strain. When the cream begins to thicken, add the cornflour, and stir continuously until ready. Pour the custard on to a dish. If a caramel top is desired, allow to cool, then sprinkle with sugar (dusting only a little of the surface at a time, as the sugar tends to be absorbed too quickly into the custard) and glaze with a glazing iron.

Cream for Filling Cakes   *Crema para rellenar pasteles*

½ pint milk
1 vanilla bean
2 egg yolks

4 oz. sugar
1¼ oz cornflour

Boil the milk with vanilla and let it cool. Cream the yolks with sugar and mix with the milk. Dilute cornflour with a little water, strain, add to the rest and mix well. Cook mixture over a low heat, stirring continuously until it thickens.

Fried Custard   *Fritos de crema*

7 eggs	1 teaspoon orange blossom water
4 oz. flour	4 oz. sugar
½ pint milk	small pinch salt
peel of ½ lemon	breadcrumbs
1 cinnamon stick	lard or olive oil

Beat two eggs, stir into them all the flour required to make a thick paste. Beat four more eggs and stir them into the paste, working until very smooth. Boil the milk with lemon peel and a small piece of cinnamon (or a pinch of ground cinnamon) strain and leave to cool. When cold, add it gradually to the paste, mix well, cook on a low heat, stirring continuously. When the custard begins to get hot, add orange blossom water, sugar and a tiny pinch of salt. Stir all the time until the custard is cooked. Butter a wide, shallow dish, pour the custard into it and leave to cool. When cold, cut into strips, squares or round or oval-shaped pieces. Coat with beaten egg and grated breadcrumbs, fry in hot lard or olive oil and drain well. Serve hot sprinkled with sugar.

Chocolate Cream Sandwiches
      Emparedados de crema de chocolate

1 small sandwich loaf	4 oz. sugar
2 tablespoons *anis* liqueur	2 oz. flour
½ pint cold boiled milk	4 oz. grated cooking chocolate
3 eggs	olive oil

Remove crust off the loaf, cut it into slices ½ inch thick, sprinkle lightly with *anis* mixed with a little milk. Put two yolks and one white of egg in a saucepan, beat a little, add sugar, flour and chocolate, mix well, gradually stir in the rest of the milk and heat gently, stirring continuously to prevent sticking. As soon as boiling is established, remove from heat and leave to cool. When cold, spread the bread slices with chocolate cream, sandwich together, coat the sandwiches with beaten egg, fry in hot olive oil until golden on both sides and drain. Arrange on a plate, sprinkle both sides with sugar and serve.

Butter Cream   *Crema de manteca*

½ pint milk
1 lb. sugar
¼ vanilla bean

3 beaten yolks
1¼ lb. butter

Boil the milk with sugar and vanilla, strain through a very fine strainer, pour slowly on to beaten yolks, stirring until well mixed. Heat the mixture on a low heat, stirring continuously. When it begins to thicken, remove from heat, add butter and mix well. This cream is used both as filling and icing for cakes.

English Cream   *Crema inglesa*

1 egg
5 oz. sugar

strained juice of 1 lemon
1¼ oz. butter

Put the egg in a small saucepan, whisk, add sugar, beat until smooth, add lemon juice and incorporate the butter, blending it in in small pieces. Cook in a *bain-marie*, stirring continuously to ensure smoothness, for 10–15 minutes.

Baked Caramel Custard   *Flan de leche*

1 pint milk
peel of ½ lemon
1 cinnamon stick
8 oz. granulated sugar

4 eggs, 3 yolks of egg
2–3 oz. loaf or granulated sugar for
    caramel

Boil the milk with lemon peel and cinnamon, cool and strain. Beat the eggs and the yolks with sugar, gradually stir in milk and mix well.

Caramelize a mould, i.e. coat it with sugar cooked to caramel degree (see note on Sugar, p. 274). To do this, heat loaf or granulated sugar, moistened with a little water, in the mould, until the sugar acquires a light brown colour. Tilt and rotate the mould to caramelize the inside evenly.

Pour in the mixture and cook in a *bain-marie* in a slow oven. To test, insert a long needle into custard; if it looks dry, the custard is cooked.

Baked Chocolate Custard   *Flan de chocolate*

1 pint milk
4 oz. grated cooking chocolate
1 small vanilla bean

6 yolks
10 oz. sugar
4 whites of egg

Boil the milk with grated chocolate and vanilla, leave to cool and remove vanilla bean. Cream the yolks with 7 oz. sugar and add to milk. Beat the whites until very stiff and fold into the mixture.

Line the mould with caramel (as described in the recipe for Baked Caramel Custard, see above), pour the mixture into it and bake in a *bain-marie* in a slow oven until set.

A depraved palate thinks sweet things bitter

Baked Orange Custard   *Flan de naranja*

10 eggs   8 oranges
12 oz. sugar

Beat the eggs with 9 oz. sugar into a smooth paste. Grate the peel of an orange and mix it in. Add the juice of all the oranges and stir well. Line the mould with caramel (see Baked Caramel Custard, p. 255), pour in the mixture and bake in a *bain-marie* in a slow oven until set.

Spanish Baked Apples   *Manzanas al horno*

2 lb. cooking apples   rum
sugar

Choose large apples, remove cores, wash and fill the apples with sugar moistened with a teaspoon rum. Put on a baking tin with a little water and bake in the oven.

Sweet Elizabeth   *Dulce Elizabeth*

6 eggs   1 lemon
9 oz. castor sugar   ¾ oz. powdered (or 6 leaves)
6 oranges   gelatine

Separate the yolks from the whites. Cream the yolks with sugar until very smooth. Squeeze the oranges and the lemon making at least ½ pint fruit juice in all, strain and add to yolks. Mix gelatine with enough hot water to dissolve it, add to sweet mixture, stir to blend all ingredients and leave until the mixture begins to set. Whisk the whites very stiff, fold into the mixture and put in a refrigerator to set. Serve in the same dish. This sweet can also be made in individual dessert dishes, or in a buttered mould and turned out before serving.

Sweet Mignon   *Dulce Mignon*

4 eggs
6 oz. castor sugar
1 gill white wine

3 gelatine leaves
2 teaspoons almond oil

Separate the yolks from the whites of egg. Blend the yolks with sugar and wine. Heat the mixture on a moderate heat, stir until it is on the point of boiling, remove from heat and leave to cool. Dissolve the gelatine in warm water and add to mixture. When it begins to set, fold in the stiffly beaten whites, pour into a mould greased with almond oil and chill until set. Dip the bowl for an instant into hot water, turn out carefully and serve.

Spanish Bread Pudding   *Budín de pan*

2 oz. currants
½ gill rum
1 pint milk
1 teaspoon grated lemon rind
4 oz. sugar

4 oz. crustless bread
4 beaten eggs
1 oz. butter
2 oz. loaf sugar for caramel

Soak the currants in rum for 4 hours. Boil the milk with lemon rind and sugar, remove from heat, put the bread into it to soften, stir until it becomes a paste, add eggs, butter and currants. Stir well and leave until cold. Line a mould with caramel (see Baked Caramel Custard, p. 255), pour in the bread mixture and bake in a *bain-marie* for 50–60 minutes either in the oven or on top of the stove. Do not turn it out until cold.

Diplomatic Pudding   *Budín diplomático*

3 oz. loaf sugar
3 tablespoons cold water
3 or 4 sponge cakes
3 oz. glacé cherries, raisins or any
   preserved fruits

5 eggs
4 tablespoons castor sugar
vanilla flavouring
12 oz. milk
2 tablespoons brandy

Boil the loaf sugar and water together until it acquires a light brown colour. Use this caramel to coat a mould (see recipe for Baked Caramel Custard, p. 255). Dice the sponge cakes and the preserved fruits and lightly fill the mould with alternate layers of sponge and fruit. Beat the eggs, add the sugar, milk and flavouring to taste and stir until the sugar is dissolved. Strain the custard into the mould and bake in a slow oven for about 30 minutes, using a *bain-marie* if the oven is too hot.

While still warm, turn out carefully on to a dish, pour the brandy over it and light.

This pudding is equally nice cold; allow to cool before turning out of the mould. When ready to serve, pour warm brandy over it and light.

Jonathan Pudding   *Budín Jonathan*

5 oz. butter	2 tablespoons kirsch
6 oz. castor sugar	5 whites of egg
5 yolks	1 teaspoon butter
4 oz. sponge fingers	1 tablespoon flour
4 oz. ground almonds	custard cream (p. 252)

Cream the butter and sugar, add yolks and mix well. Crush the sponge fingers, add them and the almonds to the mixture and moisten with kirsch. Beat the whites until very stiff and fold them in. Butter a mould, sprinkle with flour, pour in the mixture and bake in a moderate oven. (To test, insert a long needle into the pudding. If it comes out dry, the pudding is ready.) Leave to cool completely, turn out, cover with custard cream, sprinkle a layer of sugar on top, glaze with a glazing iron and serve.

A pear that makes a noise when you cut it is not worth a fig

Marzipan *Mazapán*

1 lb. almonds 1 lb. castor sugar
2 whites of egg

Mince the almonds together with the whites of egg. (If the whites are mixed with the almonds, the oil is not released in the mincing.) Stir in sugar and mix well.

Uncooked marzipan made this way should be used the same day. When it is necessary to keep it for some days, it must be cooked in the following manner: make a thick syrup by boiling the sugar with a little water, put the minced almonds into it and cook for 2–3 minutes, stirring continuously.

Yemas *Yemas*

8 oz. sugar 12 yolks
1 gill water icing sugar

Make a syrup by boiling the water and sugar. Put the yolks in a bowl, pour the syrup over them little by little, stirring continuously. Heat the mixture, stirring all the time. When it is very hot but not boiling, remove and leave to cool. Then work in as much icing sugar as needed to make a stiff paste. Take portions of it, shape into balls, place on a lightly greased plate, sprinkle with sugar and glaze with glazing iron. Serve in small pleated paper cases.

Coconut Yemas *Yemas de coco*

1 lb. sugar 1 lb. dessicated coconut
½ pint water

Make a syrup by boiling the sugar and water. When the sugar is dissolved, remove from heat, add coconut little by little, mix well, shape into balls, roll them in sugar and serve in small pleated paper cases.

Yema for Pastries   *Yema para pasteles*

12 oz. sugar   12 yolks
1 gill water

Make a syrup by boiling down sugar and water to the thread degree.* Little by little mix it with the yolks, stirring continuously. Cool before using.

Beatrice Meringue   *Pastel Beatriz*

6 eggs   4 oz. pounded roasted almonds
4 oz. butter   4 oz. candied orange
8 oz. sugar   chocolate fondant icing (p. 266)
1 tablespoon strong coffee

Separate the yolks from the whites. Cream the yolks with butter, 2 oz. sugar, coffee and almonds until the mixture is smooth. Chop the candied orange very finely. Beat the whites until very stiff,

---

* Thread degree is the first stage in the cooking of sugar. Professional practitioners often measure the degree by a saccharometer or a Baumé thermometer. Thus thread degree will be shown to have a density of 25° and will register 215°F (102°C) on the Baumé thermometer. However, there is a simple, everyday method of testing thread degree, which is easy to recognise: take a little of the sugar between thumb and index finger and stretch them apart. Little threads forming between the two show that the sugar has reached small thread degree. (see SUGAR, p. 274).

add the remaining sugar and candied orange. Beat again, for the more stiffly the whites are beaten, the better the meringue. Butter a baking tin, divide the whites into three portions, shape them into three round omelettes on the tin and bake these meringues in a slow oven. When they begin to colour, take them out and leave to cool. When cold, put the meringue shells in a glass dish, on top of each other, with a layer of the almond cream between each. Cover with chocolate fondant icing.

PASTRY, CAKES, BISCUITS

REPOSTERÍA

Puff Pastry   *Pasta de hojaldre*

1 lb. flour
13 oz. shortening
2 eggs

⅛ oz. salt
1 teaspoon lemon juice
¼ pint water

Sieve the flour on to a pastry board, make a well in the centre, add 1¼ oz. shortening, eggs, salt, lemon juice and water. Work the paste until it is very smooth, then roll out, distribute half the remaining shortening on top, fold it into three and roll out again. Repeat this once more, distribute the rest of the shortening and fold over into three. Altogether puff pastry must be rolled out six times. During rolling out, sprinkle the board and the rolling pin with flour to prevent sticking.

Pastry for Pies   *Pasta para empanadillas*

1 lb. flour   3 tablespoons water
5 oz. lard   pinch salt
1 egg

Sieve the flour on to a pastry board, reserving a little for dusting the board later. Make a well in the centre and put in lard, egg and warm water with salt. Mix well into a smooth paste and leave wrapped in a damp cloth for an hour. Sprinkle the pastry board with flour and roll out the paste to a thickness of $\frac{1}{8}$ inch.

Pastry for Tarts and Tartlets   *Pasta para tarteletas*

6 oz. flour   pinch salt
3 oz. lard   2 tablespoons water

Sieve the flour on to a pastry board, make a well in the centre, put in the lard, salt and water and knead to a smooth paste. The more it is kneaded, the better it is. Leave wrapped in a clean, slightly damp cloth for at least an hour.

Batter for Frying   *Pasta para freír*

2 tablespoons flour   pinch salt
2 tablespoons warm water or milk   1 dessertspoon olive oil
1 yolk   1 stiffly beaten white of egg

Put flour in a bowl, stir water or milk into it, add yolk, salt and olive oil. Mix well until the batter reaches the consistency of single cream. Let the mixture stand for an hour. Just before using, fold in white of egg.

Churros (1)   *Churros (1)*

2 pints water	olive oil
½ teaspoon salt	sugar
1½ lb. plain flour	

Bring water to the boil with salt and pour it gradually into a bowl containing the flour. Mix well to a very smooth paste. Fill a forcing bag with the paste and using a wide fluted nozzle, pipe it in the shape of a spiral into plenty of sizzling olive oil. Fry until golden, drain, cut to the desired length, sprinkle with sugar and serve immediately.

Churros (2)   *Churros (2)*

2 eggs	grated peel of 1 lemon
8 oz. flour	4 oz. sugar
1 pint milk	olive oil for deep frying

Beat the eggs and fold in the flour. Gradually add the milk and stir to a smooth paste. Mix in lemon peel and one tablespoon sugar.

Fill a forcing bag with the paste and proceed as in the first recipe for *Churros*.

Coca   *Coca*

2 oz. yeast	4 oz. butter
flour	1 teaspoon grated lemon rind
1 pint milk	marzipan (p. 259)
11 oz. sugar	candied fruit
4 eggs	

Dissolve the yeast in ¼ pint water and add as much flour as it will absorb; put it in a bowl, cover and keep in a warm place until it has doubled its size.

Make a sponge mixture using milk, sugar, three eggs, butter, lemon rind, and as much flour as the mixture will absorb.

Fold in the yeast, cover and leave to rise.

Flour a paste-board and roll the dough out into one, two, or more oblongs, cover with marzipan (made slightly thinner than usual by adding a little water), leaving the edges free of marzipan, place strips of candied fruit on top, put the cakes carefully on greased tins, brush the edges with beaten egg and bake in a moderate oven.

Coca Buns   *Pastelitos de coca*

Make the dough as for *coca*, place ball-shaped portions on a greased tin, remembering that they will double their size in baking; brush with beaten egg and bake in a fairly hot oven. When baked, leave to cool, cut in half, without cutting right through, and fill with custard cream (p. 252).

Bread Ring   *Roscón*

1 lb. flour   3 oz. sugar
2 eggs   3 oz. butter
2 teaspoons baking powder   zest of 1 orange or lemon
¼ pint milk

Sift the flour on to a paste-board, make a well in the middle and break the eggs into it. Add baking powder, mix well and gradually add milk, sugar, butter and zest. The mixture should be slightly spongy. Butter a baking tin, put the mixture in the form of a ring on the tin and bake in the oven.

It is delicious dipped in chocolate or whipped cream.

Airy Doughnuts   *Buñuelos de viento*

There are many recipes for making these doughnuts, but the best way is to make a paste for Spanish Cream Buns (p. 270). Taking a teaspoon at a time, drop little balls of the mixture into sizzling olive oil, deep fry until golden all over, turning with a slice, if necessary, drain and sprinkle with icing sugar.

Apricot Doughnuts   *Buñuelos de albaricoque*

12 ripe apricots	½ pint milk
2 tablespoons brandy	2 eggs
sugar	olive oil
8 oz. flour	pinch salt

Halve the apricots, stone, sprinkle with brandy and sugar to taste. Make a light batter using the flour, milk, two yolks of egg, one tablespoon oil and a pinch of salt. Leave for 2 hours, then fold in whites of egg beaten very stiff. Dip apricot in the batter, deep fry in hot olive oil, drain and sprinkle with sugar.

Apple Doughnuts   *Buñuelos de manzana*

1 lb. apples	½ pint milk
3 tablespoons *anís* liqueur	2 eggs
4 oz. sugar	pinch salt
8 oz. flour	olive oil

Peel and core the apples, cut into rings, sprinkle with *anís* and sugar to taste. Make a smooth batter using flour, milk, two yolks of egg and a pinch of salt. Leave for 2 hours, then fold in stiffly beaten whites of egg. Dip the apple rings in batter, deep fry in hot olive oil until golden, drain and sprinkle with sugar.

Pastry Flakes   *Hojuelas*

2 eggs
pinch salt
flour

olive oil
sugar or honey

Beat the eggs, add salt and half teaspoon olive oil. Gradually stir in sufficient flour to make a thick smooth paste. Roll out as thinly as possible, cut into any shape desired and fry in hot olive oil until golden on both sides. Sprinkle with sugar, or better still coat with a thin layer of honey.

Delights   *Delicias*

8 oz. flour
½ pint milk
2 eggs

sugar
pinch salt
olive oil

Sieve the flour on to a pastry board, make a well in the middle, stir in the milk little by little, add eggs, one teaspoon sugar and salt, mix to a smooth paste, roll out thinly, cut in strips ½ inch wide and 7 inches long, tie each strip into a loose knot, fry in hot olive oil and sprinkle with sugar. Serve hot.

Chocolate Fondant Icing   *Fondant de chocolate*

8 oz. sugar
¼ pint water

½ vanilla bean
4 oz. plain chocolate

Make a thick syrup by boiling together the sugar, water and vanilla. Remove the vanilla bean. Grate the chocolate into a small saucepan, dissolve it in the syrup, stir until it is quite smooth and use for icing cakes.

Tipsy Sponge   *Bizcochos borrachos*

1 sponge cake	1 gill Málaga wine
4 oz. loaf sugar	cinnamon

Slice the sponge cake and cut each slice into oblong pieces. Make a syrup with the sugar and four tablespoons cold water, boil until it turns light brown and stir in wine. Soak the pieces of sponge cake in the syrup, put on a cake rack to drain and sprinkle with cinnamon.

Eulalia Wafers   *Bollos Eulalia*

8 oz. ground almonds	6 yolks of egg
8 oz. sugar	small pinch salt
8 oz. flour	½ teaspoon cinnamon
8 oz. butter	wafers

Mix the almonds with the sugar to make a paste. Sieve the flour on to a pastry board, add butter, yolks, almond paste and salt. Stir, add cinnamon and mix well. Spread this preparation fairly thickly on wafers, put on a baking tray and bake in a slow oven.

Astorga Shortbread   *Mantecadas de Astorga*

10 oz. butter	10 oz. cornflour
10 oz. sugar	cinnamon
6 eggs	

Cream butter and sugar until very smooth, add the eggs one by one, mixing them in thoroughly. Add cornflour and a pinch of cinnamon. Fill small square cases with the mixture and bake in a moderate oven for 10 minutes.

Magdalenas   *Magdalenas*

6 eggs   10 oz. melted butter
10 oz. sugar   10 oz. sifted flour
grated rind of 1 lemon

Cream the eggs with the sugar and lemon rind until the mixture becomes white and forms a ribbon, add butter, stir, add flour gradually and mix well. Put into buttered moulds, filling them two-thirds full. Bake in a hot oven for 20–25 minutes.

Spanish Rings   *Rosquillas*

2½ lb. flour   ¼ pint milk
12 oz. butter   grated rind of 1 lemon
6 beaten yolks   ½ teaspoon bicarbonate of soda
14 oz. icing sugar

Sieve the flour on to a pastry-board, make a well in the middle, put in butter, yolks, sugar, milk, lemon rind and bicarbonate of soda. Work the ingredients together to make a smooth paste, roll out, cut into strips, make into rings, put on a buttered baking tray and bake in a slow oven.

Macaroons   *Almendrados*

8 oz. almonds   4 whites of egg
1 lb. sugar   powdered vanilla

Blanch (i.e. scald and peel) the almonds, keep a few for decoration and mince the rest with the sugar and the unbeaten whites of egg. Flavour with a little powdered vanilla. If the mixture is too thick, add another white of egg. Squeeze portions of the paste on to greaseproof paper placed on a baking tray, through a forcing bag with a plain wide nozzle, put half an almond on each macaroon and bake in a moderate oven until golden.

Almond Biscuits   *Tejas de almendras*

5 oz. butter	5 oz. sifted flour
5 oz. sugar	4 whites of egg
5 oz. finely chopped almonds	grated rind of 1 lemon

Cream butter and sugar until smooth, add almonds, flour, slightly beaten whites of egg and lemon rind. Mix well. Drop well spaced teaspoons of the mixture on to a buttered baking tray and bake in a moderate oven until golden. Immediately on taking out of the oven, roll them flat and store in a tin with a well-fitting lid. These almond biscuits can be kept for a week or two.

Tea Biscuits (1)   *Pastas para el té* (1)

10 oz. butter	3 eggs
8 oz. icing sugar	1¼ lb. sifted flour
3 oz. minced candied orange peel	

Cream the butter and sugar together, add orange peel and two unbeaten eggs, fold in flour and mix lightly without kneading. Roll out to a thickness of ¼ inch, cut into rounds, brush with beaten egg, put on a buttered tray and bake in a slow oven until golden.

Tea Biscuits (2)   *Pastas para el té* (2)

1¼ lb. sugar	3 eggs
1¼ lb. dessicated coconut	4 oz. flour

Mix the sugar, coconut and eggs to a smooth paste, add flour, folding it in without kneading too much. Drop dessertspoons of the mixture on to a greased baking sheet and bake in a moderate oven until golden.

Spanish Shortbread   *Mantecados*

8 oz. lard
3 oz. icing sugar

1 gill sherry
1 lb. sifted flour

Cream the lard and sugar together, add sherry little by little, fold in flour and mix well without kneading too much. Roll out the pastry to a thickness of $\frac{1}{2}$ inch, cut into rounds, put on a greased baking sheet and bake in a moderate oven for 15–20 minutes.

Lady's Fingers   *Bizcotelas*

8 eggs
1 lb. sugar
$\frac{1}{2}$ pint water

2 oz. flour
icing sugar

Separate the yolks from the whites. Cream yolks with sugar, add water, sift in the flour gently and, finally, fold in the stiffly beaten whites. Put a sheet of buttered greaseproof paper on a baking tray. Put the mixture into a forcing bag with a plain round nozzle and squeeze long fingers on to the paper. Sprinkle with icing sugar and bake in a slow oven until light brown.

Spanish Cream Buns   *Lionesas*

$\frac{1}{2}$ pint milk
6 oz. lard
1 oz. sugar
pinch salt
peel of 1 lemon

8 oz. flour
8 eggs
butter
custard cream (p. 252)
icing sugar

Put the milk, lard, sugar, salt and lemon peel in a saucepan, bring to the boil, remove lemon peel and pour in all the flour. Remove the pan from heat, stir vigorously to make a very smooth paste, return to heat, stirring continuously, until the paste thickens and begins to stick to the pan. Remove from heat, add the eggs, one by one, working each one in separately. (The more the mixture is beaten, the better will be the result.) Butter a baking sheet, sprinkle with flour, and using a forcing bag with a plain ¼ inch round nozzle, pipe little mounds of the paste on to it. Bake in a slow oven. When baked, slit on one side, fill with custard cream or whipped cream and sprinkle with icing sugar.

Gypsy's Arm   *Brazo de gitano*

3 eggs, separated   butter
4 oz. sugar   custard cream (p. 252) or whipped
4 oz. sifted flour   cream

Beat the yolks with the sugar and four tablespoons water until smooth. Gradually fold in flour, mixing well without working it too much. Fold in stiffly beaten whites. Cover a baking tray with a sheet of buttered greaseproof paper, spread the mixture on it very carefully, stirring as little as possible and bake in a moderate oven until pale golden.

Wet a napkin, wring out, turn out the cake on to this napkin, spread with a layer of custard cream or cream whipped with a little icing sugar, roll up quickly, carefully remove napkin and leave to cool. Before serving, dust with icing sugar.

Genovesa   *Genovesa*

6 eggs   1¼ oz. butter
8 oz. sugar   8 oz. flour
grated rind of 1 lemon

Beat the eggs and sugar together until smooth, add lemon rind, butter and, little by little, incorporate flour. Butter a cake tin, sprinkle with flour, pour in the mixture and bake in a slow oven.

Chocolate Cake   *Pastel de chocolate*

8 oz. butter
8 oz. sugar
2 yolks
4 oz. chocolate

8 oz. sifted flour
1 teaspoon baking powder
2 stiffly beaten whites of egg

Cream the butter and sugar together until smooth, mix in yolks. Melt the chocolate in a double saucepan and add to yolks. Gradually add flour and baking powder and mix well. Gently fold in the whites of egg. Butter a cake tin, sprinkle with flour, pour in the mixture and bake in a slow oven.

Victoria Cake   *Pastel Victoria*

6 eggs
8 oz. sugar
1 teaspoon grated lemon peel

8 oz. sifted flour
1½ oz. butter
apricot jam
chocolate fondant icing (p. 266)

Separate the yolks from the whites of egg. Cream the yolks with the sugar, add lemon peel, fold in stiffly beaten whites and flour. Butter a cake tin, pour in the mixture and bake in a slow oven for 30 minutes. Leave to cool, cut into three equal layers, spread each one with sieved apricot jam, sandwich the layers together and ice the cake with chocolate fondant icing.

Spanish Apple Tart   *Tarta de manzana*

puff pastry (p. 261)
1 lb. cooking apples

1 tablespoon *anís* liqueur
sugar or syrup

Roll out the pastry to a thickness of ¼ inch, cut into oblongs of any desired size and put them, well spaced, on a buttered baking tray. Peel and core the apples, slice into very fine rings and sprinkle with *anís*. Moisten the pastry lightly with a pastry brush dipped

in water, taking care not to wet the edges. Arrange the apple rings
in overlapping rows down the length of the strip (making as many
rows as the size of the pastry allows), sprinkle with sugar or, if
preferred, with a little syrup, made by boiling some sugar with a
little water. Bake in the oven until the pastry has risen and turned
golden.

Almond Sponge *Bizcocho de almendras*

6 oz. butter	8 oz. roasted minced almonds
1 lb. sugar	2 tablespoons kirsch
6 eggs	8 oz. sifted flour

Butter a cake tin, sprinkle with flour. Cream the rest of the butter
and the sugar together until smooth, add eggs one by one, mix
well, stir in almonds, kirsch and flour. Blend all the ingredients,
pour the mixture into the cake tin and bake in a moderate oven.

JAMS, FRUITS IN SYRUP AND ICE CREAMS
CONFITURAS Y HELADOS

SUGAR

Directions for Boiling Sugar Syrup

THE correct boiling of sugar is a very important factor in cookery and requires a little practice. The best method, of course, is to rely on a sugar-boiling thermometer. The points to bear in mind are these:

(1) Sugar passes from one stage to the next so rapidly that it needs very careful watching during boiling.

(2) The pan must be large enough, as sugar rises up to a great height and is liable to overflow.

There are eleven degrees of sugar boiling:

1st	Small thread	215°F.	102·6°C.
2nd	Large thread	219°F.	104°C.
3rd	Small pearl	220°F.	104·5°C.
4th	Large pearl	222°F.	106°C.
5th	Soufflé (blow)	230°F.	110°C.
6th	Feather (large soufflé)	232°F.	111°C.
7th	Small ball	238–240°F.	112–116°C.
8th	Large ball	246–252°F.	119–122°C.
9th	Small crack	264–289°F.	129–143°C.
10th	Large crack	334°F.	168°C.
11th	Caramel	356°F.	180°C.

If you have no thermometer, test sugar as follows:

THREAD DEGREE: Dip the tip of the finger and thumb into cold water, then into syrup and back into cold water. Press finger and thumb together and separate them slowly, when a fine thread is formed. The large thread can be stretched further, is slightly thicker and does not break quite so easily.

SMALL PEARL: Large bubbles can be seen on the surface of the syrup.

LARGE PEARL: The syrup is thickly covered with bubbles.

BLOW (SOUFFLÉ): Twist a wire into a loop, dip into syrup, withdraw and blow through the loop. The blow degree is reached if bubbles appear on the other side of the loop.

FEATHER (LARGE SOUFFLÉ): Is tested in the same way as Blow, but the bubbles should be bigger and should fly off like little feathers.

SMALL BALL: Drop a small quantity of syrup into iced water, leave for a second, then roll between thumb and finger, when it should form a small soft ball.

LARGE BALL: Tested in the same way as above, but the ball should be hard.

SMALL CRACK: Drop a small quantity of syrup into cold water. When cold, it should break, but will stick to the teeth when bitten.

LARGE CRACK: Tested as above, is short and brittle and does not stick to the teeth when bitten.

CARAMEL: When this stage is reached, sugar begins to turn brown. At this point the pan should be immediately removed from heat and the bottom of the pan dipped in cold water to check further cooking.

Ideally, a clear dry day should be chosen for sugar boiling, as sugar is liable to be affected by a damp atmosphere.

Angel's Hair Jam   *Cabello de ángel*

2¼ lb. peeled winter squash   1 quartered lemon
2¼ lb. sugar   stick cinnamon
1¾ pints water

Choose a squash gathered at least a year before, break it open, divide into pieces, peel, put the flesh into a saucepan with water, boil until soft, drain, put on a plate, separate the fibres, remove and discard seeds, put the fibres in a colander, rinse well, drain thoroughly and weigh them. Cook the sugar and the water with lemon and a small piece of cinnamon. When the syrup thickens, remove lemon and cinnamon, put in the squash and cook together, stirring from time to time to prevent sticking. Test for jelling point by putting a drop of the juice on a cold plate for a few minutes. If the juice hangs in a large drop when the plate is tilted, the jelling point has been reached. On the sugar thermometer, jelling degree registers 32°–33° or 235°F.

Apple Jam   *Mermelada de manzana*

2½ lb. cooking apples   pinch cinnamon
2 lb. sugar   juice of 1 lemon

Peel, quarter and core the apples. Boil with ½ gill water until soft, drain, rub through a fine sieve. Put pulp and sugar in a preserving pan, cook gently, stirring continuously with a wooden spoon and taking off scum from time to time. Add cinnamon and lemon juice and continue cooking until the syrup reaches thread degree (see recipe *yema* for pastries and note on Sugar, p. 274).

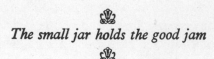

The small jar holds the good jam

Apple Cheese   *Pasta de manzana*

cooking apples   sugar
lemon peel

Wash the apples, quarter, cook in water with strips of lemon peel, drain and rub through a sieve. Weigh the pulp, put in a preserving pan with equal quantity of sugar, cook slowly together, stirring continuously to prevent sticking. Boil long enough for all the liquid to evaporate and to give the apple cheese the right consistency.

Quince Cheese   *Pasta de membrillo*

4 large quinces   1¾ pints water
2¼ lb. sugar

Choose large quinces, wash, dry well with a cloth and grate, taking great care not to mix in any seeds. Make a syrup by boiling together the sugar and water. Stir in quince pulp and cook gently, shaking the pan frequently to prevent sticking, until the cheese is transparent and firm.

Apricot Jam   *Mermelada de albaricoque*

Choose sound apricots, halve and stone them, put in a pan with just enough water to cover, boil for 10 minutes, drain and rub through a sieve. Weigh the pulp, put in a preserving pan with equal quantity of sugar, cook over moderate heat, stirring constantly, until the setting point is reached and the syrup reaches thread degree. (See recipe *yema* for pastries, p. 260, and note on Sugar, p. 274.)

Plum Jam   *Mermelada de ciruelas*

Scald plums with boiling water, skin, stone, put in a pan, cover and place over a very low heat. When liquid is released, drain, weigh the pulp, add 1½ lb. sugar to every pound of pulp and cook together until jelling point is reached. (See recipe for Angel's Hair Jam, p. 275.)

Tomato Jam   *Mermelada de tomate*

Choose large, ripe, firm tomatoes. Put them in a bowl, scald with boiling water, peel, remove all seeds, wash well, drain and weigh the pulp. Make a syrup by boiling together 1¼ lb. sugar and 8 oz. water to each pound of pulp. When the syrup reaches thread degree (see note on Sugar, p. 274) add tomatoes and the juice of two lemons. Stir continuously to prevent sticking. The jam is ready when the syrup is thick and the tomato transparent.

Orange Jam   *Mermelada de naranja*

Allow 1½ lb. sugar to 1 lb. of oranges. Scrape the surface of the oranges lightly with a grater and boil them whole in plenty of water until they yield to a light pressure with the fingers. Drain and leave to cool. When cold, halve them, remove seeds and, using a very sharp knife, slice the oranges as finely as possible. Make a syrup by boiling together ¾ pint water to every 1½ lb. sugar. When the syrup reaches thread degree (see recipe *yema* for pastries, p. 260, and note on Sugar, p. 274) add oranges and cook until the syrup is thick and the fruit transparent.

Orange Jelly   *Gelatina de naranja*

6 oranges   grated rind of 2 oranges
1 lemon   4 leaves gelatine
12 oz. sugar

Squeeze the oranges and lemon, put the juice with equal quantity of water into a pan with the sugar and rind, bring to the boil over a moderate heat, skimming from time to time. At the first bubble, remove from heat and strain through a muslin bag. Melt the gelatine in a little hot water, stir it into the syrup, pour the jelly into a buttered mould and chill to set.

Oranges in Syrup   *Naranjas en almíbar*

Allow 1½ lb. sugar for every pound of oranges. Scrape the surface of the oranges lightly with a grater, cook the fruit whole in plenty of water until soft to the touch, drain, leave to cool, divide each orange into six or eight slices and remove seeds.

Make a syrup by boiling together a pint of water to every 1½ lb. sugar. When it reaches thread degree (see recipe *yema* for pastries, p. 260, and note on Sugar, p. 274) add oranges, boil gently until they become transaprent.

Peaches in Syrup   *Melocotón en almíbar*

Peel the peaches and cut them up. Make a syrup by boiling together 1¼ lb. sugar and ¾ pint water for every pound of fruit pulp. When the syrup reaches thread degree (see note on Sugar, p. 274) add fruit, let it boil, stirring continuously, until the syrup is thick and the peaches transparent.

When a man's belly is full, cherries taste bitter

Quince in Syrup — *Membrillo en almíbar*

2¼ lb. quinces
2¾ lb. sugar

1¾ pints water

Peel and core the quinces, cut into pieces, cook in water until soft, drain and leave in cold water. Make a syrup by boiling together the sugar and water until it reaches thread degree (see note on Sugar, p. 274). Drain pieces of quince and put into syrup. Cook until the fruit becomes red in colour and the syrup is thick and transparent.

Vanilla Ice Cream — *Helado de mantecado*

6 yolks
1½ pints milk
1 teaspoon vanilla

pinch salt
10 oz. sugar
½ pint single cream, whipped

Beat the yolks and dilute with a little milk. Scald the rest of the milk with vanilla, salt and sugar, boil to dissolve, stirring from time to time. Remove from heat, add yolks gradually, transfer to a double saucepan, cook for 7–8 minutes, stirring all the time. Take the pan out of hot water, stir to cool, strain, add cream and freeze. Lemon juice may be used as flavouring instead of vanilla.

Ice Cream with Candied Fruit
Helado de mantecado con frutas

Prepare the ice cream mixture as described in the previous recipe, add 8 oz. finely chopped candied fruit, cool and freeze.

Harlequin Ice Cream — *Helado arlequín*

¾ lb. choice strawberries
½ lb. sugar

vanilla ice cream (see above)

Hull and rub the strawberries through a sieve, stir in ¼ pint water and strain through a cloth, squeezing to extract all the juice. Make a syrup by boiling this juice with the sugar to thread degree (see Sugar, p. 274), cool and freeze. Separately prepare Vanilla Ice Cream, using half the quantity given in the recipe. To serve, put half vanilla and half strawberry ice cream in fruit cups.

Hazel-Nut Ice Cream   *Helado de avellana*

Make vanilla ice cream mixture (p. 280), add 8 oz. blanched ground hazel-nuts and freeze.

Fancy Ice Cream   *Helado caprichoso*

12 bananas	2 tablespoons kirsch
juice of 6 oranges	vanilla ice cream (p. 280)
6 tablespoons sugar	candied fruit for decoration

Peel and mash bananas, add orange juice and sugar, sprinkle with kirsch and leave to macerate. Make Vanilla Ice Cream and freeze. Rub the fruit mixture through a sieve, put into champagne goblets, filling them half-way, top with ice cream and decorate with small pieces of different coloured candied fruits.

Quick Lemon Ice Cream   *Helado de limón rápido*

1 lemon	½ pint double cream
1 orange	1 yolk
1 egg white	3–4 oz. sugar

Squeeze lemon and orange. Whip separately the white of egg, the cream, and the yolk with sugar. Strain fruit juice into yolk mixture, stir well. Fold in the cream, then the white of egg, and freeze in the ice tray of the refrigerator.

A variety of flavours may be obtained by using the juice of other fruits. With sweeter fruit, use less sugar.

Chocolate Ice Cream   *Helado de chocolate*

6 oz. grated chocolate

1½ pints milk

6 yolks

1 teaspoon vanilla

pinch salt

10 oz. sugar

½ pint single cream, whipped

Dissolve the chocolate in the milk and proceed to make the ice cream as described in the recipe for Vanilla Ice Cream (p.280). Freeze in the usual way.

Meringue Ice Cream   *Helado de leche merengada*

1¾ pints milk

8 oz. sugar

1 teaspoon vanilla

4 whites of egg

grated chocolate

Bring the milk, sugar and vanilla to the boil, leave to cool, pour into the ice cream tray and put in the freezer. When almost frozen, fold in the whites of egg beaten to a stiff froth and finish freezing. Serve in goblets sprinkled with grated chocolate. This ice cream is also good flavoured with lemon instead of vanilla, but in that case, substitute powdered cinnamon for the grated chocolate.

Ice Gâteau   *Biscuit glacé*

5 oz. sugar

½ pint water

1 teaspoon vanilla essence

8 yolks and 1 whole egg

4 oz. whipped cream

ice

4½ lb. freezing salt

Make a syrup by boiling together the sugar, water and vanilla. Put the yolks and the egg into a bowl and, while beating them, add the hot syrup, a little at a time. When all the syrup has been incorporated, continue beating until the mixture rises. Add whipped cream very slowly, otherwise it will cause the mixture to subside.

Pour the mixture into a round mould and hermetically seal it with greaseproof paper under a tightly fitting lid. Place the mould in a container of at least the same height and completely surround the mould with well compressed pieces of ice alternating with layers of freezing salt. (The container should have a hole at the bottom for drainage.) At all times during the freezing the mould must be kept completely surrounded and covered by ice. As it melts, add more ice and salt. Three or 4 hours are necessary to freeze the ice gâteau *glacé*. Do not remove from the mould until the moment of serving. Before lifting the lid, wipe it carefully to prevent salt falling into the gâteau.

NOTE. Ice gâteau can also be frozen in ice trays in refrigerator.

GLOSSARY

AU GRATIN: Dishes with a thin crust on the surface formed when they are browned in the oven or under the grill. Usually covered with sauce, breadcrumbs or grated cheese.

BAIN-MARIE: Vessel containing hot water in which dishes and sauces can be kept hot without coming into contact with direct source of heat. The temperature of water in a *bain-marie* should be kept near boiling point.

BOUQUET-GARNI: A faggot or bunch of herbs. Normally it consists of three sprigs parsley, including stems, one sprig thyme and a small bay leaf. To make it easier to remove them from soups, stews, sauces, etc., tie together in a piece of muslin.

CARAMEL: Sugar cooked until it turns brown. Used for coating moulds (caramelizing) and for colouring.

CHORIZO: Hard Spanish paprika-spiced sausage, available in all good delicatessen shops.

CHURROS: A dough mixture piped into hot olive oil.

COCA: A dough cake.

COURT-BOUILLON: Aromatized liquid for cooking meat, fish, vegetables, offal, etc. Usually it consists of salted water, with the addition of wine, vinegar or lemon juice, a *bouquet-garni*, carrot, onion, a few peppercorns.

CROÛTONS: Bread cut in dice or sliced, of any shape or size, fried in oil, butter or other fat, toasted under the grill or dried in the oven. For soups they are usually cut into dice $\frac{1}{4}$ inch square, fried crisp and golden and dusted with fine salt (see recipe p. 51).

FAT SALTED PORK: Pork fat cured with salt and sometimes smoked. Obtainable in delicatessen shops—also known as *speck*.

FINES HERBES: Finely chopped herbs used for seasoning and stuffing. In classical cookery, it is a mixture of equal parts of chopped parsley, tarragon, chives and chervil.

FRITOS: Popular Spanish speciality. There is a great variety of *fritos*, but whilst the ingredients suitable for fritos range from ham and mushrooms to prawns and artichoke hearts, the method is always the same—deep frying in sizzling hot oil.

FUMET: Liquid used to give flavour and body to stocks and sauces. They are made by boiling down almost to nothing foodstuffs of various kind either in stock or wine and should not be confused with essences, extracts or concentrates.

GALANTINE: Boned and stuffed meat or poultry, served cold with sauce or glazed.

LARDING: Threading lardoons of varying thickness into meat, fish, poultry or game, with a larding needle.

LARDOONS: Strips of bacon or fat salt or fresh pork used for larding.

MACERATE: Steep in liquid.

MAGDALENA: A sort of biscuit.

PAELLA: Large frying pan with two handles, which has given its name to the delicious rice dish.

PAPILLOTES (EN): Cooked in greased papers.

PARBOIL: Boil in enough water to cover for 5 to 10 minutes. Salt pork and bacon are often parboiled to remove excess salt,

PURÉE: A pulp of mashed or sieved fruit or vegetables; meat. fish or other food pounded and sieved. Thick soup.

RAMEKIN: A mixture served in small paper or china cases, either oval or round.

REDUCE: Boil down a liquid to concentrate its flavour or to thicken it.

RIBBON (TO): To work sugar and egg mixture until it ribbons as it flows from the spoon.

ROUX: A mixture of butter (or other fats) and flour, cooked for varying periods of time, used for thickening soups and sauces.

SIMMER: Cook very, very gently so that the mixture bubbles but cooks at a temperature just under boiling.

SOBRASADA: Soft paprika sausage.

TORRIJA: Sliced bread dropped in eggs and milk and fried in oil.

YEMA: Candied yolk of egg.

ZEST: The outside rind of orange, lemon, tangerine or citron, without any of the white pith, often finely chopped or shredded and used as flavouring.

ENGLISH INDEX

(*For* Spanish Index, *see page* 306)

SPANISH INDEX

(*For* English Index, *see page* 289)
ÍNDICES DE FÓRMULAS